Translating Apollinaire

Besides providing a new appraisal of Guillaume Apollinaire, the foremost French poet of early Modernism and WWI, *Translating Apollinaire* aims to put the ordinary reader at the centre of the translational project. It proposes that translation's primary task is to capture the responses of the reader to the poetic text, and to find ways of writing those responses into the act of translation. Every reader is invited to translate, and to translate with a creativity appropriate to the complexity of their own reading experiences.

Clive Scott is Professor Emeritus of European Literature, University of East Anglia. He is a Fellow of the British Academy and 2014 President of the Modern Humanities Research Association.

Also by Clive Scott and published by University of Exeter Press

Translating Baudelaire (2000)

"Clive Scott's *Translating Baudelaire* offers exhilarating perspectives on the practice of (verse) translation. ... His unrivalled ability to analyse French verse and his remarkable talents as a wordsmith, indeed as a poet, combine to produce compelling renderings of some of Baudelaire's finest verse." *Times Literary Supplement*, 27 April 2001

Translating Rimbaud's Illuminations (2006)

"[Clive Scott's] passion and enthusiasm for an experimental translation which defamiliarises and destabilises make this an exciting tour de force and a significant contribution to the field of translation studies." *Forum for Modern Language Studies*, 43, July 2007

"Clive Scott's highly original study forges innovative lines of inquiry, while being a pleasure to read thanks to its fluid prose, thorough research and clear presentation of the translation techniques." Denise Merkle, *Target*, 21:1, 2009

Translating Apollinaire

Clive Scott

UNIVERSITY
of
EXETER
PRESS

First published in 2014 by
University of Exeter Press
Reed Hall, Streatham Drive
Exeter EX4 4QR
UK
www.exeterpress.co.uk

British Library Cataloguing in Publication Data
A catalogue record for this book is available
from the British Library.

Paperback ISBN 978 0 85989 895 9
Hardback ISBN 978 0 85989 894 2

Typeset in 10.5pt Plantin Light, by Carnegie Book Production, Lancaster
Printed in Great Britain by Short Run Press Ltd, Exeter.

for M.-N., who else

Contents

Illustrations

The front cover reproduces a portrait of Apollinaire by Irène Lagut (1893–1994), frontispiece of *Guillaume Apollinaire* (1919) by Roch Grey [Hélène d'Oettingen].

Acknowledgements

I would like sincerely to thank editors and publishers for permission to make further use of the following materials: an earlier version of the first part of Chapter One appeared as 'Apollinaire and Madeleine Pagès: Translating the Photography of a Relationship', in *Forum for Modern Language Studies*, 2002, 38/3, 302–14; some part of Chapter Two, including the translations of 'Marizibill' and 'Annie', appeared in 'Genetic Criticism, Text Theory and Poetry', in Susan Bassnett and Peter Bush (eds), *The Translator as Writer* (London: Continuum, 2006), 106–18; a first treatment of 'Chantre' (Chapter Three) was offered in 'Experimenting with a Single String: Apollinaire's "Chantre"', *Norwich Papers: Studies in Translation*, 2009, 16, 72–87, while the translations of lines 121–34 of 'Zone' and of '1909' (Chapter Four) were first published in 'Our Engagement with Literary Translation', *In Other Words*, 2008, 32, 16–29; the translation of 'Les Fenêtres' (Chapter Five), with modified commentaries, was published first in 'Translating the Art of Seeing in Apollinaire's "Les Fenêtres": The Self of the Translator, the Selves of Language and Readerly Subjectivity', in Paschalis Nikolaou and Maria-Venetia Kyritsi (eds), *Translating Selves: Experience and Identity between Languages and Literatures* (London: Continuum, 2008), 37–51, and subsequently in 'The Windows: Translating Apollinaire's "Les Fenêtres"', in Eugenia Loffredo and Manuela Perteghella (eds), *One Poem in Search of a Translator: Rewriting 'Les Fenêtres' by Apollinaire* (Bern: Peter Lang, 2009), 234–47; the idea of approaching a translation of 'Le Voyageur' through an experimental language related distantly to Russell Hoban's Riddleyspeak (Chapter Six) was first tested in 'Intermediality and Synaesthesia: Literary Translation as Centrifugal Practice', *Art in Translation*, 2010, 2/2, 153–70; an early and rather shorter tabulation of the differences between the linear and the tabular—see Appendix II—is to be found in 'From Linearity to Tabularity: Translating Modes of Reading', *CTIS Occasional Papers*, 2009, 4, 37–52, an article which also included a translation of 'La Porte' (Chapter Three).

The photographs, including the photographic copies of other photographs, were either taken by myself or are fragments of unattributed photographs.

I would like to express my deep gratitude to Simon Baker, publisher and managing director at the University of Exeter Press, for his unfailing and sympathetic understanding of this project, and for his tireless oversight of its publication. I would also like to offer my warm thanks to Rachel Clarke and the production team at Carnegie Publishing for so elegantly solving the manuscript's typographical problems and producing so handsome a volume; and to Sarah Harrison for her meticulous and helpful editing of the text. Any remaining shortcomings are wholly my own.

A Note on the Text

The use of the acronyms ST, TT, SL and TL, for 'source text', 'target text', 'source language' and 'target language' respectively may strike some readers, to begin with, as unnecessarily jargonistic. The full terms themselves ('source text', 'target text', etc.) are standard currency in the literature of translation studies, and avoid the ambiguities and unwanted implications of alternatives such as 'original', 'translation', 'translated text', 'language of the original'; for these reasons, it is desirable that they should be used consistently throughout the text. The use of acronyms for these terms is, again, standard practice in the field, and, once accustomed to them, the eye does, I hope, instantly and painlessly identify them, without their repetition becoming cumbersome. From time to time in the text, readers are reminded of the keys to the acronyms.

In the matter of translations of critical and poetic texts, where no reference is given to standard translations they are my own.

Prefatory Remarks

This book is the last volume in two converging trilogies. First, along with *Translating Baudelaire* (2000) and *Translating Rimbaud's 'Illuminations'* (2006), it constitutes the final stage of a journey from my beginnings in literary translation to my present practices and convictions; some of these convictions are laid out in the Introduction. However much my ideas may have modulated in the course of this three-station itinerary, my underlying concern has always been to elaborate a practice which allows and encourages literary translation to develop its own literariness, its own literature, rather than seeking to regurgitate the literariness it finds in the source text (ST). An important part of my argument has always been that it is not translation's business to preserve the literariness of the ST, since textual preservation runs counter to translation's propulsive or projective instincts; if the ST's literariness does not 'naturally' survive in translation, then it is because the ST's survival depends on its capacity to become different from itself, to inhabit a condition of constant becoming. And that becoming different necessarily entails a relocation of literariness, which literary translation, the translation of the literary into another literary, is expressly designed to achieve.

The second trilogy that this book completes has, as its first two volumes, *Literary Translation and the Rediscovery of Reading* (2012a) and *Translating the Perception of Text: Literary Translation and Phenomenology* (2012b), which seek to shift the task of translation from that of interpreting texts to that of capturing the phenomenology of reading. By 'capturing the phenomenology of reading' I mean both capturing reading as a whole-body, psycho-physiological response to text *and* writing that response back into the translation of the ST. The achievement of this end entailed two fundamental and closely related changes in what I took to be the 'standard' approach to literary translation, namely: (i) radically to enlarge the translator's ability to put him/herself at his/her own disposal as a reader/writer, and (ii) to increase the range of languages, both national and textual, available to the translator. This enterprise entailed many other shifts of translational emphasis: it entailed translating the textual towards the performative; the linguistic towards the paralinguistic; the linear towards the tabular; the perspectival towards the planar; the single towards the multiple; *langue* towards *langage*. By this last, I mean that if translation desires to bring many more languages into play than the standard dialogue of the source language (SL) and target language (TL), then specific languages (*langues*) must learn to immerse themselves in the totality of language, in the raw, undifferentiated medium that includes all forms of language (*langage*).

There is, then, a danger that, in translating Apollinaire, I shall fail to do justice to his poetry in its every detail, because my eye is on a larger target—the business of translation—even though doing full justice to the ST has long been one of translation's perennial preoccupations. Apollinaire's verse in this book may seem to act primarily as a platform for exploratory thinking about translation and about, among other things, the relationship, in translation, between text and photographic fragment. Can it be claimed that the book addresses problems specific to the translation of Apollinaire? Yes, it can, but it certainly does not pursue a systematic programme of investigation. Rather, it uses what it perceives as the habits of Apollinaire's writing as an inspiration and justification for the translational attitudes it wishes to promote. Thus it passes back and forth between the two collections of poetry published in Apollinaire's lifetime—*Alcools* (1913), *Calligrammes* (1918)—and only implicitly indicates patterns of development in Apollinaire's creative thinking; it does not provide a careful history of Apollinaire's writerly career. Instead, the pattern of poems treated, their various groupings, are governed by the affinities that the practices of reading and translating discover or engender among them.

And there is one further caveat to be registered. This book incorporates photography into the majority of its treatments of individual texts; but it is not a book which deserves the subtitle 'Translation and Photography', a fascinating project yet to be undertaken. It does not deserve this subtitle for two reasons. First, photography is only one of the many resources upon which the translations offered here draw. Photography is one element—and a virtually untried element at that—in a practice that remains steadfastly experimental and multifarious. Second, I am not concerned with whole photographs so much as with collages of photographic fragments, or of contact prints. Indeed, it is the degree to which these fragments and contact prints are not standard photographs which make them, for me, a particularly expressive and 'involved' supplement and response to the written text.

I should add that this adventure in translation periodically adverts to the work of Gilles Deleuze and Félix Guattari, not because that work concerns itself with the problems of translation—it does not—but because it circles round concepts the thinking of which is peculiarly fruitful for the kinds of translation I have in mind. Among those concepts one might mention: the critique of interpretation; the rhizomatic; deterritorialization (minor literature); language as continuous variation (metamorphosis/becoming); stuttering; the logic of sense; the nomadic; difference and repetition. Fundamental to my translation of the textual into the performative is the desire to achieve a reversal of the Saussurean perception that *langue* precedes and underpins *parole*, or the Chomskyan perception that deep structure generates surface structure. Both of these perceptions depend on the stable concertedness and the differential equilibrium of the underlying language system. But, like Deleuze, I believe that language is not a homogeneous system, in or close to equilibrium, but a heterogeneous assemblage in perpetual disequilibrium (Deleuze, 2003: 343–5; 2007: 370–2). Thus 'une langue ne se décompose pas en éléments, mais en langues à l'infini [...] la langue n'a pas de constantes, elle n'a que des variables' (2003: 344–5) [a language cannot be broken down into its [permanently constitutive] elements; it can be broken down into diverse languages ad infinitum; [...] language has no constants, only variables (2007: 372)]. National languages thus constantly release 'foreign' languages within themselves; *parole* infinitely revises *langue*; translation as performance is always moving into variation, into the multilingual (including the languages of typography and of different media), into *langage*.[1]

And if I have made Deleuze and Guattari periodic companions to my translational thinking it is also because I have in view not a (another) *theory* of translation but rather a *philosophy* of translation; that is to say, I do not want to develop methodologies based on putative translational functions or objectives; I want to imagine what translation is as a form of knowledge, as an existential undertaking, as an adventure in perception, as a mode of engaging with the world; I want to understand by what concepts translation should be animated. Translation is clearly an activity greater than the texts it translates. In my view, as will become apparent, it is concern for the monoglot reader which confines translational thinking to theory, to textual questions and cruces; correspondingly, it is the polyglot reader who liberates translation into its philosophical fullness as a particular kind of writerly enterprise or opportunity that can take us to places in language that other kinds of writing have left untouched. Philosophy assumes that translation is not a specialized activity with its own conducts and standards, but an integral part of the creativity of us all, a natural impulse or energy which can play a more important part in our intellectual formation, in our perceptual habits, in our resources of self-expression. It is for this reason that my Appendix II, on the differences between the linear and the tabular, is of some significance: these two notions have attached to them implicit visions of, and attitudes towards, the nature of textual being and of textual activity, to which it would be singularly inappropriate to attach the term 'theory', and whose ideological implications far exceed the limits of any particular translational application; the linear and the tabular are divergent systems of thought.

Correspondingly, then, if I make mention of Deleuze and Guattari as writers whose spirit comes periodically to haunt these pages, I should also summon Mallarmé, since all adventures in paginal space take us back unerringly to *Un coup de dés* (1897). Valéry, who believed himself to be the first to have seen this work, gives us an invaluable account not only of the manner in which Mallarmé read it—'d'une voix basse, égale, sans le moindre "effet", presque à soi-même' (1957: 623) [in a low voice, even, without the slightest 'effect', almost to himself]—but also of the capacity of the text's layout to project 'la figure d'une pensée' [the tracery of a thinking mind]:

> Ici, véritablement, l'étendue parlait, songeait, enfantait des formes temporelles. L'attente, le doute, la concentration était *choses visibles*. Ma vue avait affaire à des silences qui auraient pris corps. Je contemplais à mon aise d'inappréciables instants: la fraction d'une seconde, pendant laquelle s'étonne, brille, s'anéantit une idée; l'atome de temps, germe de siècles psychologiques et de conséquences infinies,—paraissaient enfin comme des êtres, tout environnés de leur néant rendu sensible
>
> (1957: 624)

> [Here, truly, space spoke, thought, engendered temporal forms. Expectation, doubt, concentration were *visible things*. My sight was engaged with silences which had become substance. I considered at leisure imperceptible instants: the fraction of a second during

> which an idea is surprised into existence, shines, is erased; the atom of time, germ of psychological centuries and infinite consequences—appeared at last like beings surrounded by their nothingness made tangible].

In the space of the page Valéry finds transcribed, made visible, the temporality of a living psyche, in all its motions, where silences hang heavy on the air, not as vacancies, but as pressures, fullnesses, pushing themselves into existence, and where the human voice is somehow 'prise au plus près de sa source' (1957: 623–4) [captured as near as possible to its source]. Armed with these kinds of insight, and armed, too, with Mallarmé's guiding principle that the variable disposition of words and word-groups on the page should reflect the 'subdivisions prismatiques de l'Idée' (1998: 391) [prismatic subdivisions of the Idea], we may be better able to develop our own sense of paginal layout both as a mapping of the field of energies released in and from the ST by translation and as the choreography of the changing movements and dynamics of the reading mind.

Introduction

1. The Project and Apollinaire

I have recently been preoccupied with the formulation of a translational philosophy and practice adapted to my needs as a literary reader (2012a; 2012b). In brief, this philosophy involves shifting the task of translation from that of interpreting the source text (ST) to that of capturing the phenomenology of reading. For me, *literary* translation is about the creation of a literature of reading literary texts. By 'capturing the phenomenology of reading' I mean both capturing reading as a psycho-physiological experience of text, as an adventure of consciousness and perception in reading, and *writing* that experience, that consciousness and perception, *back* into the translation of the ST. The pursuit of this end necessitates the multiplication and extension of the linguistic, graphic and pictorial resources available to the translator, which in turn entails an approach which is multilingual and at the same time anti-semiological: that is to say, the dialogues between different languages, whether verbal or visual, encourage each language constantly to re-adapt itself to new relationships and new expressive demands, and thus undo any sense of its codedness, of its systemic stability, and this in turn draws all languages (*langues*) towards the inclusive totality of the medium (*langage*). Apollinaire himself anticipates an enterprise like this when he writes, in a letter to Jeanne-Yves Blanche of 30 October 1915: 'Le moment de revenir aux principes du langage n'est pas encore venu, mais il viendra, et à ce moment la pureté de telle ou telle langue ne pèsera pas lourd' (1966a: 676) [The time to return to the first principles of language [*langage*] has yet to arrive, but it will, and when it does, the purity of any language [*langue*] will count for little].[1]

The multiplication of resources is designed, as I put it in the Prefatory Remarks, 'radically to enlarge the translator's ability to put him/herself at his/her own disposal as a reader/writer', and it includes the incorporation into translation of those modes of graphic self-representation—handwriting, crossing-out, doodling in ink and paint—which have access to the unconscious, to reverie, to the impulses and spontaneities of the reading body, and the harnessing of the languages of text (punctuation, typefaces, margins, diacritical marks, layout) to embody the paralinguistic features of voice (tempo, tone, intonation, pausing, loudness, emphasis, accent, voice-quality) and the physical kinaesthetics brought to bear on the ST by the reader. These preoccupations seem doubly appropriate in a book about Apollinaire: his own handwritten calligrams, whether they constitute the decorative dedications of copies of his own works, or derive from wartime correspondence (on postcards, in letters), or form part of a catalogue for other artists (Léopold Survage/Irène Lagut), have become an important part of his output, together with his other typographical experiments, thanks to the resourcefulness of modern printing technology. How far these new languages might also incorporate into translation the larger reading environment, the ambient world, continues to exercise me; in my view, it should certainly be a significant element, almost a form of guarantee, in translation's effort to 'recontextualize' the ST.

The pursuit of the multilingual entails the supercession of the bilingualism which governs most translational transactions. The translator feels able to draw on all languages, including dialects, jargons, pidgins, creoles and even science-fictional languages, to register those associations of sound, of orthography, of textual fragment which are generated in the reader by the ST. Translation elbows aside the ethnocentricity, the atavisms, the territoriality of national languages in its desire to generate new linguistic maps, new forms of linguistic nomadism, new morphings of culture, new versions of the cosmopolitan. Apollinaire's own multilingualism springs not so much from the serious study of languages as from a creative attraction towards the curious kinships and modulations that languages develop, and from a fearless cultivation of linguistic variety (Décaudin, 1973: 10–11, 14–15). He looks for the same variety of linguistic background, and of social and human condition, in his readers:

> Moi je n'espère pas plus de 7 amateurs de mon œuvre mais je les

> souhaite de sexe et de nationalité différents et aussi bien d'état: je voudrais qu'aimassent mes vers un boxeur nègre et américain, une impératrice de Chine, un journaliste boche, un peintre espagnol, une jeune femme de bonne race française, une jeune paysanne italienne et un officier anglais des Indes
>
> (letter to Jeanne-Yves Blanche, 19 November 1915; 1966a: 680–1)
>
> [I don't hope for more than 7 fans of my work but I want them to be of different sexes, different nationalities and of different social standing too: I would like my poetry to be enjoyed by a black American boxer, a Chinese empress, a German journalist, a Spanish painter, a young French woman of good breeding, a young Italian peasant woman and an English officer from the Indies].

Implicit in these wishes is a rejection of monoglottism and the monoglot reader.[2] My own wishes for translation are motivated, as must already be apparent, by the desire to break the monopoly of a translation geared to the monoglot reader, in the belief that this kind of translation, against its own will perhaps, not only perpetuates monoglottism but is an implicit argument for the dispensability of knowledge of foreign languages, produces a disempowered reader, endorses fossilized notions of national cultures and prevents translation from prosecuting its own distinctive literariness/literature. Translation for the polyglot reader, on the other hand, for the reader who is acquainted with the source language (SL), develops a deeply embedded relationship with the text, a relationship which involves listening to, and speaking, the ST across languages and into languages: that is, across and into the languages of the reading experience itself, the languages which give expression to readerly perception and readerly consciousness. This in turn facilitates the inhabitation of the multicultural and the re-drawing of linguistic and cultural geographies.

There are many senses in which Apollinaire makes the ideal subject for a translational enterprise driven by a restless and proliferating phenomenology of reading and writing. Not surprisingly, it took scholars and editors a long time to catch up with Apollinaire's *Nachlass* of occasional epistolary pieces, poems put aside, poems published but uncollected. It is only posthumously that the collections *Il y a* (1925), *Poèmes à Lou* (1947; initially *Ombre de mon amour*), *Le Guetteur mélancolique* (1952) and *Soldes* (1985) were rather arbitrarily 'constructed' for publication. I want to foster this sense of translation as a form of ongoing daily intercourse with texts, as a form of dialogue with others and with self, of the experimental search for an adequate language. A translation is a formal project, yes, but also a journal of reading, an album of try-outs, an intimate letter to its own readers, which multiplies drafts, sketches, casual snapshots.

In line with this readerly/writerly *désinvolture*, and with the structural habits of the poet of *Alcools* (1913), who pays no heed to chronology or to a carefully mapped existential itinerary, my own chapters select their materials not chronologically, but in the order in which they become appropriate to the translational issues raised. And there is a further, textual aspect of this attitude by which my approach is equally informed: Apollinaire has little sense, it seems, of the inviolability of texts or of their impatience to be finished: he might, at the last minute, dismantle a decasyllabic line into a tetrasyllable followed by a hexasyllable ('Sous le pont Mirabeau'), or radically reduce a passage of verse (e.g. the East European Jewish emigrants of 'Zone'), or plunder longer unpublished poems for shorter publishable ones (both 'L'Adieu' and 'La Dame' are fragments of 'La Clef'), or turn a three-stanza poem into a five-stanza one ('Spectacle' > 'Crépuscule') or, conversely, a five-stanza poem into a three-stanza one ('Les Saltimbanques' > 'Saltimbanques'), not to mention the plethora of other textual variants. In his hands, the text is infinitely malleable, rarely satisfied with being itself, always in transition, always heading off somewhere, or, abruptly, somewhere else. Texts are unquiet things, always full of their being still to be fully imagined, and it is perhaps this very unsettledness which gives them their energy, the dynamism of the temptation to be other. This improvisatory habit may also have connections with Apollinaire's devotion to the aesthetics of collage, his growing resistance to syntactical continuity, his cultivation of expanded fields of consciousness at the expense of local cohesion.

And there are other important respects in which Apollinaire seems to be the fitting objective and agent of the kind of translation I wish to essay. In his work, as we have already intimated, the printed, the calligraphic and the graphic live in easy intercourse with one another. We learn from his notebooks and proofs how existentially important were the gestural self-embodiments of handwriting, doodling, drawing, watercolour painting, trying out alphabets and scripts and signatures; as Peter Read tells us, these various 'decorations' 'constituent un prolongement de son œuvre écrite et une facette essentielle de son imaginaire' (Debon and Read, 2008: 67) [constitute an extension of his written work and an essential facet of his imaginary]. Despite the fact, as Michel Décaudin reports (2002: 90), that 'Apollinaire a toujours soutenu que les techniques de la peinture ne s'appliquaient pas à l'écriture et qu'il n'y avait pas de "cubisme littéraire"' [Apollinaire always maintained that the techniques of painting were not applicable to writing and that there was no such thing as 'literary cubism'], his verse contradicts this view, as we shall see, and we should not overlook, of course, his collaborations with other artists: with Derain for *L'Enchanteur pourrissant* (1909), with Dufy for *Le Bestiaire ou Cortège d'Orphée* (1911)—after the failure of plans with Picasso—and the unrealised project for *Odes* with Picasso. An integral part of this extension of writing into the gestural and spatial, this projection of utterance into a visual field, is, for me as translator, the projection of the linear into the tabular (see Chapter Three).

Given my persuasion that translation should translate from the textual towards the performative, from the linguistic towards the paralinguistic and kinaesthetic, it is fitting that Apollinaire should make much of the *oral* composition of his verse; as in improvisatory jazz, or aleatory or indeterminate music, performing *is* composing. In a letter to Henri Martineau (19 July 1913), Apollinaire tells us that perambulation and composition are natural partners, and that rough draft usually turns out to be final copy, a comment to be taken more as a vindication of writing 'd'un seul jet' than as the truth (see Burgos, 1973: 35):

> Mes vers ont presque tous été publiés sur le brouillon même. Je compose généralement en marchant et en chantant sur deux ou trois airs qui me sont venus naturellement et qu'un de mes amis a notés. La ponctuation courante ne s'appliquerait point à de telles chansons.
>
> (1966a: 768)

> [My poems have almost all been published from the draft itself. I usually compose as I walk, singing two or three tunes which have come naturally to me and which one of my friends has noted down. Current punctuation would not be appropriate to such songs].

The creation of verse for Apollinaire is, it seems, less to do with writing-on-the-page than with in-the-head-composition. On the evidence of his manifest and tireless tinkering with drafts, and of his calligrams, and of all his doodling, we might want to question this claim. But it is important as an assertion of the primacy of the lyrical in his poetic make-up. However much one might wish to see in Apollinaire's abandonment of punctuation an acknowledgement of Futurist sympathies—Marinetti had called for the discarding of punctuation in his *Technical Manifesto of Futurist Literature* of 1912[3]—and, particularly, sympathies with the Futurists' assault on the constraining machinery of syntax, Apollinaire jibbed at their dismantling of the lyric partnership of voice and verse-line, and remained in two minds, to judge by his poetic practice, about their banishment of the psychological 'I'. In 'Nos amis les futuristes' (*Les Soirées de Paris*, 15 February 1914) he welcomes Marinetti's 'words-in-freedom', but finds in them a propensity for the descriptive and didactic, which confirms the continuing need for the rhythmic articulations of phrase and line for the purposes of self-expression:

> Certes, on s'en servira pour tout ce qui est didactique et descriptif, afin de peindre fortement et plus complètement qu'autrefois. Et ainsi, s'ils apportent une liberté que le vers libre n'a pas donnée, ils ne remplacent pas la phrase, ni surtout le vers: rythmique ou cadencé, pair ou impair, pour l'expression directe.
>
> (1991: 971)

> [Certainly, they [words-in-freedom] will be used for everything which is didactic and descriptive, so as to depict forcefully and more completely than hitherto. And thus, even if they introduce a freedom which free verse has not provided, they will not replace the phrase, nor, above all, the line: rhythmic or cadenced, even- or odd-syllabled, for direct expression].

2. Translation and Projection

While translation may seek, as its primary task, to translate the phenomenology of reading, it also has the task of projecting the ST into its future, into its renewed engagement with the world. The struggle towards the future is a constant preoccupation of Apollinaire's work after 1908 (Davies, 1973), a struggle because its boundless promise is countervailed by equally boundless uncertainties, and because it seems to necessitate the sacrifice of that past of memory and suffering which constitute the poet, and constitute, too, his particular lyric gift. It can never be sufficiently insisted that translation is an act of writing, of resuming that never-ending investigation of language's expressive capacity, so that one can both write one's readerly responses into the ST and write the ST into what lies ahead of it and which it has no power to foresee. This approach is very close to the heart of Yves Bonnefoy and necessarily takes his translational thinking in the direction of co-authorship, the harnessing of someone else's thought processes to one's own, and vice versa, to produce collaborative work (2000: 7–15). This idea of reading a poem to write with it, both as record of a linguistic experience and to take it forward, coincides with my own persuasions. Bonnefoy calls this 'une lecture écrivante', a relative of Roland Barthes's notion of the *scriptible* (1970: 9–12; 1974: 3–6).

Bonnefoy's vision of the relationship between co-authors is one in which a process of intimate recognition, based on the sharing of a certain essentialist, presence-filled vocabulary, is enhanced by the fact that the foreign language of the ST sets this vocabulary differently, in territories to which the translator has not had access in his own language. A foreign language is a new consciousness applied to the world. Additionally, the translator's relative ignorance of the SL sharpens his sense of the compact density, the intensity of the ST's words. Bonnefoy's abiding preoccupation remains the pursuit of the immediacy that lies buried in words. However much I may be of the translator-as-co-author persuasion, I do not share Bonnefoy's ideology of partnership; I am more of the view that the translator's task is to help the ST to be different from itself, to do justice to the time and space it has traversed since it was first published. While criticism practises a constant process of re-interpretation of works, assimilating new reading conditions and intellectual contexts to ensure the continuing relevance of the work in question—that is, practises an updating at the level of consumption—translation, as I imagine it, is an updating at the level of production, and involves imagining not how a work can best be interpreted to suit prevailing conditions but what its own potential for change is, how that potentiality might best be caught.

But here, again, Bonnefoy's position is really not so far from my own. He argues that the reader is superior to the poet he analyses in the sense that, with much greater lucidity, he sees what the text is capable of being and becoming:

> En bref, l'auteur, ce serait celui qui croit, ou a cru longtemps, qu'il se tourne vers le monde, comme serait celui-ci en lui et autour de lui, et cela pour en découvrir la vérité: alors que monde et vérité ne sont que des constructions de ses mots et pour une part des mirages. Et ainsi il perdrait de vue ce foisonnement de virtualités de son texte qu'il faudrait que l'on tienne pour la puissance de la parole, tandis que son hardi interprète percevrait, lui, ces ambiguïtés, ces polysémies, et en saurait la valeur, comprenant

> même qu'elles sont la seule réalité dans un univers qui n'est constitué que de signes en perpétuel mouvement
>
> (2000: 22–3)
>
> [In short, the author is one who believes, or has long believed, that he addresses the world, as it exists in him and around him, and that in order to discover its truth: whereas world and truth are only what his words construct and are to some extent mirages. And thus he loses sight of that proliferation of virtualities in his text which must be attributed to the power of language, while his bold interpreter, for his part, sees these ambiguities, these polysemies, and knows their value, even understanding that they are the only reality in a universe which is made up only of signs in perpetual movement].

In his preface to his translation of twenty-four of Shakespeare's sonnets into French sonnets of anything up to eighteen lines, Yves Bonnefoy returns to a topic which has consistently exercised him in his translations: the relationship between form and content. To treat the one as a variable and the other as a given is to subject the variable element to an undue and inertial constraint. Instead, one needs to generate a dialectical relationship between two variables (within certain parameters of recognizability), such that translation, like poetry itself, becomes a search, a search for what is most creatively immediate in us, a search for a territory this side of ready-made concepts, before the involuntary has ceded too much ground to approved equivalences. And metre is no more a safeguard of the spirit of poetry than fixed forms are. The adoption of a freer form enables the translator not only to listen to the ST more intensely but also to draw out of the ST potentialities which may have been stifled by its own formal constraints. 'Comprenons bien', Bonnefoy writes, 'car c'est cela l'essentiel: le matériau du traducteur, c'est moins le "sens" qu'a le texte [...] que son expérience propre de celui-ci' (1995: 59) [Let us make no mistake, for this is at the heart of the matter: the material of the translator is less the "meaning" possessed by the text [...] than the translator's own experience of this meaning' (trans. Antony Rudolf; Bonnefoy, 2004: 254)].

In entertaining the idea that the translator might outdo the source author, Bonnefoy reveals an affinity with Borges, an affinity which extends to the manipulations and undoings of form. Among the items in the literary remains of Borges's Pierre M[é]nard is a transposition into alexandrines of Paul Valéry's decasyllabic 'Le Cimetière marin' (2000: 35). This is actually not so surprising, since Valéry himself tells us that the decasyllable he had chosen for 'Le Cimetière marin', a line little used in modern verse, seemed to him 'pauvre et monotone' [poor and monotonous], particularly in relation to the alexandrine; thus it is that to Valéry, too, '[l]e démon de la généralisation suggérait de tenter de porter ce *Dix* à la puissance du *Douze*' (1957: 1503) [the demon of generalization suggested the attempt to raise this *Ten* to the power of *Twelve*]. Thus it is that, often, a translation, in finding a new formal garb for its ST, is only bringing to realization what the ST may itself already dimly suggest, may already dimly desire.

In order to distinguish between a translation that is retrospective and one that is prospective we need to make a distinction between meaning and sense. Meaning is something which is seen to inhere in language by virtue of lexical and cultural embeddedness. It is something which, however ambiguous, however plural, must be respected and cannot be denied, something which has claims to make. But we must be careful, or else meaning will subdue the translator, demand its dues overbearingly and without right. Because meaning is, in fact, in a permanent state of obsolescence. Sense, on the other hand, has constantly to be made. But it is elusive; it multiplies, diversifies, escapes, or holds itself at a distance, just beyond our grasp. It is an integral part of the ST's progress through time and space, a guarantee of that progress, and both sense and progress are dependent on the efforts that the readers and translators of the ST are prepared to make in pursuit of them. Translation, then, is not the extraction of meaning from a text in order to perpetuate it. Translation is an account of a sense-making of the ST by the translator, a sense-making which has written into it the activity of the readerly consciousness and the play of the readerly senses. And if the ST has to be made sense of, repeatedly, it is because STs cease to be comprehensible to themselves shortly after their production, and progressively lose their meaning. STs are nomadic texts, in search of themselves, in search of a 'place' in the world, in search of an ever-renewed expressive energy. In a word, then, translation does not recuperate meaning but generates sense, as it generates the future of the ST.

3. Poetry and Photography

On occasion, Apollinaire makes disparaging reference to photography's purely imitative, uncreative relationship with nature: in the first section of *Méditations esthétiques* (1913), for example, 'Sur la peinture', he declares: 'Chaque divinité crée à son image; ainsi des peintres. Et les photographes seuls fabriquent la reproduction de la nature' (1991: 8) [Each divinity creates in his/her own image; so it is with painters. And photographers alone manufacture the direct reproduction of nature]; and, in similar vein, in the preface to *Les Mamelles de Tirésias* (1918), he speaks of the need to 'revenir à la nature même, mais sans l'imiter à la manière des photographes' (1965: 865) [return to nature itself, but without imitating it in the manner of photographers]. But, as we shall discover in Chapter One, the camera's ability to capture the light reflected off the subject and thus become the instrument and mirror of nature is a boon to the soldier away at war; Apollinaire sorely needed the photograph's unimaginative indexicality to fire his own imagination, to make present to himself the charms of Madeleine Pagès. And, beyond this, Apollinaire had much hope invested in the creative possibilities of those new technologies of moving photographic images and recorded sounds, the cinema and the phonograph:

> Quant aux *Calligrammes*, ils sont une idéalisation de la poésie vers-libriste et une précision typographique à l'époque où la typographie termine brillamment sa carrière, à l'aurore des moyens nouveaux de reproduction que sont le cinéma et le phonographe
> (letter to André Billy, quoted by Butor, in 1966b: 7)
>
> [As for the *Calligrams*, they are an idealization of free-verse poetry and a typographic culmination at a time when typography is bringing its career to a brilliant close, at the dawn of new means of reproduction represented by the cinema and the phonograph].

Inasmuch as our affair is with the absorption by translation of collaged photographic fragments (see below), the contribution of cinematic thinking to our argument is not inconsiderable.

In the course of the pages following I want to pay particular attention to the part photography might play in a translational enterprise. This intention has already been initiated in previous work: in *Literary Translation and the Rediscovery of Reading*, my translation of Apollinaire's 'Marizibill' is accompanied by a photocollage (2012a: 61–7), and I construct 'photo-poems' from two passages in 'Zone' (2012a: 162–5). I return to both of these poems in the present work. But in this book I want to take the opportunity more thoroughly to examine the relationship between both text and photography, and translation and photography, without, however, trying to theorize any fixed typology of interaction.

It is easy to suppose that, since Apollinaire's poetry is already in existence, the incorporation of photographs into a translation would entail a kind of reverse ekphrasis: rather than a linguistic commentary on, or description or narrative of, a picture, we have a pictorial account of a poem. But such a supposition would be mistaken for two important reasons: the relation between poetry and photography may be a co-textual one (i.e. juxtapositional or reciprocal or competitive) rather than a metatextual one. And secondly, the assumed order of events—Apollinaire's poetry > photographic commentary—is undermined by the natures of the media involved. Even though photographs, in their taking, in chronological terms, may post-date the event or text they bear witness to, in the relation between photograph and text the photograph *sensorily predates the text.* A photograph predates text because the photograph is a primary material, a raw sensory material, in a way that writing cannot be, because, in Peircean terms, the indexical of the image predates the symbolic of language. Writing is always too late. Photographs cannot be called upon to authenticate or represent writing.

But the more distance (of subject, attitude, etc.) there is between poem and photograph, the more the fatality of precedence is lifted: image and poem can enjoy a simultaneity of origin, which is held in place by letting them go their own ways, by letting them interact as they wish, aleatorily, without forcing any dependencies, or priorities, or meta-positions. As John Berger says of the text and images in O'Grady and Pyke's *I Could Read the Sky* (1998: n.p.): 'And so they work together, the written lines and the pictures, and they never say the same thing. They don't know the same things, and this is the secret of living together'. This is not an argument to polarize their specific ontologies as media, but to maximize the fruitfulness of their relationship, of the tensional ground between them.

These arguments tacitly presuppose the use of full photographs, constituted as wholes by their rectangular frames, frames which endow their images with autonomy, guarantee them a significance (without, however, indicating what it might be) and bespeak an expressive control (without necessarily meaning compositional integrity). We shall have more to say about the frame as the book unfolds (see particularly Chapter Four), but for the moment we should recognize that framed wholeness will tend to diminish the photograph's ability dynamically to interact with the poem's structural energies, its processes of self-constitution. The full photograph is, in many respects, already beyond reach, an inert tableau which only the spectator can re-activate, which only the spectator can massage into a relationship with the text. All photographic theory, one might claim, is based on the full photograph, because a photograph is only a photograph by virtue of being a full photograph. It is only through the full photograph that we can construct a notion of authorship, of intention, even of vision, of seeing and framing. Is a hand excised from a photographic portrait still a photograph? And if it is not, have we ways of thinking about the photographic fragment which will allow us to recompose our expectations, our responses, our creative impulses, around that hand? And in our argument about the sensory precedence or temporal priority of the photograph in relation to text, does a photographic fragment have the power to exercise any visual imperatives, and does it have any stable relationship with temporal orders?

There are some immediate remarks we might make about the photographic fragment. It is an action on a photograph that already exists, just as translation itself is an action on a text that already exists. But immediately a qualification is necessary: a target text (TT) may be produced which looks to question whether the ST is already a foregone conclusion, that looks to cast doubt on the ST's finishedness, on its stability. This is the kind of TT that wishes itself a genetic event, a re-geneticization of the ST. The TT is, as it were, another play of variants that the ST has spawned in the process of its own composition. In similar, but by no means identical, fashion the photographic fragment, as a translational accompaniment or complementary language, might have the ability to suggest or project other pieces of photograph which do not add up to the photograph from which the fragment was initially excised. Photographic fragments, like word-choices or typographic choices, may generate a floating visual/textual field which promises infinitely to ramify and modulate rather than to return home to its origins. This is certainly not to say, however, that a photographic fragment, like a textual fragment, may not operate as a quotation from, or allusion to, an original text, as a metonymy for an originating work, but this citational function must not be allowed to obscure the more compelling motive of fragmentation, which is precisely to expand the metonymic field, the metonymic 'influence' of the image, far beyond its original photographic environment.

The photographic fragment requires the eye to look more fleetingly, less possessively, less insistently, with a more dynamic responsiveness than it does with the full photograph. The eye does not stare or gaze, because such a perceptual mode is unproductive; the eye traverses, flickers, glimpses, intuits, guesses, constantly feeding itself on new patterns of circulation. This is the art of 'looking among' (see Chapter Four). Photographic fragments install the nervous, mobile spectator, whose relationship with the image is piecemeal, distracted, incomplete, ever-renewed. Through these photographic clusters and interpolations the reader does not submit to the meditative time of the text, or rather does not allow it a meditative time; he/she looks instead for the restless activity of the text, its being-in-progress, the progress of self-formation, of making sense. The time of perceiving looks to oust the time of reporting, or describing, or representing. Writing itself, under the influence of photographic fragments, might become a performance of perception in writing, just as translation is a performance of linguistic glimpsing, intuiting, traversing, sense-making, as it constantly reinvents the circulation of languages.

It might be thought that the 'straight' photographic image is hostile to performance, in that it has no tactility, in that it seems to arrest time rather than propel it, in that there seems to be no presence of the photographer's body in the image. We might argue that there is performance in the blurred and the out-of-focus, or in the radical camera angle, or in photographic 'errors' more generally, or indeed in the very act of framing the shot. There is, after all, a performative eye, a performative eye which is also at work in the contact sheet (see Chapter Two), and which photographic fragmentation brings into full presence and activity; the photographic fragment has the power to translate the visual given, back into something virtual or latent, something which has yet to realize itself in all its possibilities; which is perhaps to say that the photographic fragment more effectively performs the pulsions and movements of the unconscious than the whole photograph (see Chapter Six). At the very least, one might claim that the cluster of photographic fragments is peculiarly adept at capturing the intimate workings of a sensory consciousness at several levels.

But we must not forget that the photographic fragment is produced by cutting, and it is the process of cutting that not only brings the performative eye into existence but also redefines the photograph's field of play, releases it into a specialized activity on the page, makes it available for collage. What the cut first of all produces is a rupture in and with the whole image, so that the initial rupture established by the frame itself, and which established the photograph's autonomy in relation to its environment, is nullified. Thereafter, as we have already intimated, the cut acts to produce both a photographic quotation, an allusion to a visual intertext, and, transcending that, the photographic fragment's peculiar capacity for fictionalization, a capacity to bond intimately with other images, a capacity to open up an infinitely extendable and diversifiable blind field,[4] a capacity not enjoyed by the whole photograph, which has particular obligations to its blind field. We speak of re-geneticizing the text, but we need also to imagine what one might call post-compositional editing and modification: given that a TT has been arrived at, in what ways might one wish to modify it (in terms of disposition, additional materials, added textual notations, etc.) in order better to contextualize it, or to free its synaesthetic or multisensory possibilities, or to increase its own performative energy, or to prepare it for performance? Here again the photographic fragment, in the form of collaging, might become both a model and an indispensable resource, the cut constituting a significant stylistic and expressive decision, that act by which the whole photograph sacrifices its autonomy, its own language (*langue*),[5] in order to contribute to the formation of a more inclusive, more experientially and sensorily complex miscellany (*langage*).

4. *Structure of argument*

Chapter One ('Styles and Margins') begins in biography, with Apollinaire's wartime correspondence with Madeleine Pagès and the significance of the photograph in that epistolary exchange. The chapter's initial destination is the poem 'Photographie', in its two versions, the first sent to Madeleine in October 1915, the other appearing in *Calligrammes*. The issues raised by the translation of these two versions revolve around the capturing of different visual styles (Pictorialist/Symbolist and Cubist) and the expressive manipulation of margins. This latter constitutes the central preoccupation of the chapter's second objective, the translation of another poem addressed to Madeleine, 'Chevaux de frise' (*Calligrammes*). As throughout the book, the various translations offered include renderings which incorporate photographic fragments as a way of adding expressive density or complexity to the translated text, or of extending its experiential reach. If this first chapter sets out to show that photography is not only able to act in counterpoint to textual margins but also to explore the margins of reading, the textual incorporation of marginalia is part of the enquiry undertaken in Chapter Two.

This second chapter ('Choices, Variants and Variation') argues that translation should be a process of continuous variation and becoming, which slips outside the mechanisms of choice, variant and intertext into those of metamorphosis and resists meaning in the interests of sense. These ideas are developed in translations of Apollinaire's 'Marizibill' (*Alcools*) and 'Annie' (*Alcools*). In the photographic versions of these texts, the Benjaminian issue of 'aura' is examined in relation to Impressionism and the photographic fragment ('Marizibill'), and the expressive significance of contact-sheet photographs is integrated into the play of textual ambiguities ('Annie'). The final excursion into the chapter's principal themes is provided by a short sequence of versions of 'La Nuit d'avril 1915' (*Calligrammes*). Throughout the chapter, the writings of Deleuze and Guattari act as points of reference and elucidation.

Chapter Three ('The Linear and the Tabular') examines the ways in which the principle of metamorphosis makes its peace with the principle of montage, principally through translation's transformation of the linear into the tabular. Apollinaire's cultivation of montage has much to do with the dis-assigning and redistribution of consciousness, an underlying modernist concern which manifests itself in, among other things, the fascination, shared by his contemporaries, with alternative geometries and the fourth dimension. Apollinaire's own vision of the fourth dimension is not always easy to determine, but we attempt to incorporate the multi-dimensional in translations of 'La Porte' (*Alcools*) and the *poème-conversation* 'Lundi rue Christine' (*Calligrammes*). It is not only the tabular which promises the reconciliation of the metamorphic and the montaged, the cinema does too, and the versions of 'Lundi rue Christine' engage with the cinema of Dziga Vertov and his theory of intervals. The photographic accounts of these two poems also address the notion of the disembodied consciousness (the acousmatic) and exercise a problematics of looking. The chapter closes with a final example of the tabular's capacity to negotiate between metamorphosis and montage in a photographic translation of Apollinaire's single-line poem 'Chantre' (*Alcools*). A separate and more methodical case for making the tabular an indispensable translational resource is argued in Appendix II.

As its subtitle 'Frames and Blind Fields' suggests, Chapter Four investigates processes of framing and deframing, in all their variety of guise and significance. The structure which informs the chapter's argument moves from metrico-rhythmic framing in the line, through features of formal framing—rhyme and disposition—which govern the line-group, to the framing which orders a whole poem, a framing which here involves frames within frames (temporal, typographical). The first two of these steps take passages from 'Zone' (*Alcools*) as their subject, while the whole-poem frame is explored through '1909' (*Alcools*). The translations which accompany these steps either seek to maintain the unframings and opening of blind fields that Apollinaire himself engineers, or use translation itself to liberate text into the blind fields of reading experience and extra-textual repercussion, as part of the ongoing 'politics' of the translation of the linear into the tabular. In fact, we might claim that translation *is* the blind field of the ST. Cinematic and photographic framing provides other models, other relationships to the blind field, and these are worked into the argument and into the translations as the chapter proceeds.

Chapter Five is devoted to the production of a translation of 'Les Fenêtres' (*Calligrammes*), Apollinaire's 'tribute' to the 'Windows' paintings (1912) of Robert Delaunay. Pierre Francastel claims that 'Au fond, Apollinaire pas plus que les futuristes ne comprit vraiment la portée des recherches de Delaunay' (Francastel, 1957: 29) [In reality, Apollinaire no more understood the implications of Delaunay's researches than the Futurists]. Delphine Bière-Chauvel declares that 'Le poème *Les Fenêtres* n'est pas une tentative d'illustration des toiles de Delaunay ni une recherche d'équivalence verbale' (2005: 199) [The poem *Les Fenêtres* is not a an attempt to illustrate Delaunay's canvases nor a quest for a verbal equivalent]; but she does concede that the poem lets the reader drift, so as to liberate him/her from meaning and to 'mettre l'accent sur les mots dont les rythmes et les sonorités correspondent à des contrastes presque "simultanés"' (2005: 199–200) [to concentrate on the words whose rhythms and sonorities correspond to almost 'simultaneous' contrasts]. My contention is that, despite his wish to corral Delaunay in the Cubist enterprise, albeit with a distinctive 'Orphism' tag, Apollinaire deeply understood the directions of Delaunay's work, and, in 'Les Fenêtres' successfully found a linguistic homologue for them.

Chapter Six sets out from an interpretative analysis of 'La Victoire' (*Calligrammes*), with its call to tap new linguistic sources in the body, haunted by anxieties though the poem is. The chapter then goes on to consider how the language of translation might renew itself, might become a medium of discovery, and overcome those linguistic features which obstruct our engagement with the perceptually unfamiliar. Part of the solution lies in the diversification of modes of presentation (handwriting and graphism, the tabular). But translations of 'Le Voyageur' (*Alcools*) experiment, too, with new linguistic formations, drawing on Russell Hoban's Riddleyspeak as a point of comparison. A painted and photographic account of the poem is constructed around image-clusters, designed to suggest new morphologies of the image, their elements looking to re-morphologize themselves with other image-clusters. Finally, the chapter turns to translations of 'A travers l'Europe' (*Calligrammes*), a poem dedicated to Marc Chagall. Here the argument explores back-translation, the filtering through each other of different languages, as a way of making the TL strange to itself, particularly in its syntax. The last of these versions is a multilingual back-translation, accompanied by a photographic patchwork which feathers fragments of paintings by Francis Bacon into Chagallian fragments, so that they translate into each other their own very different visions, in seamless metamorphic continuity.

Drawing on Deleuze's *Différence et répétition* (2011; 1st pub. 1968), the Conclusion explores the relationship between difference, diversity, repetition and the notion of representation in the practice of translation. This enquiry is concerned to develop the idea that translation is a projective enterprise, a proposal which has already found its first formulation in this Introduction.

But I should end this Introduction, and at the risk of already repeating myself, with a word of defensive clarification. It might be felt that the approaches to translation and the translational strategies canvassed here are attempts to undo, or at least undermine, that translational practice built on maximal linguistic transparency and transferability between two languages, a practice which established its credentials long ago and which for centuries has proved its worth. I am far from wishing to oust this tradition. But I am anxious to argue that a complementary alternative should be developed, and that principally for three closely related reasons. First, the transparency of the existing translational model is required, is justified, by the assumed monoglottism of its readers; the monoglot reader needs a text which is a reliable and snugly fitting image of the ST. But if the reader is polyglot, if the reader can comfortably read the ST for him/herself, then a transparent translation serves no purpose. What the polyglot reader requires is not something that might act as a surrogate for the ST, but a response to the ST in his/her own language, or rather an enactment of the creative nature of his/her reading of the ST, an enactment of the dynamics and inventiveness of the reading consciousness. This, in turn, makes it possible to imagine that literary translation can be literary not by virtue of transferring the literary features of the ST into the TT but by virtue of creating its own literariness, its own kind of literature, the literariness of the ST re-imagined, the literariness of the reader's experience of the ST. This would then be a literariness *peculiar to translation*; and it would be a literariness born of the associative resourcefulness of the translating reader. And this brings me to my third reason for establishing a 'complementary alternative', a reason with pedagogical implications: if it is possible to argue for a translation which seeks to do justice more to the reader than to the text, then inevitably it is possible to argue that every reader should be a translator, that translation is a natural way to express one's reading, to embody and communicate it. This is an argument I have already made (2012a), and I have tried to show how it might operate with both intralinguistic and interlinguistic translation. Translation is no longer primarily a test of, an exercise of, the translator's linguistic skills and intercultural competences; it is a challenge to the reader's critical-creative resourcefulness, it is the challenge to give textual shape to those associations, memories, hypotheses, fantasies, which standard criticism treats as inadmissible, as impressionistic or anecdotal, as disqualified by their own idiosyncrasy. But our argument is that literary education, indeed that literary criticism, should find a way of admitting and incorporating the experience of reading, not as interpretation but as phenomenology, not as analytical discipline but as responsive experience, as existential engagement. This view further entails the debunking and eradication of that pernicious prejudice, still to be found, alas, in Don Paterson's 'Appendix: Fourteen Notes on the Version' (2006: 73–84) to his translations of Rilke Orpheus sonnets, whereby poets who translate, by virtue of being poets, have special translational dispensations ('the version'), while translators, naturally inhibited (!) by their own linguistic knowledge and their reflex care for various kinds of fidelity, plough their uncreative and dogged furrow, often as groundwork for elaboration by monoglot poets. In our view, reading naturally intends that readers should become writers, through the agency of translation.

1

Styles and Margins

This chapter begins with a story in two parts. The first part takes place between New Year's Day 1915 and 13 October 1915. On 1 January or 2 January 1915,[1] on a train between Nice and Marseille, Apollinaire made the acquaintance of Madeleine Pagès. He was returning to his artillery regiment at Nîmes, having just taken leave of Louise de Coligny-Châtillon[2] on Nice station. Madeleine was on her way back, via Marseille, to her family and her teaching post in Oran. On the train Apollinaire made known to her that he was a poet and offered to send her a copy of *Alcools* (1913); he took her address.

Apollinaire's first letter to Madeleine, an illustrated postcard in fact, was written on 16 April 1915, explaining that he could not send her a copy of *Alcools* after all, because his publisher was away at the war. From the very first letters exchanged, Apollinaire makes Madeleine feel the responsibility of letter-writing, responsible for maintaining the contact at the right temperature and with the right frequency: 'Songez que vous avez pris une responsabilité en me répondant, petite fée … la responsabilité de m'écrire souvent, très souvent. Je vous le demande; bien plus, je l'exige de votre bonne grâce' (3 June 1915) (2005: 53; hereafter just page references are provided). [Bear in mind that you have taken on a responsibility by replying to me, little fairy … the responsibility of writing to me often, very often. I ask you to do it; much more, I demand it of your good grace]. Elsewhere, he has no scruple about taxing her with the brevity, or the relative coolness, of a letter.

Photographs were another way of applying pressure. He first asked Madeleine for a photo in a letter of 11 May 1915. This request was made in the spirit of a medieval knight asking his lady for a favour, in the courtly sense: he would 'wear' the photograph on his left side, the side on which he carried his sabre and revolver, so that 'sur le cœur de votre poète ce portrait pourrait jaser avec des armes et serait ainsi en bonne compagnie' (40) [lying on the heart of your poet this portrait might chatter with arms and would thus keep good company]. As was customary among First World War soldiers in the service of a lady, Apollinaire fashioned for Madeleine an aluminium ring inscribed '1915', from a German 77 shell (28 May 1915),[3] the first of a string of such 'trophies' (other rings, an inkwell, paper knives, a heart, a penholder), and in the same letter sent a small photograph of himself, cut from a larger group (this practice of excision and fragmentation is, of course, central to my own incorporation of photographs). It was on 3 June 1915 that he acknowledged receipt of his first photograph of Madeleine, 'la jolie personne aux yeux profonds au nez mutin' (52) [the pretty person with the deep eyes and impish nose], and on 23 June he received two more, so that he could now describe the three photographs in his possession: in one, Madeleine is seated in an armchair, in another she is at her desk and in the third on a balcony (67). A further photograph is acknowledged in a letter of 25 June.

We often speak of the photographer taking possession of his subject through the photographic act. Handing over one's photograph is correspondingly a surrender of self, principally to language: that is, to gossip, speculation, aspersion, insinuation.[4] At the same time, the photograph keeps a secret, in its muteness, inaccessible to all violations.[5] Conversely, the person who yields the photograph may wish something to be seen; but so weak in intentionality is the photograph that the receiver may choose to see something else, indeed may choose to see what is not visible. At all events, Apollinaire wastes no time in exploiting the photographs sent to him, in three ways: to endow Madeleine with a character, to confirm an obedience and to enjoy a body. On the receipt of the two photographs (23 June 1915), Apollinaire exults as follows:

> Dieu, que ma petite fée est charmante—Je suis bien heureux des deux photos. Le joli joli visage si grave, si sérieusement, si profondément voluptueux. Petite fée, encore encore de vos photos! Que j'aime cette gentille, cette bénévole obéissance de Madeleine! (66)
>
> [God, how charming my little fairy is—I'm very happy with the two photos. The pretty pretty face so serious, so gravely, so deeply voluptuous. Little fairy, more more photos! How I love this kind, this unstinting obedience of Madeleine's].

'Sérieux', 'profond', 'voluptueux', these are the qualities which recur under Apollinaire's pen as the parameters within which Madeleine can develop: 'avec votre air étonné sérieux et impénétrable mais voluptueux à l'extrême' (74–5) [with your surprised serious and impenetrable but extremely voluptuous look]. If Madeleine is to become Apollinaire's desired *épistolière*, she must inhabit familiar paradoxes: while deploying her natural and charming 'pudicité'[6] in relation to the world, she must explore an exquisite and equally charming 'impudicité' as Apollinaire's correspondent; she must learn to master her erotic impatience—Apollinaire will get leave neither soon nor often—and yet, verbally at least, she must give free rein to that impatience. And this regime requires an obedience from Madeleine which Apollinaire harps upon ('ce que j'aime le mieux c'est de vous avoir rencontrée, vous que je cherchais, le cerveau sororal du mien, la plus grande beauté, la plus tendre obéissance attentive' (30 July 1915) (99) [what I like most is having met you, the one I was looking for, the mind which is a sister of mine, the greatest beauty, the tenderest and attentive obedience] and which is guaranteed by the surrender of those hostages, photographs.

The erotic exploitation of photographs begins perhaps with a photograph whose receipt is first acknowledged in a letter of 10 July and which is referred to again in a letter of 12 July—'Vous ne pouvez imaginer le plaisir que m'a causé la petite photo où ma fée chérie en peignoir se balade entre des massifs d'anthémis et de géraniums' (77) [You cannot imagine the pleasure given me by the small photo in which my beloved fairy in a negligee strolls among the clumps of anthemis and geraniums]—and again at the end of a letter of 22 July:

> Maintenant pour finir, je vous aime, j'aime vos cheveux sur le dos, j'aime vos seins que révèle le peignoir, j'aime le front, les yeux, la bouche et tout ce qui est vous, qui est ma Madeleine (91)
>
> [Now to finish, I love you, I love your hair falling down your back, I love your breasts which your negligee reveals, I love the forehead, the eyes, the mouth and all that is you, who are my Madeleine].

One might equally cite, among many others, Apollinaire's reference to a photo received on 8 October 1915:

> Je t'adore ma chérie et baise ta bouche. Je baise aussi tes seins dont la photo d'hier m'a donné l'alliciante presquevision et tes cheveux qui m'ont fait surgir de si troublantes correspondances, exprimées

> par les vers que j'ai cités du poème de Baudelaire: 'Les Promesses d'un visage'.
>
> (9 October 1915) (244)
>
> [I adore you my beloved and kiss your mouth. I kiss your breasts, too, of which yesterday's photo has given me a tempting (?) glimpse and your hair which has summoned up in me such troubling associations, expressed by the lines I quoted from Baudelaire's 'Les Promesses d'un visage'].

The photographs thus become the justification of, and connive with, those modernist versions of the *blason* which are 'Les neuf Portes de ton corps' (21 September 1915), 'Le Deuxième Poème secret' and 'Le Troisième Poème secret' (9 October 1915) or 'Pour Madeleine seule' (13 October 1915) (and the many similar poems addressed to Lou). Apollinaire, studying these photographs with a magnifying glass ('j'épie au moyen de la loupe les mille détails de mon amour...' (211) [I spy on the thousand details of my love with the help of a magnifying glass]), itemizes body parts made beautiful and cohesive by the sheer fact of being possessed by Madeleine, who is herself a putative being at the point of convergence of a string of possessive adjectives. Do the photographs warrant her self being taken for granted, after her voluptuousness has been identified? Evidently, for Apollinaire, the sequence of photographs is a sequence of opportunities to read the same body more clearly, rather than a sequence which makes the self ever more problematic ('Ta photo nouvelle te montre longue comme tu dis et que je ne savais pas encore car tes vêtements de voyage le dissimulaient et tes autres photos ne le montraient pas, surtout l'exquise longueur de ta jambe' (202) [Your new photo shows you tall as you say and that I hadn't realized because your travelling outfit concealed it and your other photos did not make it clear, above all the exquisite length of your legs]).

In view of this precipitate eroticization of Madeleine's image, on the visual evidence of parts of a body all invested with a certain voluptuousness—in the first of the three photographs mentioned in the letter of 23 June 1915, 'le menton' is 'si voluptueux', while in the second 'le nez est voluptueux', and the third shows 'l'air voluptueux de Madeleine' which 'dépasse toute imagination' (67) [exceeds all imagining]—it is surprising to find the poem entitled 'Photographie', sent to Madeleine on 13 October 1915 (255–6), so elusive, so indirect, so ambiguous:[7]

1. Ton sourire m'attire comme pourrait m'attirer une fleur 17 (3 > 3 > 5 > 3 > 3)
2. Photographie tu es le champignon brun de la forêt qu'est sa beauté 19 (4 > 7 > 4 > 4)
3. Les blancs y sont un clair de lune dans un jardin pacifique 16 (2 > 6 > 5 > 3)
4. Plein d'eau vive et de jardiniers endiablés 11 (3 > 5 > 3)
5. Photographie tu es la fumée de l'ardeur qu'est sa beauté 16 (4 > 5 > 3 > 4)
6. Et il y a en toi Photographie des tons alanguis 15 (6 > 4 > 5)
7. On y entend une mélopée 9 (4 > 5)
8. Photographie tu es l'ombre du soleil qu'est sa beauté 15 (4 > 3 > 4 > 4)

We might suggest several reasons for Apollinaire's withdrawal from sensual explicitness to this dignified, oblique and muted treatment. In his poem 'Plainte', sent to Madeleine on 8 October 1915, he had already envisaged Madeleine as an image expressly created to fill his solitude:

Existes-tu, ma Madeleine,

Ou n'est-tu qu'une entité que j'ai créée sans le vouloir

Pour peupler la solitude

Es-tu une de ces déesses comme celles que les Grecs avaient créées pour moins s'ennuyer

Je t'adore, ô ma déesse exquise, même si tu n'es que dans mon imagination

Mais tu existes ô Madeleine, ta beauté est réelle

Je l'adore

Malgré la tristesse de la craie et la brutalité incessante des coups de canon (234)[8]

[Do you exist, my Madeleine,/Or are you no more than a being I created without wishing to/To populate the solitude/Are you one of those goddesses that the Greeks created to diminish their boredom/I adore you, o my exquisite goddess, even if you are only a figment of my imagination/But you exist O Madeleine, your beauty is real/And I adore it/Despite the sadness of the chalk and the incessant brutality of cannon fire].

Apollinaire's ignorance of Madeleine's nudity generalizes itself into a belief, at least, in the reality of her beauty, and it is this that 'Photographie' sets out to capture, not through any physical attributes, but through metaphors from the natural world. Beauty, Apollinaire has also admitted (17 September 1915), is precisely what escapes the camera, because its superlativity is not reducible to what a mechanical device might be able to register. Where elsewhere Apollinaire has allowed that the camera might capture all that is exquisite, fine and perfect in Madeleine, where he has implied that a photograph might at least project a latent Madeleine, he is here careful to make no such claims:

> Certes je ne confonds pas tes photos avec toi-même. Je sais que les photos ne donneront jamais l'image de ta beauté qui est trop parfaite, trop royale trop subtile pour être interprétée par un appareil aussi parfait soit-il.
>
> (17 September 1915) (182)

> [Certainly I do not confuse your photos with the real you. I know that the photos will never give the image of your beauty which is too perfect, too regal too subtle to be interpreted by a machine however perfect].

The poet, it seems, wishes to compensate for photography's shortcomings by managing to encapsulate Madeleine's beauty in a verbal snapshot.

What kind of photography, then, does Apollinaire have in mind in 'Photographie', and what kind of photographer does he wish to be? And that he is now the 'photographer' has its own possible significance: he is now the one who is putting an image into the hands of others, and has set himself the task of creating an inaccessibility, of shaking off those who might want to colonize the poem with salacious suggestion or vicarious possession. In short, Madeleine's body disappears into her beauty. More particularly, we might argue that Apollinaire wants to wrap Madeleine in the 'flou', in a photographic tradition which lacks resolution, which blurs contours, which cultivates continuity of atmospheric space, which diffuses focus, the photographic tradition of the Pictorialists, of photographers such as Robert Demachy and Constant Puyo, the masters of manipulative techniques such as gum bichromate, bromoil, transfer. One reason for my making this proposal is the sense we may derive, from these photos of Madeleine on the terrace, or on the balcony, or, most especially, 'en peignoir [...] entre des massifs d'anthémis et de géraniums', of those women in white, in poses of meditative self-collection, distant but domestic, spirits of the hearth and garden, so dear to Symbolist photographic iconography (in addition to Demachy and Puyo, one thinks of images by Antonin Personnaz, George Seeley, Clarence Hudson White, Paul Burty-Haviland, or, more particularly, of Alvin Langdon Coburn's *The Garden by Moonlight* (c. 1907)).

Mystery inhabits this poem in other ways. Is it about photography or about a photograph? Phrases within the poem could as well refer to an individual image as to the photographic process as a whole (e.g. 'le champignon brun de la forêt' = sepia; the 'mélopée' = monochromaticism; 'l'ombre du soleil' = negative/positive process; and if the 'tons alanguis' are treated as a visual rather than musical reference, then there is a certain languidness, or lack of energy, or drained coloration, in the grey tones). If 'photographie' means 'photograph', is this a single photograph seen several times or several photographs, each heralded by the click of the shutter ('photographie' as onomatopoeia)? If the third-person possessive adjective ('sa beauté') refers to Madeleine, is the second person to be identified as photography/a photograph (what then of 'Ton sourire'?), or are third and second persons one and the same (i.e. photography/a photograph *is* Madeleine, and vice versa), fused in metaphoric identity? If the latter is true, then we are back with a photography and a Madeleine that are equal to each other, or with a Madeleine whose only existence is photographic (let us note that the line-initial tetrasyllabic measure 'Photographie' is three times answered by the line-terminal tetrasyllabic measure 'qu'est sa beauté', as a sustaining refrain).

The very length of the poem's lines may suggest a continuity of atmospheric space, but an atmospheric space which refuses to be framed—the line-lengths create no perceptible scheme—and floats off into an imaginary blind field. The indeterminacy of frame and contour is reinforced by the fact that overall syllabic numbers are more often odd than even, and the lines, when they rhyme, do so only weakly, either by repetition ('beauté') or by *rime pauvre* (/e/) or by assonance ('pacifique/alanguis'). Lack of resolution is also contributed to by the absence of punctuation, which, one might argue, elasticates temporality in the way the 'flou' does in Symbolist photography—punctuation, like sharpness of focus, delivers an image into history, into temporal units and voice-spans carefully measured.

In keeping with this general vision of the poem, my scansion counts mute e's in the traditional way. This gives us the supple, stretching liaisons of the first line:

> Ton souri:/re m'atti:/re comm*e* pourrait/ m'attirer/un*e* fleur

and supplies the softening fade in ll. 3 ('lun*e*'), 7 ('un*e* mélopée') and 8 ('l'ombr*e*'). The rhythmic dynamic derives not so much from the length of individual measures, their repetitions and variations, as from the number of measures per line: all lines beginning 'Photographie' are, in my reading, tetrametric, as is line 3. Across this recurrent figure occurs a gradual reduction of measures, from the relatively dynamic pentametric first line—verbal activity in 'm'attire' and 'pourrait m'attirer', where, elsewhere, the verb is usually a bare copula—to the constative trimetric lines (4 and 6) and finally to the dimetric line 7, a line of the acoustic, of a verb of participation, of a single noun, of doubled phonemes (/ɑ̃/ and /e/). This metric reduction might be likely to produce a soothing deceleration of vocal tempo, as a gesture of compensation. At all events, the final line re-establishes the tetrametric constant.

My own version increases the poem's metaphoric drive: it uses the absence of punctuation to make 'Photo(graphy)' as much a predicate as an apostrophe, and it increases appositional juxtapositions by removing Apollinaire's relative clauses:

PHOTO(GRAPHY)

1. Your smile's spreading lips a flower draw me towards you
2. You are Photo(graphy) the brown forest mushroom her beauty
3. Your pools of white are moonlight in a peace-enduing garden
4. Full of lively water and demon-smitten gardeners
5. You are Photo(graphy) the smoke of her fire her beauty
6. The ear picks out in you Photo(graphy) falls softly dying
7. Wistful lament
8. Photo(graphy) you are the sun's shadow her beauty

These 'syntactic' adjustments produce a poem in which fusion is an effect not of liaisory materials but of substantival insistence and a consequent perceptual disorientation. This disorientation is rhythmic, too. Rhythmic uncertainty is inscribed in the very title—Photo (/x); Photography (x/xx)—and no bearing rhythm declares itself: the fourth line feels principally trochaic, and the third seems to have iambic in mind, but there is no conviction in these impulses, because there is no contextual support. On the other hand, I have tried to parallel the source text's weak rhyme-structure by installing rhythmic echoes across line-endings: the choriamb (/xx/) of 'Wistful lament', for example, can also be heard at the end of line 1 ('me towards you') and in an adonic variation (/xx/x) in lines 2 ('mushroom her beauty'), 6 ('falls softly dying') and 7 ('shadow her beauty'), while lines 3, 4 and 5 end with a tri- or di-trochaic cadence. As far as the distribution of measures is concerned, I have made a tri-phrasal line my standard unit: thus lines 1 (5 > 2 > 5), 2 (6 > 6 > 3), 3 (4 > 3 > 8), 5 (6 > 5 > 3), 6 (6 > 4 > 5), 8 (4 > 6 > 3), the only exceptions being the two-measure line 4 (6 > 7) and the single-measure line 7 (4). One cannot, therefore, speak of a cross-pattern of progressive reduction with the same persuasiveness that one could in the ST, but line 7 is still able to act as a point of dreamy stasis, of aural transfixation in the otherwise self-renewing string of images.

My photographic version of this text (Fig. 1) attempts to capture, in its visual dislocations, something of both the imaginative difficulties of creating physical continuities in memory and the scopophilic fetishization that Apollinaire's correspondence bears witness to. Normally, we do not think of a photograph as something that needs to be put together: it is already there in its entirety. Language is less able to build it up than to unravel it, to enumerate the elements of its achievedness, the *blason*, for reasons we have already adduced: the photograph has a temporal priority over any writing attached to it. And this may indeed perfectly suit the image of Madeleine, of the *givenness* of her beauty. But the fragmented photograph is able to reverse our 'law' of temporal priority and may express the *constructive* processes of memory; or, rather perhaps, it will place the photographic image ambiguously on the cusp between construction and unravelling. But this is where we want the photograph to be, partly because Apollinaire's poetry is a living and undecided process of montage and *démontage*, and partly because translation itself is, in our view, a process of unravelling, of associative proliferation, which makes possible different, coherent journeys back through its constituents.

But the photographic pieces are not there purely to serve either Apollinaire's *modus scribendi* or the spirit of translation; they also belong to the reader, they are part of a readerly response and input. This is true in two senses. The photographs I have cut up and arranged are photographs of photographs; to have cut the originals would have been

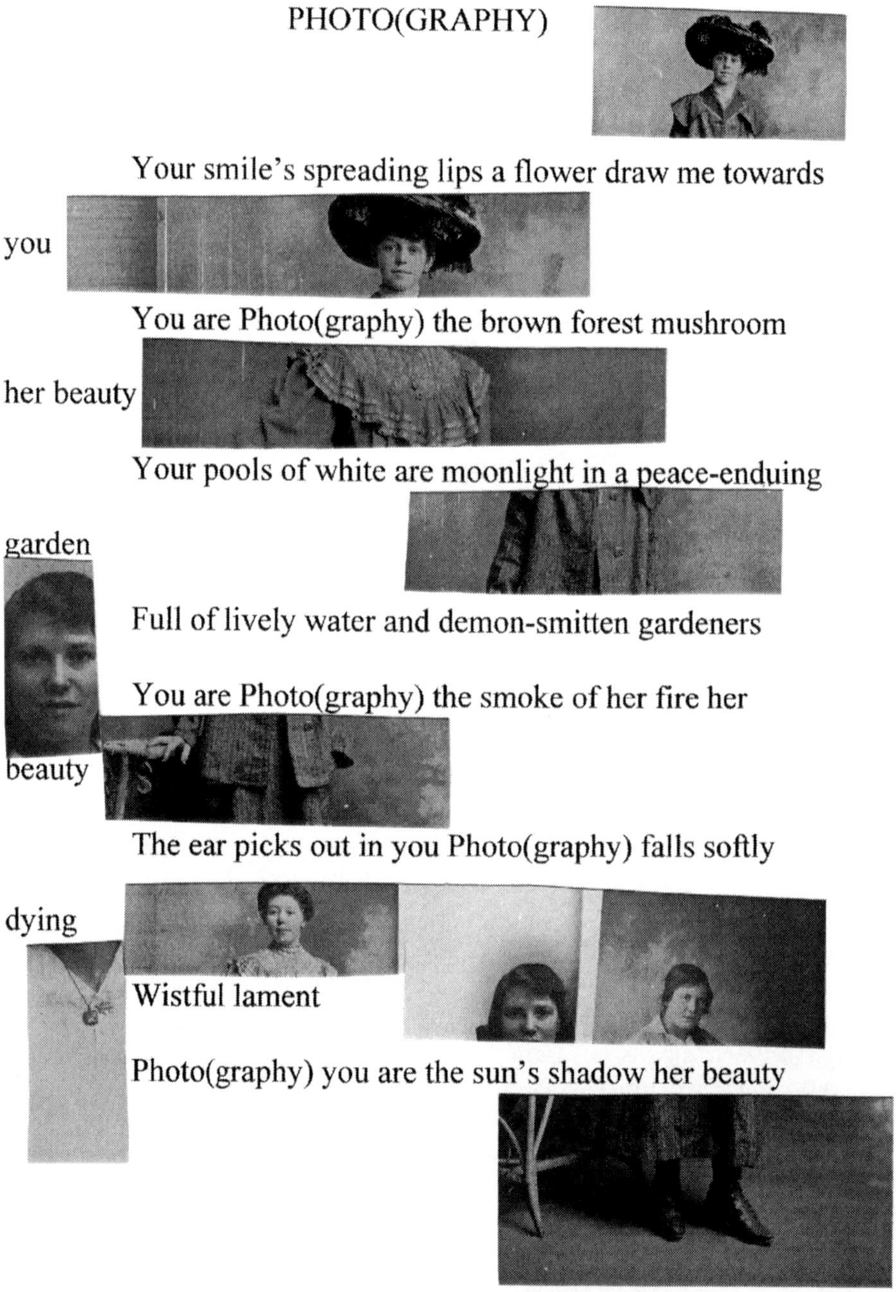

Figure 1: Translation, with photo-collage, of 'Photographie'

a desecration; the wholeness of the photograph spells respect for the image, the sanctity of the duties of memory, the talismanic value of the remembered. These fragmented photographs presuppose whole photographs, originals, and are, so to speak, a desecration to prevent a desecration. They are a necessary desecration precisely because, as readers, we cannot set out from the wholeness of the original, because that would be to accept it as given, to read it off rather than read into it. The text of the poem is an exhortation to fragment the photograph, so that we can come into possession of a text which is not originally our own. And to fragment is not only to scan and construct but also to let other images in.

And, relatedly, the cusp of reconstruction and deconstruction, the cusp between memory and re-fabulation, is the point at which the reader looks back in order to look forward. The photograph is literally scattered, disseminated, multiplied, in its search for other contexts in which it might become imaginatively fruitful. If fragmentation loosens the photograph from the blind field of its taking, it is to make it available to the interferences of collage and the expressive pressures of other blind fields.

One of our tenets for translation is that the source text (ST) should be translated towards performance, so that, among other things, it is reinserted into a vivid here and now as an active intrusion. Thanks to its indexicality, photography might be regarded as a convenient way of investing text with an acute temporality. But what if that temporality is 'anachronistic', what if the images are portraits taken during WWI? Here, fragmentation is a way of updating their presentness, since fragmentation is a performance of the photograph, the incorporation of the photograph into a gestural dynamic, into a particular embodiment of vision. These photographic fragments accommodate themselves to the text, are in counterpoint to the text, polyphonize the text, are played by the text and play the text; what I see as a reader is not just images answering the text but a self-improvising and ongoing conflict of agencies, mute and voluble, repetitious and variable.

* * * * * * * *

The second part of this story begins on 24 November 1915, when Apollinaire announces his transfer to the infantry as a second lieutenant, and ends with the publication of *Calligrammes* in April 1918. The nub of this second part is the gradual attrition of his relationship with Madeleine—his last letter to her is dated 16 September 1916—after he had spent his Christmas leave with her and her family (26 December 1915—10 January 1916). Once he is back with his regiment, the erotic content of the letters decreases, although the expressions of love do not. A variety of reasons for this change can be adduced. Apollinaire himself mentions increased censorship ('On lit tellement les lettres en ce moment que je n'ose plus me livrer à mes épanchements comme avant' [12 February 1916] (426) [At the moment there is so much censoring of letters that I no longer dare surrender to my outpourings as before]) and the new pressures of military existence ('Mon petit amour n'attends en ce moment rien de très amoureux dans mes lettres. Je t'adore, mais n'ai ni loisir ni expression pour l'exprimer' [10 February 1916] (412) [My little love don't expect anything very amorous in my letters at the moment. I adore you but have neither the time nor the words to express it]). And, of course, criticism has suggested that the Madeleine Apollinaire found in Oran was altogether more constrained or inhibited than the epistolary Madeleine he had constructed for himself.[9] But, whatever we suppose, Apollinaire's days in the infantry engendered, with increasing frequency, a mind-set, a fatigue, a dazed empty-headedness, unconducive to erotic fantasy: 'Il me semble que je traîne mes pieds dans la boue des grands chemins depuis un temps infini. Je deviens un automate, sans pensée véritable' (23 February 1916) (435) [I seem to have been dragging my feet through the mud of the highways for ever. I am becoming an automaton, with no real thoughts in my head]. On 18 March 1916 Apollinaire sent Madeleine a barely legible card, in pencil, telling her of his having been wounded by a 150 shell splinter the previous day. Thereafter, there are short communications telling of hospitalization and convalescence, complaining repeatedly of fatigue, expressing continuing affection; the final postcard is dated 9 October 1916.[10]

What is interesting from our photographic point of view is the effect of the replacement of an erotically manipulable image by an image which does not condone fantasy beyond certain limits set by the leave in Oran and by the physical conditions of warfare. A photography that has lost its power to generate fictions of the flesh and future consummations is suddenly restored, one might say 'reduced', to its task of *aide-mémoire*, its talismanic force of pure presence. And, in this guise, the sheer survival of the images (rather than the specificity of what they depict) is what matters. Apparently, some of the images have not been properly fixed—'Pour les photos il y en a qui m'ont dit qu'elles ne sont pas virées demande à Louise Décor car je n'y connais rien' (12 February 1916) (424–6) [As for the photos, I've been told that they are not properly toned ask Louise Décor because I know nothing about these things]—and there had already been ominous signs of this vulnerability even before the Christmas leave: 'J'ai regardé aujourd'hui tes photos. La dernière qui me plaisait tant, s'est entièrement effacée. Les petits ne doivent pas savoir virer leurs photos. C'était arrivé déjà pour la toute première photo' (14 November 1915) (331) [I looked at your photos today. The last one, which gave me so much pleasure, has entirely faded. It must be that the little ones do not know how to tone their photos. It had already happened with the very first photo]. And, bearing in mind the terms of his first request for a photograph (11 May 1915, already quoted), we may find his final reference to photos all the more poignant: the war, and more particularly its weather, have found their way into the last refuge of the cherished image, the tutelary talisman:

> J'aime ton amour, ma chérie ma chérie, tes photos (une de Narbonne et celle où tu avais 18 ans) se sont collées et complètement abîmées dans ma poche ... Je suis assez fatigué en ce moment. Il pleut tout le temps; l'humidité, le froid et [la] perspective de recoucher par terre tout cela n'est guère engageant [...]
>
> (20 February 1916) (432–3)

> [I love your love, my beloved my beloved, your photos (one of Narbonne and the one in which you are 18) have stuck together and been completely ruined in my pocket ... I'm pretty tired at the moment. It never stops raining; the wet, the cold and the prospect of another night on the ground is hardly appealing].

It is perhaps not surprising, then, that when Apollinaire came to revise 'Photographie' for publication in *La Grande Revue* (November 1917) and subsequently in *Calligrammes* (1965, 257), the poem should have undergone a radical transformation, which spirits us from the Pictorialist/Symbolist to the Cubist:

1.	Ton sourire m'attire comme	8 (3 > 3 > 2)
2.	Pourrait m'attirer une fleur	8 (5 > 3)
3.	Photographie tu es le champignon brun	11 (4 > 2 > 5)
4.	De la forêt	4
5.	Qu'est sa beauté	4
6.	Les blancs y sont	4
7.	Un clair de lune	4

8.	Dans un jardin pacifique	7 (4 > 3)
9.	Plein d'eaux vives et de jardiniers endiablés	12 (3 > 6 > 3)
10.	Photographie tu es la fumée de l'ardeur	12 (4 > 2 > 3 > 3)
11.	Qu'est sa beauté	4
12.	Et il y a en toi	6 (4 > 2)
13.	Photographie	4
14.	Des tons alanguis	5 (5/2 > 3?)
15.	On y entend	4
16.	Une mélopée	5
17.	Photographie tu es l'ombre	7 (4 > 3)
18.	Du Soleil	3
19.	Qu'est sa beauté	4

It is not necessary here to rehearse all the critical work that has been done on Apollinaire's Cubism; it is a facet of his poetry which, however variable the manner of identifying and interpreting it, can be taken for granted. The letters to Madeleine themselves give us no privileged access: Cubism is mentioned only twice, and then in general, non-poetic terms (19 November 1915 (341); 5 February 1916 (407–8)). Anyway, it is clear that differences in poetic form, in layout and rhythmic distribution, affect not only the nature and degree of focus but also the framing and 'depth' of the image.[11] While the 1915 version favours a backward-looking, verbally and rhythmically diffused and diffusive style (though the line-lengths are by no means familiar), which expands time and minimizes the dynamism of the image in favour of the unfolding envelope of discourse, the 1917 revision cultivates a nervous, fragmented and improvised treatment, which juxtaposes or combines familiar rhythmic units/lines in alienating configurations. The tetrasyllabic lines, for example, are all on the same margin, but their initially uncontested possession of that margin is soon disputed by lines of six, five, and three syllables, units which are not a perfect fit, which create effects of non-coincident double exposure. Equally, the first margin is shared by two lines of twelve syllables, but also by one of eleven, and the second and third margins each share an octosyllabic line with a heptasyllable. These four margins are all different perspectives on the subject, different modes of discourse, different rhythmic projections. But within each of these margins there are other adjustments, variations, so that our overall impression is of sets of imbrications, of overlapping planes, most of which are interwoven with another. Thus, for example, in the sequence of lines 10–16, lines 12–16 provide the musical metaphor, but aside from the alternating pattern 4.5.4.5. of lines 13–16, there are external and internal rhymes on /i/ ('il', 'y', 'photographie', 'alanguis', 'y') and /ɑ̃/ ('en', 'alanguis', 'entend'). The /e/ ending of 'mélopée', however, takes us both back and forward to 'beauté', which relates to other image fields ('la fumée de l'ardeur', 'l'ombre/Du Soleil'). And rhythmically the 4 > 2 of line 12 echoes the 4 > 2 of the first hemistich of line 10 ('Photographie tu es'), whose own 2 > 3 ('tu es la fumée') is picked up in 'Des tons alanguis' (l. 14). The typographical disposition of the poem as a whole may look like a figure trying to emerge from an encumbrance of masking distortions and slippages of outline—why is it, for example, that the first two lines, which are both octosyllables, are not on the same margin?

The impression of the reorganization of the space of discourse into isolated components treated analytically, into discontinuous, if imbricated, verbal planes, is contributed to by the fate of the e mutes of the original version. While many of these survive, those of 'comme', 'lune' and 'ombre' have become extra-metrical by virtue of being line-terminal. This syllabic demotion, this removal of liaisory function, is above all symbolic: those phonetic elements designed to make the surface of the image more fluid, unbroken, viscous, elusive in outline, are disempowered by the planar structure, the lineation, and become instead markers of the 'femininity' of the line, in a poem in which gender is not apparently a structuring factor, but in which the feminine ('Photographie') is the central player. Thus, while the metaphorical relationship between 'her' and 'photography'—she is the spirit of photography, photography has all her qualities—grows, in the Pictorialist photograph, from the seamless flowing together of adjacent elements, it is explored, in the Cubist poem, by superimposition, by non-coincident frames being laid one over the other, so that one level of perception is dimly visible through another. Correspondingly, while the Pictorialist photograph, by its 'frayed' lack of right-hand justification, implies a blind field of fantasy, erotic, oneiric, spiritual, the Cubist version seems more centripetal, more concerned to construct an autonomous reality, by continually folding referentiality in on itself, by replacing the possibility of a single subjective viewpoint with a multiplicity of viewpoints which do not correspond with each other, and thus oust the viewer, remove a viewing position, but at the same time endow the viewed with a complex and unstable density of being.

My translation of the Cubist 'Photographie' looks to establish the Cubist experience by means which differ from Apollinaire's:

your lips x/
spread in a smile /xx/
draw me /x
a flower x/x
photo(your flower)graphy /xx/x/x
draws your beauty /x/x
brown mushroom of the forest //xxx/x
the white smiles patches x///x
spreading a moonlight /xx/x
in a pacific /xx/x
garden /x
full of white-hemmed water and demon-driven /x///xx/x/x
gardeners /x
photo(lips brown)graphy /xx//x
smoke of burning /x/x
mushrooming beauty /xx/x
garden /x
and in you photo(browning)graphy xx//x/x/x
languid, languishing tones /x/xx/
threnody /xx
photo(enfolding)graphy(slow melody) /xx/x/x//xx
dark-brown shadow dusk-laden forest /x/x/xx/x
of the sun's sunshine xx//x
your (lips spreading x//x
flowers dark /x/
brightness) /x
beauty /x

In this rendering I develop an indication already present in Apollinaire's layout: although his poem has margins, it seems visually to be pushing towards a symmetrical figure with a medial axis. In realizing this tendency, I have removed margins—which also entails the substitution of line-initial lower-case letters for capitals—and thus the principal source of Apollinaire's imbricative system, the planar armature.

Instead, I have resorted to lexical imbrication at the same time as I vary the lexemes' grammatical status. Ultimately this has the effect of ambiguating parts of speech: in line 8, for example, it is difficult to know whether 'smiles' and 'patches' are plural nouns or present-tense verbs; in line 14, 'brown' might be a present-tense verb, a post-posed adjective, a free-standing adjective, or a free-standing noun. I have also ensured a number of rhythmic overlaps, which may occur at the level of either the word (e.g. 'garden', 'brightness', 'beauty'; 'melody', 'threnody', 'mushrooming') or of the phrase (/xx/ or /xx/x: 'spread in a smile', 'photo(your flower)', 'spreading a moonlight', 'in a pacific', 'photo(lips brown)', 'mushrooming beauty', 'languishing tones', 'photo(enfolding)', 'dusk-laden forest'. My version is more clearly than Apollinaire's an analytic Cubist construction, withdrawing towards the centre of the canvas, denying the frame. This denial of the frame—that is to say, denial of the problematic of the relation between the work of art and a reality external to it, which the frame dramatizes—may leave my version too 'conceptual', too self-regarding in its play. But, at the same time, the self-surrender of the reader, which my version might entail, allows perhaps a less inhibited, a less cautious exploration of the expressive layerings of this quiet paean. And while Apollinaire's disposition has a certain calligrammatic legibility—a human figure 'interrupted' by skeins of mist (?)—my medial axis gives the figure at once a more specific, detailed shape and at the same time a greater elusiveness, which it more teasingly challenges the reader to make sense of.

The photographic version (Fig. 2) compels an abandonment of the medial axis, although it may still strike one as a medial-axis poem occasionally knocked out of true by the incursions of photographic image-clusters, so that the overall centripetal gravitation is from time to time frustrated by a centrifugal counterthrust. These image-clusters get no nearer to authentic Cubist visual experience than did, say, Pierre Dubreuil's *Interprétation Picasso: Le Rapide* (1911), or the machine/architectural photos of Paul Strand and Morton Schamberg (see Coke, 1975), or, indeed, those of Albert Renger-Patzsch and László Moholy-Nagy, or the vortographs of Alvin Langdon Coburn (1917), or the polaroid 'joiners' and SLR photocollages (1980s) of David Hockney. But there is a sense in which these image-clusters have Cubist ambitions and a sense in which they do not.

Like Cubism they are intended to capture a process of optical palpation. But they do not ask us to look at a pre-given object—guitar, fruitbowl, newspaper, human figure—as constituted by changing,

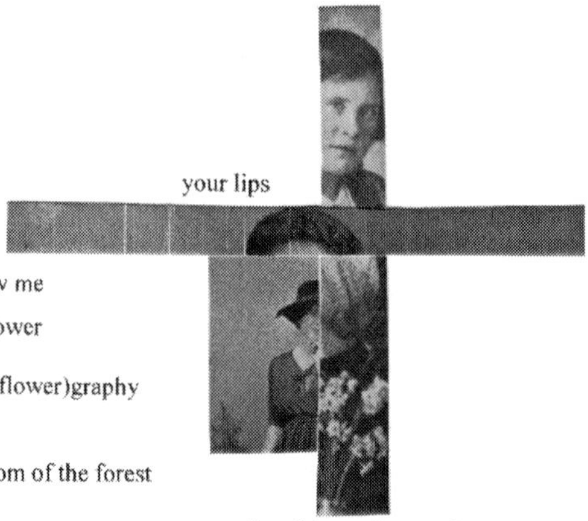

your lips
spread in a smile
draw me
a flower
photo(your flower)graphy
draws your beauty
brown mushroom of the forest
the white smiles patches
spreading a moonlight

in a pacific garden
full of white-hemmed water and demon-driven
gardeners
photo(lips brown)graphy
smoke of burning
mushrooming beauty
garden

and in you photo(browning)graphy
languid, languishing tones
threnody
photo(enfolding)graphy(slow melody)
dark-brown shadow dusk-laden forest
of the sun's sunshine
your (lips spreading
flowers dark
brightness)
beauty

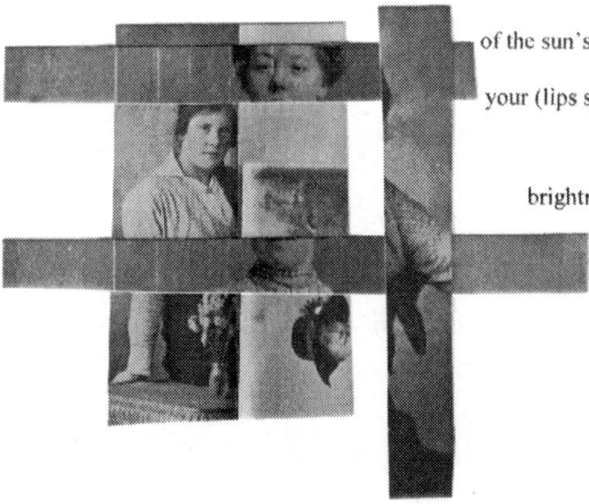

Figure 2: Translation, with photo-collage, of 'Photographie'

overlapping planes and angles of vision, but rather to look at suggestive shapes/configurations as constituted by the planes and angles of vision of an associative and interrupted memory. As the eye scans over and (re-) constructs these visual sculptures, so it re-embodies them in a confusion of visual hallucinations. The shapes themselves are ill-formed, or deformed, structures of the battlefield: 'chevaux-de-frise', crosses, fences, the stepping of trench-walls, a dejected human figure. The Cubist planes and angles are therefore not spatial notations but temporal and affective ones, whose very unsteadiness paradoxically creates, or is created by, the shadowy forms they are called upon to corporealize.

But this semi-Cubist dimension is not the disposition's only sense. War shatters images, images of wholeness, just as surely as it suggests them. Apollinaire struggles to keep his images intact, quite literally, and this poem is precisely a procedure of reconstruction, whose target is the wholeness expressed in the refrain 'Photographie ... sa beauté'. But it is as if the poet has had to withdraw into the photograph itself, into its own terms of reference and metaphors, to achieve this unity. The poem, we might say, is like a visit to the darkroom where the poet can develop and print his own image, decide on degrees of contrast, on whether to dodge or burn in. He observes the image's emergence in the developing bath, in its latencies and actualizations. But I, as translator, remove the image from this refuge and subject it to the contingencies of war, to another space, the battlefield. There, it must contend with the turbulent whirlwind of competing photographic images, with the depredations of the weather and rough handling, with fragmentation. In these circumstances these fragments are likely to become a poignant detritus, bits and pieces blown together in chance accumulations which, derisively, find the rough shapes of the machinery that are responsible for them. The centripetality of the darkroom is invaded by a centrifugal force impatient with the darkroom's self-absorption; war is an ever more extended scattering of ruptured lives, whose number no statistics can do justice to.

Apollinaire's re-disposition of 'Photographie' might look like a gesture designed to remove the poem from Madeleine's constraining influence and restore it to the milieu of avant-garde Paris. And it is certainly not difficult to believe that the path from the Madeleine letters to the publication of *Calligrammes* was a path from a lexicon and imagery flirting dangerously with the cloying and trite, and from a formal practice based on linearity and a properly respected left-hand margin, to something altogether crisper, more abrasive, more inventive and experimental. But such an impression is by no means entirely true. Apollinaire was not afraid to send Madeleine calligrams, even on birch-bark, and many of the poems are maintained in their original form for *Calligrammes*. All in all, he sent fifty-eight poems to Madeleine;[12] of this fifty-eight, thirty-one appeared in *Calligrammes*, and of that thirty-one, twenty-three transfer from the letters to the collection with relatively few revisions. What revisions there are do not seem to pursue any consistent agenda, although there is some systematic removal of references to Madeleine (see 'L'Inscription anglaise', 'Dans l'abri-caverne', 'Chef de section', 'Fusée', 'Il y a'). What one does notice is the textual unsteadiness of these poems: lines are broken into shorter segments; further indentations are introduced; there are shifts between lower and upper case, italic and roman; there is evidence of collage thinking in the occasional reordering of lines, in the ease with which 'versets' and stanzas can be added or omitted (see 'Il y a', 'Fusée', 'Le Vigneron champenois', 'Un oiseau chante', for instance); and Apollinaire's habit of placing asterisks between 'versets' or stanzas—more marked perhaps in his letters to Lou—throws into question structural relationships and ambiguates the degree of autonomy of each of the units concerned.

Despite these observations, critics have plausibly argued that some of the poems sent to Madeleine sacrifice quality to the recipient's conception of poetry.[13] Boschetti (2001: 201) numbers my next subject, 'Chevaux de frise', among a group of poems cultivating the 'verset prosaïque' and epic ambitions, and further finds in it 'les poncifs de la poésie sentimentale et érotique' (2001: 203) [the clichés of sentimental and erotic poetry]. Claude Debon has the same disparaging opinion:

> Aucun poème ne fait davantage sentir l'effort, l'exercice, que 'Chevaux de frise', avec ses images banales, son parfum de cantique des cantiques, ses anaphores [...]
>
> (2004: 134)
>
> [No poem makes one more aware of effort, of exercise, than 'Chevaux de frise', with its banal images, its Song of Songs odour, its anaphora (...)].

In Apollinaire's defence, a case might be made for the archness of his apparent submissiveness, a piquant blend of the bleak, the Biblical and the erotically facile in a love-token poem sent to Madeleine on 18 November 1915. Alternatively, one might regard it as a necessarily (self-) indulgent relief from the muddy, snowy conditions which

Apollinaire has just come through, described in the accompanying letter; in the relative comfort of the battery's new position, the erotic can make a return, as can the floral and ecclesiastical imagery with which, in these letters, it is so often associated.

The task of the translator, faced with the 'Chevaux de frise', might then well be seen as a minimization of the saccharine and the prosaic, without any jeopardization of the poem's lexicon. This may involve some paring down of verbiage, some lightening of syntactic machinery (conjunctions, relative pronouns). But the principal resource to be drawn on will be layout, and more especially the pattern of margins.

In regular verse, we think of margins as indentations, to mark changes in rhyme perhaps and thus spatially to choreograph the rhyme-scheme; or to indicate a shortening of lines, the shift, say, from decasyllables to octosyllables to hexasyllables. It is as if these indentations were given by the text itself, dictated by its innate structure.

As we move to free verse, the source of margin shifts from textual structure to expressive design or enunciatory mode. We might describe the margin as the location of consciousness, the will that drives utterance, a will which, as margins multiply and move inwards, unravels and becomes subject to subconscious pulsions. The view that margins perform different levels of consciousness/subconsciousness exercises the voice, encouraging it to find that flexibility of articulation which allows the speaker to move between the confidently out-loud and the vocal emergence of half-suppressed or surprised materials. The layout of free verse thus becomes a mapping of mentality, whose potential diversity urges the voice to find new dimensions of itself, to cope with different degrees of psychic pressure, different affective impulses, like variations of touch on a piano keyboard.

With the version of 'Photographie' to be found in *Calligrammes*, we made another suggestion: that margins are different (optical) perspectives on a subject, or the instruments of multi-planar organization, to achieve Cubist ends. My translation adopted other means to attain these ends and transformed Apollinaire's margins into radiations from a medial axis designed to underline the centripetal forces at work in the (high-analytic) Cubist art-object. In my translation of 'Chevaux de frise' I want to pursue another agenda: the 'anarchization' of margin, margin as an agent of disorder, of tonal instability, tirelessly recentring experience.

The 1952 edition of *Tendre comme le souvenir* prints 'Chevaux de frise' with four margins (1997: 276–7), as does Campa's 2005 edition

(336–7) but in ways which disagree with the 1952 edition. The printing in *Calligrammes* (1965: 302–3) has seven margins, which I follow in my initial translation (see Appendix I (i) for French text):

Chevaux-de-Frise

In the white nights of November
As the shell-splintered trees
Aged on under the snow
And hardly seemed chevaux-de-frise
Enfolded in rolling waves of barbed wire
My heart revived like a tree in spring
A fruit tree whose blossoms are
                    Flowers of love
In the white nights of November
While the shells intoned their terrible wail
And earth's dead flowers exhaled
                    Their fatal perfumes
I described my love to Madeleine each single day
The snow pins pale blossoms on the trees
        And fleeces the sawhorses with ermine
            You see them everywhere
                Abandoned baleful
                    Dumb horses
        Not Barbary but barbed
            And suddenly I bring them to life
        A herd of pretty piebald horses
Trotting towards you like white breakers
                On the Mediterranean
            They bring you my love
Roselily opanther odoves bluestar
                    OMadeleine
I delight in my love for you
If I think about your eyes I dream of fresh springs
If I think of your mouth roses appear
If I linger in thought on your breasts the Paraclete descends
            Odoubledove of your breast

And loosens my poet's tongue
To tell you again
Iloveyou
Your face is a bunch of flowers
Today I see you not as Panther
But Allflower
And I breathe you in omyAllflower
All the lilies rise up in you like Songs of Songs and of Lightness of Being
And these poems in flight towards you
Carry me to your side
In your comely Orient where the lilies
Change into palm trees whose fair hands
Beckon to me
The rocket unfolds its petals nocturnal flower
When it is dark
And falling scatters them like a rain of lover's tears
Happy tears pricked by joy into flowing
And I love you just as you love me
Madeleine

As one shifts from one translation to the next, from one draft to the next, so one correspondingly shifts from interlingual to intralingual translation, from translation to transcription in a musical sense: a piece for seven margins becomes a piece for, say, fifteen margins, a completely different instrumentation. In re-addressing this translation, I have already tried to diminish some of the sentimentality by resorting to *scriptio continua*, particularly in the apostrophes, as if these elements were to be delivered *sotto voce*. And in contrast to the convention of the leftmost as the first margin (the 'anchor' margin), I want to embed the first margin deeper within the text, so that it can diversify leftwards as well as rightwards, without its becoming a medial axis. Above all, by tireless shifts of margin, I want to capture a prodigal and aperiodic scattering of verbal energy, a dynamic in which forward momentum is constantly distracted by the wayward and self-diversifying, and a nomadism of associations and images in the territory of the page:

Chevaux-de-Frise

In the white
nights of November
As the shell-splintered
trees
aged on under the snow
and hardly seemed chevaux-de-frise
enfolded in rolling
waves of barbed Wire
My heart revived like a tree in spring
a fruit tree whose blossoms
are
Flowers of love

In the white
nights of November
while the shells intoned
their terrible wail
And earth's dead flowers exhaled
their Fatal perfumes
I described my love to Madeleine each
day
The snow pins pale
Blossoms on the trees
and Fleeces
the saWhorses with erMine
You see them everywhere
Abandoned baleful
Dumb horses
Not Barbary but barbed
And suddenly I bring them to
life
a herd of pretty piebald horses
Trotting towards you like
white breakers
On the Mediterranean

They bring you my
love
roselily opanther odoves bluestar
OMadeleine
I delight in my love for
you
If I think about your eyes I dream of Fresh springs
If I think of your mouth
roses appear
If I linger in thought on your breasts the Paraclete descends
Odoubledove of your Breast
and loosens my poet's tongue
To tell you again
IloveyouYour face is
a bunch of flowers
Today I see you not as Panther
But Allflower
and I breathe you in omyAllflower
All the lilies rise up in you like Songs of Songs and of Lightness of Being
and these poems in flight towards you
Carry me to your side
In your comely Orient where the lilies
Change into Palm trees whose
fair hands
Beckon to me
The rocket unfolds its petals
nocturnal flower
When it is dark
and falling
scatters them like a rain of
lover's tears
Happy tears pricked by joy
into Flowing
andIloveyoujustasyouloveme
madeleine

We usually treat margins to the left of the poetic margin as prose margins, used for the overflow of overlong prose *versets*, for example, and here that may help to maintain that hint of the prosaic which beds the poem in the everyday particularities of battlefield writing and epistolary exchange. This impression is perhaps strengthened by our sense of materials from outside the poem's perceptual field or purview demanding admission, insinuating themselves, from the left, into the poem's consciousness. And quite clearly this leftmost margin creates its own vertically moving poem of notations—predominantly noun phrases—a web of floral, nocturnal, marine and chromatic values with an ultimate destination in human response. There are two other such vertical strings; the one is a kind of naïve, verbally minimal toast to the beloved ('each day/everywhere/to life/my love/for you') and the other, which touches the rightmost limit of the page, treats of the transformation of the forbidding and death-giving into the light-spirited and affirmative.

These three vertical sequences constitute three different aspects of the poetic persona, different experiential capacities, a heteroglossia of separated voices. They also form an outer 'stage' for the poem, whose inner stage is occupied by the turmoil of fluctuating margins, incorporating the vertical sequences into their unpredictable progress. The principal margin, now strictly speaking the third, maintains its dominance by its frequency relative to other margins and by its periodic capitalization of initial letters. But this dominance is put under threat by other margins with periodic capitalization and by the play of capitals more generally: as the poem proceeds capitals are decreasingly a sign of structural 'firstness' or of syntactic beginnings and become an autonomous language creating trans-linear connections of their own, which pull the text into other shapes and begin to compose a covert abecedary. At the same time, capitalization remains an apparently arbitrary, intermittent condition, a momentary elevation from lower case, as words, or indeed parts of words ('saWhorses', 'erMine'), fleetingly accede to proper, as opposed to common, status, and thereby draw attention not to what they here denote or designate, but to other semantic modalities, or other vocabularies, within them. But the reverse route, from proper to common, is also taken: behind Madeleine is to be found Proust's little cake. The exception to this possibility is 'I', the self as shifter, a transferable identity which, unlike other personal pronouns, will not surrender the essential vanity or vainglory of its capital, or right to a certain semantic prestige, unless in 'white', say, or 'while' we faintly hear an imprisoned, enslaved and unnoticed ego. All in all, and to draw on a Deleuze/Guattari terminology, we move from tree-structure taxonomy, distributing utterance in a kind of classificatory tabulation across a series of margins designed to relate meaningfully to each other, towards a rhizomatic vision of margins in which confident taxonomy gives way to a refusal of taxonomy and in which margins are tangled together, misapplied, interchangeable, in a world of moving goalposts and ever-variable orders and series.

Has this experiment achieved what it set out to: an increase in the poem's complexity and elusiveness, with a concomitant decrease in its facility? Does it manage to mitigate, even rebut, Renaud's charge (1969: 418–24) that 'Chevaux de frise' is a short-lived theatrical illusion, kept alive by rhetorical inflation and sleight of imagination, which makes of Madeleine a convenient poetic puppet? Only the reader will be able to judge. But the play with margins has allowed us to variegate consciousness, multiply voice and response to phenomena, make images more tentative and apostrophes more involuntary, less contrived, catch the changing rhythms of attention, the changing degrees of verbal relief (capitalization). At the same time we have been able to exploit two other functions of the multiplied margin: a pointing up of lexical articulation, by dramatizing the encounter between line endings and line beginnings; and the heightening of enunciatory and perceptual relationships between whole segments. Text is a space through which the body makes its way. Where one-margin linearity will tend to make this movement more abstract by deproblematizing the journey from point to point, multiplied margins turn the page into difficult readerly terrain and thus make its materiality obtrusive, obstructive even. Linear verse encourages us to see things in their madeness, so that readings are rehearsals of what is already there, the road from A to B. Multi-margined verse emphasizes reading as traversal, whose value lies in encounter and negotiation rather than in recuperation (not the road from A to B, but all the narratives that happen along the way). Criticism is bad at capturing this experience of picking one's way through a text, this surrender to the unpredictable, the digressive, the distracting. Criticism must see the whole thing at once, the end as well as the beginning. One of the huge benefits of the tabular, as we shall have occasion to reiterate in the course of this book, is that there are no conventions for either writing it or reading it; the art cannot be taught. Instead, each reader must find his/her own way of navigating the word-field, of deciphering its energies and directions, and must activate his/her own resources of paralanguage, both verbal and visual. Unfortunately, this challenge is frequently not risen to, and the dispersed language is quickly, and literally, brought back into line, to linear reading.

As a final gesture, and more particularly as a conclusion to this consideration of the tabular as a dramatization of reading consciousness, as the record of the progressive and arduous inhabitation of a text, I would like to present 'Chevaux-de-Frise' accompanied by a photographic commentary (Figs 3–4), as if the photographs were marginalia, and could not but be marginalia. While the readerly/translatorial imagination transforms the text into a play of consciousness, into the multi-sensory, into a psychosomatics, photographs sit on the edge, the camera apparently disempowered by text, unable to read. And yet the camera *is* able to explore that area of readerly experience whose significance we are happy to acknowledge but do not know how, quantitatively or qualitatively, to capture: the experience of text as a physical object, as a part of a reading environment. How shall I read 'Chevaux-de-Frise'? Wearing corduroy trousers? Sitting on a patio? And in what edition? With the design of the cover, and/or the weight of the paper, and/or the typeface, etc., as points of reference? These points of reference are also points of resistance: how they act on perception, what 'atmosphere' they insinuate, are very difficult to define. Can the camera help me to evaluate this ambient world? One might think not, since it turns depths into surfaces and individual experience into common visual denominators. Some of these partial images present the camera as a thwarted predatory animal: lens, film, lens cap prey on a victim, a text, they do not know how to tackle; the lens, in particular is a puzzled, alien eye, mesmerized by what it cannot fathom. But can the camera do justice at least to the events and contexts of reading? Caught between the machinic and human eye, its sight may run quickly out of focus, may catch the object at an odd angle, may polarize near and far, may give unexpected attention to the peripheral and interstitial, may have an uncanny fixatedness. And if this eye is a psychism, then it may produce the circumstantiality of reading, its accidents and offguard daydreaming stare, its abstracted re-scanning of titles, its adjustments of the page or book, its cross-textual glimpses. James Elkins tells us that '[…] photography also always shows us things we would have preferred not to see, or don't want to see, don't know how to see, or don't know how to acknowledge seeing' (2011: 98). A photography outside the text brings us face to face with an ambient world full of our restiveness, our breakings off from the text, our manipulations of the book, our fussy orderings of the site of reading, the vulnerabilities of our attention. Criticism assumes a reading in which the reader is engrossed by the text, gives to the text an attention which operates at uniform levels, at consistent speeds, with a consistent capacity to register the 'right' kinds of detail. What at first looks like a tracking of the camera's readerly impotence becomes the vindication of the camera as the agent of a searching critique of our assumptions about reading.

It is this transmutation which perhaps justifies the camera's apparent supercession of the text in the final, centered, non-fragmented photographic still life, of the Pléiade edition of Apollinaire's poetry, open at 'Chevaux de frise' and leaning against a kitchen window, through which graduated storage pots and a plant, or bunch of flowers, are visible. The surrounding pebble-dash wall has been roughly patched. This photograph, because not fragmented, has a real environment, temporal and spatial, as its blind field; its indexicality is correspondingly more pressing. Correspondingly, too, the poem, or our potential reading of it, is an element in a particular conjuncture, a particular social setting and a particular life. Accordingly it is not the reader who serves the significance of the poem, lends it a voice, but the reverse: the poem lends itself to the voice of the reader, is an event in that voice, and draws its significance from its position or role in a life. How does 'Chevaux de frise', in this particular edition, relate to storage pots, to the sunlight of a certain afternoon, to the reader's familiarity with a certain kitchen, or patched wall? How are we to find an account of a text which does true justice to both its inwardness and its outwardness, to both the absorption in reading and the peripheral, or distracted, or interrupted extensions of reading, if not by giving both the text *and* its extra-textual margins, both the text as the door to an other-side of reality *and* the photograph as the ineradicable this-side of the text, no less fully inhabited by the reader. If translation sets out to do justice to the reader rather than the text, to readerly experience rather than to linguistic meaning, then it must develop those kinds of 'language' capable of suggesting the perceptual totality of that experience. And any doubts we might have about the centrality of that task would be dissipated were we merely to revisit the first paragraph of Proust's 'Journées de lecture' (1971: 160) or his account of Marcel's reading in the garden at Combray, where he lovingly traces 'du dedans au dehors les états simultanément juxtaposés dans ma conscience' (1987: 86) [from the inside to the outside these states simultaneously juxtaposed in my consciousness (2003: 89)].

Chevaux-de-Frise

In the white
nights of November
As the shell-splintered
trees
aged on under the snow
and hardly seemed chevaux-de-frise
enfolded in rolling
waves of barbed Wire
My heart revived like a tree in spring
a fruit tree whose blossoms
are
Flowers of love

In the white
nights of November
while the shells intoned
their terrible wail
And earth's dead flowers exhaled
their Fatal perfumes

I described my love to Madeleine each
day

The snow pins pale
Blossoms on the trees
and Fleeces
the saWhorses with erMine
You see them everywhere
Abandoned baleful

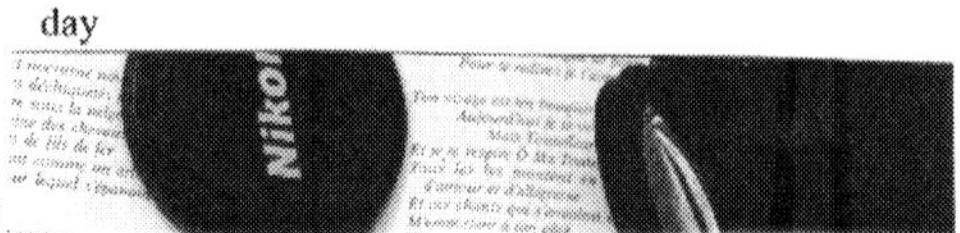

Dumb horses
Not Barbary but barbed
And suddenly I bring them to
life

a herd of pretty piebald horses
Trotting towards you like
white breakers
On the Mediterranean
They bring you my
love

roselily opanther odoves bluestar
OMadeleine
I delight in my love for
you

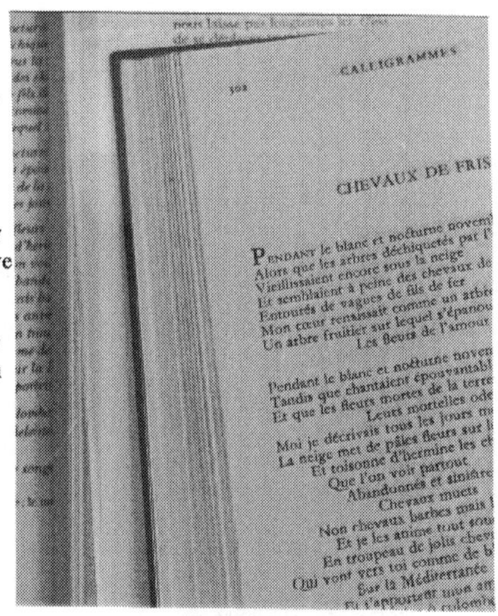

Figure 3: Translation, with photo-collage, of 'Chevaux de frise'

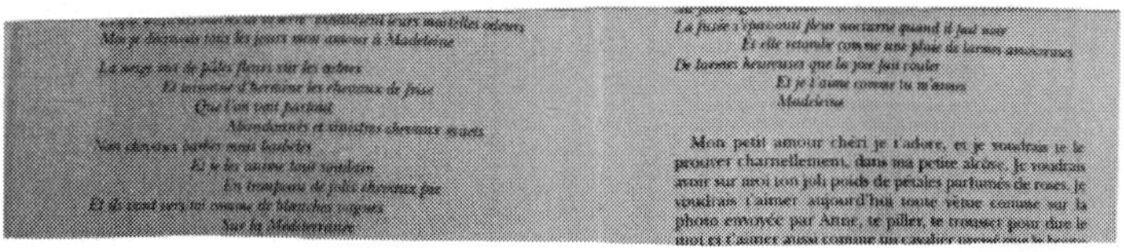

If I think about your eyes I dream of Fresh springs
If I think of your mouth
roses appear
If I linger in thought on your breasts the Paraclete descends
Odoubledove of your Breast
and loosens my poet's tongue
To tell you again
IloveyouYour face is
a bunch of flowers
Today I see you not as Panther
But Allflower
and I breathe you in omyAllflower
All the lilies rise up in you like Songs of Songs and of Lightness of
Being
and these poems in flight towards you
Carry me to your side
In your comely Orient where the lilies
Change into Palm trees whose
fair hands
Beckon to me
The rocket unfolds its petals
nocturnal flower
When it is dark
and falling
scatters them like a rain of
lover's tears
Happy tears pricked by joy
into Flowing
andIloveyoujustasyouloveme
madeleine

Figure 4: Translation, with photo-collage, of 'Chevaux de frise'

2

Choices, Variants and Variation

For Pierre Garnier, one of the crucial watchwords of 'spatialist' verse is: 'Le processus de création du poème est devenu le poème lui-même' (1968: 144) [The process of the poem's creation has become the poem itself]. Neither complete nor incomplete, the text is caught up, along with both writer and reader, in a state of perpetual movement and becoming. This chapter explores what we might mean by translation's being a process of creation rather than a product (the fairest of fair copies), using as its point of departure the proposition that translation translates the ST into a draft, an *avant-texte*, and that it can do this only by offering an alternative to the exercise of choice and decision-making which seem to be at the very centre of the translational enterprise.

As a first step we have to imagine a text, the source text (ST), as something living *into* its own multiplicity and undecidability. The ST does not already have this multiplicity; it is invested with a multiplicity by its reader/translator, and this in turn generates an increasing undecidability. Some version may indeed be put down on paper, but one might think of this as a *pis-aller*, an unwanted actualization and immobilization of the pure morphing of spontaneous linguistic invention. But the translator has two ways of outwitting this move to immobilize: by multiplying translations themselves, or by producing a kind of translation—and this indeed is a literariness specific to translation—whose materials and techniques keep, or set, the text in motion, make the text *textually proliferative*. Multilingualism (*langage*) is one of the agents of this proliferative form of textual being. Tabular, rather than linear, disposition is another. A text must become rather than mean; must produce sense rather than have a sense; must find its way out of the mechanisms of choice. We must try, then, to capture translation as an intrinsic and never-ending process, as a certain way of being with a text and with language, as a certain way of translating the language of the text (*langue*), not into another language (*langue*), but into *langage*, into the very processes of thinking language, thinking across languages and testing linguistic boundaries. Much of what we propose will have affinities with Deleuze/Guattari positions; but I should say from the outset that while Deleuze conceives of style, or the minoritarian (transgressive and subversive), as a language *within* the national language,[1] I imagine translation as the consumption or digestion of the national language by a linguistic Being which far exceeds it.

Let us suppose that the literary, as an attributed value, is the excess of the signifier over the signified: the signifier has an excess of acousticity, graphicity, expressivity, sense, fictionality, paralinguisticity in relation to any meaning ascribed to it. Addresser and putative addressee become locked in a relation of reciprocal improvisation of which a textual event, the ST, acts as a trigger. In other circumstances, the addressee tries to understand (drawing on his own (literary) competences) what the addresser means to say. In our case, however, communication is not what is at stake; what is at stake is the operation of language in a particular textual arrangement. Reciprocal competence is replaced by a rather aleatory exercise of reciprocal intuitions and associations. In circumstances such as these, it would simply be misguided for the translator to regard himself as the interpreter of the ST, as the one who mediates the ST's comprehensibility to the reader. My argument will be, in part, that it is the translator's task to maintain, or indeed increase, the innate incomprehensibility of the ST; the translator should not be subject to the apparent truism 'one cannot translate what one does not understand', simply because the translator's task is to deflect the reader from the effort to understand towards the effort to produce sense. The repositioning of translation envisaged here entails the establishing of links between translation studies and both genetic and textual criticism (for a valuable overview, see Greetham, 1999), links hitherto regrettably neglected.

But this transformation of ST into *avant-texte* has other, related consequences, equally crucial. It 'unfinishes' the ST, multiplies its possibilities of becoming, by introducing into it the passage of time. If the Impressionist painting always seems unfinished, whatever the facts of the matter, it is because time is factored into the painting, is made visible in the gestures of the brush; in the Impressionist painting, as in the *avant-texte*, are inscribed the ongoing movements of perceptual consciousness. We tend to read *avant-textes* in the perspective of the definitive text, as steps in a certain teleology. But constructing causes and effects is a retrospective activity. At the time of the *avant-texte* itself, the definitive text was not in view and might never have emerged. If the translator speculatively imagines the ST's own *avant-textes*, then the ST is no longer predicted, no longer has its own realization particularly in view. If, alternatively, the translator treats the ST as an *avant-texte*, then it is by no means evident what form the target text (TT), either as a text or another *avant-texte*, should take. Behind every manuscript there lurks any number of other, lost manuscripts, and any number of unrecorded hours of mental activity. A text is always what it might be or what it might have been.

What underlies this line of argument is the assumption that translation is not an act of preservation (of a definitive text), nor an act of recall (of a text that inevitably belongs to the past), but an act of forward propulsion and of reimagination. And it is in pursuit of these convictions that I would like to offer a first version of Apollinaire's 'Marizibill' (Fig. 5; see Appendix I (ii) for French text).

I have explored the potential significance of handwriting for translation elsewhere (2012a; 2012b), but would mention here two particular effects. First, handwriting helps to blur the line between what is properly textual and what is marginal (the 'shift right' bracket around the final stanza is a threat to demote that to the margins). The marginal, in textual work, is the space of ongoing reflection, of unpremeditated response, of metadiscourse pressing to be discourse, of unworked possibility. It is what feeds the ephemerality of associative thinking back into the text. Secondly, handwriting makes less certain where we are in the order of things, where we are in textual time. Are these scribblings post-textual or pre-textual? What is certain is that handwriting inscribes in the text its own temporal passage, its own contingency, its own improvisatory nature, its own inhabitation of an unfolding here and now. And it is handwriting, in this rendering, that is the principal motor of linguistic variation; the hand is itself the reactive-creative process, spinning out the associative lines, variants, thought about textual presentation—in short, expanding the *sense* of the text.

Here we should begin to make distinctions, because some of the associative lines are lines of potential replacements (variants) (e.g. shady, zwielichtig, sordid, malfamed), while others are slippages into other lines of thought and cannot be thought of as replacements (e.g. eau de, ô de, Öde, oh dear, aquavit, aqua vitae). The latter might seem to condone receptive anarchy, but anarchy is an inappropriate

MARIZIBILL

in the Hohe-Straße

in Köln (ô de, Öde)

pé

ripat enne ellefaisait

étici le trottoir

EAch

Evening not one to say no

a real poppet

and when shE'd had enough

of her bEAt

shE'd drink –

a night owl

in sEEdy bars

she clEAned herself out

for a pimp

pink-faced

ginger-haired

A garlic-scented Jew who'd

shanghaied her from a brothel in Shanghai

starboard home

from

Formosa

I know types of every ilk
Who can't quite match
What they might be
Shiftless, unfixed, like dead leaves
Their eyes are dying embers
Not quite out, their hearts
As restive as their unclosed doors

Figure 5: Translation, with handwritten comments, of 'Marizibill'

concept for two reasons: (a) because while a text may, through, say, its formal characteristics, indicate what it deems to be areas of appropriate attention, there can be no prescriptions about what kind of attention a reader brings to what textual details; in my translation I have picked out the /i:/ repetitions, but I might equally have singled out the oscillation between /p/ and its voiced partner /b/, or the insistent /I/, or any relation between sounds; the only sound principle for reading is to read in such a way that the text is maximally fruitful; (b) because readerly reception, by its multifariousness rather than anarchy, expresses the text's possession of sense but not of comprehensibility; the reader enriches the text in ways that the text cannot predict. The ST willy-nilly travels beyond its own comprehension of itself; as it travels through time, it becomes constantly discrepant with itself and it is this discrepancy that the translator translates. In 1912, Apollinaire's 'Marizibill' did not know what space and time it would traverse; it has encountered the poetries which post-date it and by which the world has been variously re-imagined, and which are an inextirpable part of the translator's consciousness.

An equally potent source of linguistic variation is, of course, intertextuality. Intertextuality denotes the textual traffic into and out of a text. Intertextuality belongs primarily to a postmodernist vision of the unowned text, of the kaleidoscopic nature of the literary, and thrives on the linguistically permutable. There is no independence for the literary text, however self-reflexive its ambitions. Intertextuality is part of the excess of the signifier, and is another point at which the author hands over authority to the reader. Translation is inevitably intertextual by generical condition, standing as it does at the crossroads between plagiarism, citation, pastiche, parody, imitation, adaptation. Intertextuality is part of the very dynamic of translation, the hearing of voices across languages, the hallucinations of heteroglossia. Within this dynamic, the ST is not a *terminus ad quem*, but a *terminus a quo*: the intertexts we find in the ST, in our translation of the ST may well postdate it. Thus, the voices I hear in Apollinaire's 'Marizibill' are those of Brassaï ('péripatéticienne'), a Lancôme ad ('ô de'), Wagner through Eliot ('Öde'), Eliot ('seedy bars'—'sawdust restaurants' and 'one-night cheap hotels' are just around the corner), Verlaine and John Donne ('shiftless, unfixed, like dead leaves'). Translation restores the ST to the flow of time, but time itself becomes multi-dimensional, or a cluster of competing temporalities.

As we see, the sources of linguistic permutation are manifold. It may spring from cross-language synonymies, from paronomasia (ô de,

Öde, oh dear), from new morphological segmentations (pé/ripat/étici/enne), from old etymologies (poppet < puppet). And with this materiality re-awakened, the tabular page is more likely not only to make real the incursions into the text of the paralinguistic (tone, pausing, tempo, intonation, degree of stress, etc.) but also to encourage experimentations with the voice, the recovery of vocality/orality as geno-textual interferences and eruptions. 'Glossolalia' catches the perfect paradox of translation: in religion, it is the gift of tongues, the manifestation of the Holy Ghost, the *properly* incomprehensible text; in psychiatry, it is a pathological babbling in a non-existent language. This is the gamble taken by the tabular text which restores to language its full materiality.

If we then think continuous variation along *another* axis—along the axis, that is, not of language, but of paralanguage (tone, intonation, tempo, loudness, pausing, relative emphasis, etc.)—we open up another infinity, not a lexemic infinity, but an infinity of vocal effects, most of which can achieve an enunciatory reality, but some of which remain stubbornly infra-vocal or ultra-vocal. Translation is as much about performance values as it is about textual ones. Put another way, we have to activate the languages of textual presentation just as much as national languages, we have to exploit the multilingualism of typefaces, font sizes, typographic layouts, margins, punctuation, diacritical marks, which are, in their turn, all parts of the medium *langage*.

We then have three choice-mechanisms: (a) first-order creation: variant, which belongs to the ST. Variants are private. Variants are a chronological series of self-superseding steps, a temporal progression that arrives at a place, the definitive text. Variants establish textual history, during which the text was subject to the pressures of time, the need to produce a version for publication, to revise for further publication, and so on. After these initial pressures, the text enjoys temporal invulnerability. (b) second-order creation: choice which belongs to the TT. Choices are imaginable as surface-structural transformations of the deep-structural 'meaning' of the foreign lexeme or syntagm. Choice is public and manifest. Choices occur in suspended time; they are not attempts to establish a temporality or a creative route. The supposed simultaneity of choices presupposes a different kind of disposition, one which maps options in spatial relationships of proximity and distance. (c) both first-order and second-order creation: intertextuality, which belongs both to the ST and to the TT. Other texts that the ST may be deemed to activate. Other texts which the translator associates both with the ST and with the unfolding TT. Intertexts, therefore, may be allusions or quotations within the text or may inhabit the text's blind field, if they are a non-actualized part of the reading consciousness. All texts are metonymies of a potentially inexhaustible stock of intertexts.

We are looking for an attitude to textual variation which has something of all these mechanisms: a set of variations which have the temporality of variants, but the cumulative simultaneity of choice; a set of variations none of which, by very virtue of being thought, can be excluded; a set of variations which, because of their unforeseeability, have no teleology; a set of variations which mix variant and intertext on the same level of activity (no distinction between first-order and second-order creation); a set of variations which allow marginalia to become text, blind field to enter the picture, and vice versa. But, above all, while choice offers only what *langue* makes available, our variations draw on *langage*. While choice offers an array of alternative resources, our variations are a delirium of language, a path of experience, not, as with choice, the object of critical judgement, but the vitalistic flow of the phenomenology of reading. The model for this version of translation might be found in the story by Borges, so dear to Deleuze, 'The Garden of Forked Paths', the title of a novel written by the Chinese sage Ts'ui Pen and described thus by the Sinologist Stephen Albert to Ts'ui Pen's great-grandson:

> In all fictions, each time a man meets diverse alternatives he chooses one and eliminates the others; in the work of the virtually impossible-to-disentangle Ts'ui Pen, the character chooses—simultaneously—all of them. *He creates*, thereby, 'several futures', several *times*, which themselves proliferate and fork (2000: 83).

Four further observations should be made about this proliferating series of variations. First, they are the becoming, in time, of the ST. They take the ST deeper into *langage*, into the multilingual, and thus take the TT further to the edges of the target language (TL)—that is to say, to the edges, and beyond, of the particular historical conjuncture that obtains in the TL at the moment of translation, and to the edges and beyond of the particular *episteme*, the particular body of knowledge and belief, embodied in the TL at that same moment. Translation must aim to be a destabilizing intervention in a status quo. Secondly, the entertaining of paradigmatic variations of the kind we are envisaging belongs peculiarly to the reading of the written rather than to the listening to of the spoken: this is an elaboration of text that needs time, even though it may occur spontaneously. It tends to be an activity peculiar to the reader/translator (rather than the writer), because the reader is not bound by the desire to say, or by the intention to mean, but simply by the freedom to respond. Thirdly, Jakobson relates the paradigmatic (the axis of selection or similarity) to the metaphoric in his essay on aphasia 'Two Aspects of Language and Two Types of Aphasic Disturbances' (1956: 76–82); but metaphor represents jump-thinking (getting from A across to B, across a distance); I would relate this paradigmatic elaboration not to processes of substitution but to metamorphosis, another manifestation of morph thinking (sliding from A to B). Metaphor preserves territories in order to give its jumps their intensity; metamorphosis deterritorializes, or annexes territories into its own continuum. Metaphor, the juxtaposition, let us say, of ST and TT, depends on its elements signifying, on its ability to create collisions and unisons of signification. Metamorphosis, on the other hand, refuses to mean, in favour of an infinite process of making, expanding and projecting sense. The opposition between metaphor and metamorphosis is briefly developed by Deleuze and Guattari in their work on Kafka; for them metamorphosis dissolves barriers and hierarchies, is rhizomatic and the best example of 'un *usage intensif* asignifiant de la langue' (1975: 41) [intensive, non-signifying use of language (1986: 22)]. Thus, as I proceed through transmutations, I increase the pointlessness of asking which word is the right one; the number of possibilities comes to exceed the ostensible requirements of the text. I increasingly let the spray of sense supersede the particular needs of meaning. Fourthly, and consequently, we are pursuing a view of language (*langage*) that aligns itself with the Deleuze/Guattari view of language as 'variation continue' (1980: 119) [continuous variation (1988: 94)]; and, as they point out, our espousal of this view manifests itself not in choices and exclusions but rather in the encompassment of an ensemble of potentialities:

> [...] l'ensemble des énoncés se trouve présent dans l'effectuation de l'un d'eux, si bien que la ligne de variation est virtuelle, c'est-à-dire réelle sans être actuelle, continue par là même et quels que soient les sauts de l'énoncé. Mettre en variation continue, ce sera faire passer l'énoncé par toutes les variables, phonologiques, syntaxiques, sémantiques, prosodiques, qui peuvent l'affecter dans le plus court moment de temps (le plus petit intervalle)
>
> (1980: 119)

> [[...] all of the statements are present in the effectuation of one among them, so that the line of variation is virtual, in other words, real without being actual, and consequently continuous regardless of the leaps the statement makes. To place the statement

> in continuous variation is to send it through all the prosodic, semantic, syntactical, and phonological variables that can affect it in the shortest moment of time (the smallest interval) (1988: 94)].

When we say that linguistic variations, virtualities, exceed the ostensible requirements of meaning, we must go carefully: these variations are not a disposable, dispensable surplus, products of a sub-Joycean game played beyond the necessary. These variations are *constitutive* of the language of translation inasmuch as it is *langage*, a mooted but as yet undefined totality of all languages. Language is in a constant process of constituting itself; it is not chosen from. Translation, accordingly, is not a series of choices made from a given repertoire, but the making of language as the act of producing the sense of the ST; or, put another way, the passage through the constituents of language as the very act of language's constitution:

> Il y a des mots de passe sous les mots d'ordre. Des mots qui seraient comme de passage, des composantes de passage, tandis que les mots d'ordre marquent des arrêts, des compositions stratifiées, organisées. La même chose, le même mot, a sans doute cette double nature: il faut extraire l'une de l'autre—transformer les compositions d'ordre en composantes de passages
>
> (Deleuze and Guattari, 1980: 139)
>
> [There are pass-words beneath order-words. Words that pass, words that are components of passage, whereas order-words mark stoppages or organized, stratified compositions. A single thing or word undoubtedly has this twofold nature: it is necessary to extract one from the other—to transform the compositions of order into components of passage (Deleuze and Guattari, 1988: 110)].

The last sentence of this quotation might act as a definition of translations: to translate the potential coercions of the ST, the coercions to choose right ('mots d'ordre'), into the constant slide of linguistic transition ('mots de passe'). We do not choose between options, we pass through them, in our becoming. Put another way, we cannot make choices (a) because of the principle of linguistic proliferation and (b) because of the principle of continuous interactive modification among the elements of the proliferation.

So, correspondingly, we must be careful not to identify this multiplication of options with a sequence of alternatives: A *or* B *or* C *or* D; that is precisely the process of choice. The metamorphic series governed by 'and'—A *and* B *and* C—is a series in which each item changes the sense of all the others by forging unavoidable relationships. Choice may be arrived at by a process of relating, of comparing, but the implementation of choice seems to spell the dispensability of relationship, the exclusion of others, the release of a particular word into its own autonomy, into the identity of its meaning. Maintaining the 'and' of reciprocal relationship changes the way in which words matter, or make sense; and sense thus formed is not something we can tie down or possess; it envelops us and we inhabit it.

Photographic presence in text perhaps makes it easier to understand what sense is: not meaning, but an associative irradiation of text. My photographic version of Apollinaire's 'Marizibill' (*Alcools*, 1913) (Figs 6–7) is made up of photographs taken in Norwich and Bristol and is to a degree thematized—passing women, hair, feet, chairs, signs. It may seem that I create sense through particular proliferative series; and certainly I do: these images have sources in my experience (memory, association, fantasy, the personal unconscious); they are hallucinations, less inventions than inescapable resonances. But sense quickly supersedes any individuated genesis. Sense is a world of available and potential experience which a particular utterance might be said to generate and in which that same utterance comes to participate; in other words, an utterance produces a sense which, by virtue of its readers, is larger than it can then absorb or actualize. TTs record that proliferation of sense, and write it back into the ST.

At this point we need to return to our reflections about the photographic cut initiated in the Introduction, the cutting of the image which goes hand in hand with the textual cuts introduced by tabular dispositions (cuts between words, within words, between typefaces, and so on). The photographic cut opposes itself to formal edges (the frame in its many manifestations) and in so doing minoritizes the photograph in a Deleuze/Guattari sense, because it undoes, or at least obstructs, the photograph's drift towards a semiotic, the achievement of codability. That semiotic is, for the photograph, put in place by a 'standard rectangularity', which is the first step in the act of framing. This frame establishes the signifying connections between masking frame and blind field, viewfinder frame and composition, and between wholeness of image and completeness of memory, confirmation of identity and value as keepsake. This wholeness or integrity of the photograph (standard rectangular size) also establishes the right to authorship and the image's self-sufficiency.

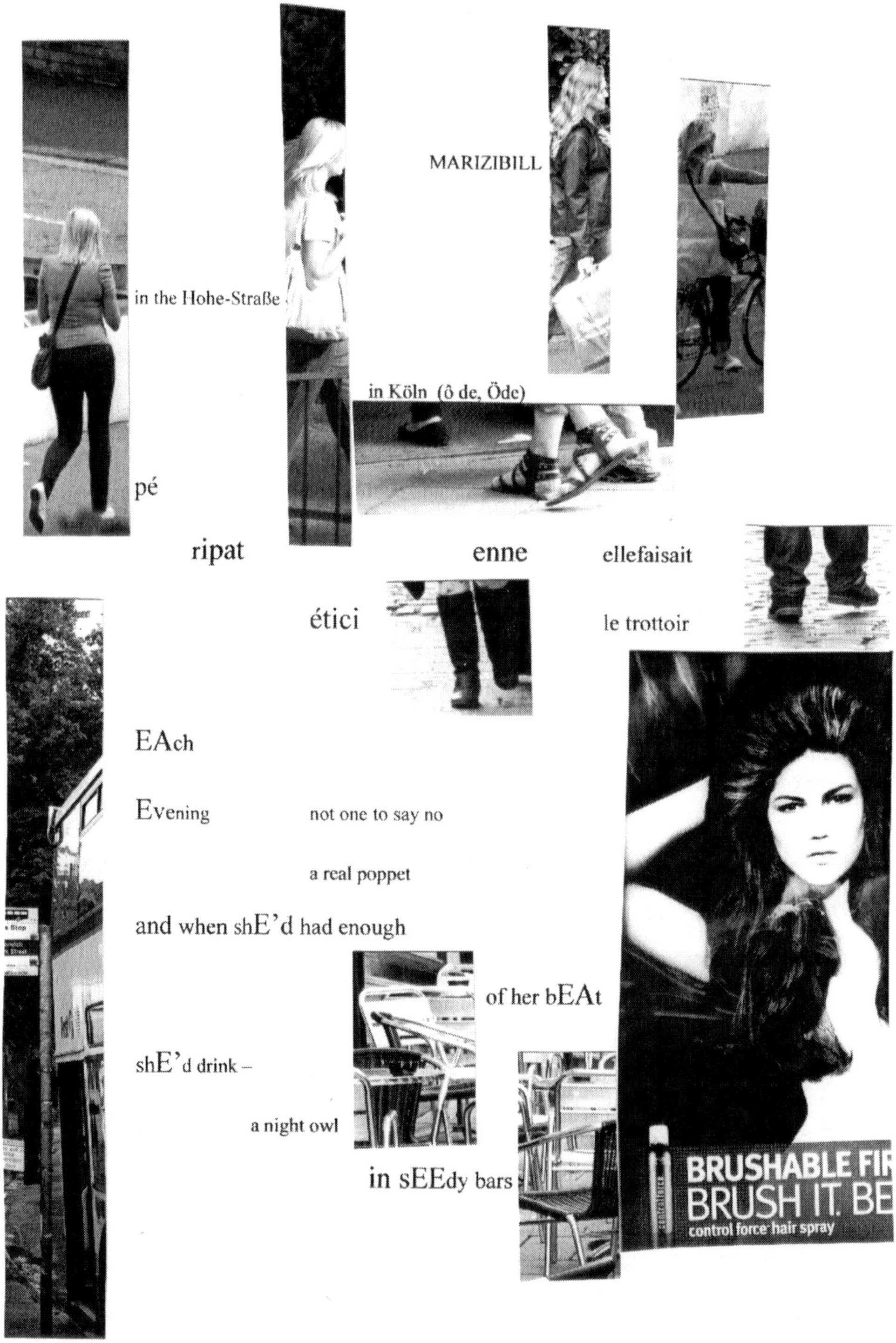

Figure 6: Translation, with photo-collage, of 'Marizibill'

she clEAned herself out

for a pimp

pink-faced

ginger-haired

A garlic-scented Jew who'd

shanghaied her from a brothel in Shanghai

starboard home

from

Formosa

I know types of every ilk
Who can't quite match
What they might be
Shiftless, unfixed, like dead leaves
Their eyes are dying embers
Not quite out, their hearts
As restive as their unclosed doors

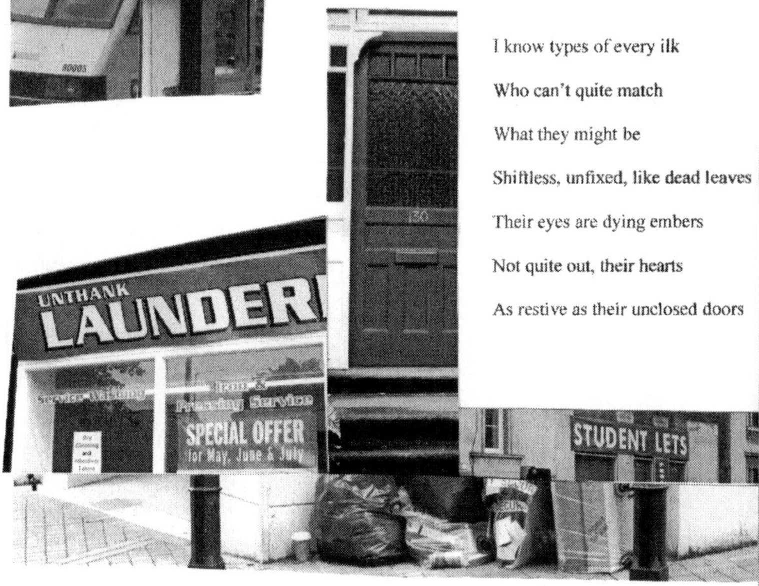

Figure 7: Translation, with photo-collage, of 'Marizibill'

Cutting the photograph foregrounds and makes critical a paradoxicality which the whole photograph tends to conceal. Cutting is, on the one hand, an act of appropriation and an intensification of ocular fixation (fetish, trauma, *punctum*, *hasard objectif*, involuntary memory). The prostitute is potentially the selling of the body for this kind of cutting and appropriation. The city, too, prostitutes itself for this kind of cutting. And where we make any such excision (from newspaper or magazine, for example), we willingly sacrifice context and the circumstantial to free the fragment into the longer and less defined temporalities of inner duration. But at the same time, and on the other hand, cutting is a cutting loose, in the sense of a simple liberation or *détournement* (cutting and collage are intimate bedfellows), in order that the photograph does not 'return home' to its single context, but is able to hunt out new contexts, to discover other futures for itself. Here cutting deprives the whole photograph of its authorship in order to put the fragment in the hands of an unassigned consciousness. This is to shanghai Marizibill, and the elements of her life, but not to another brothel; it is rather to invite her to recontextualize herself, to translate herself into new sense. The excised fragment, without the anchor of its past context, becomes nomadic, re-involves itself in becoming, in continuous variation, in metamorphosis. Of course, *détournement* may re-imprison the fragment in signification, in a programme; Marizibill might become definitively a hairstyling model or a worker in a launderette. But we should also argue that, when cut, photographs cease to make claims on truth. It is not that they toy provocatively with falsehood, as a digital image might; the truth/falsehood issue simply disappears, because it requires the corroborations or claims of a visual context no longer available. Accordingly, the photographic fragment can multiply fictions and search for new truths never corroborated, always in flight, like Marizibill herself. So the photographic fragments create Deleuze/Guattari lines of flight or continuous variation which 'conduisent au désir, aux machines du désir et à l'organisation d'un champ social de désir [...]. Faire passer des flux, sous les codes sociaux qui veulent les canaliser, les barrer' (Guattari in Deleuze, 1990: 32) [open up desire, desire's machines, and the organization of the social field of desire [...]. Opening up flows beneath the social codes that seek to channel and block them' (Deleuze, 1995: 19)]. The codes are the pink-faced pimp, the small rooms and the lost opportunities. But the final stanza, for all its pathos, leaves ajar the door through which the liberating photographic series might slip to re-kindle the dying embers.

The drift of the photographic fragment towards uncoded and

heterogeneous flows of becoming depends very much on the open-mindedness and nomadism inherent in tabular layout. The tabular page takes the space of the page as something not to be measured out and used as efficiently as possible but as a space responding to the particular solicitations of a particular text, making room for additions and revisions, alerting the reader to the play of virtualities and to the spontaneous impulses of mind and hand. By resorting to the tabular, we wish to make the experimental process that reading is complex and ramifying; we wish to re-invest the written with the oral—that is to say, with paralanguage and the readerly body. Lexical access to a written script is maximized by 'straight-line' syntax (word-order syntax) and spaces between words, identifying boundaries, generating a more or less homogeneous rhythm of lexical encounter and facilitating optical anticipation of words by extending parafoveal and peripheral vision. Saenger tells us that the ancient world saw no advantage in swift, silent reading; its cultivation of *scriptio* (or *scriptura*) *continua* (unseparated words), necessitating the manipulation of phonetic material to find the words, was geared to a reading world 'focused on a limited and intensely scrutinized canon of literature' and which 'relished the mellifluous metrical and accentual patterns of pronounced text' (1997: 11). If the mechanisms of reading have far-reaching implications for the aestheticization of text and govern the nature of the cognitive processes involved, then translation should incorporate this awareness into its own poetics and promote modes of printing and layouts that diversify the difficulty of reading and constantly re-sensitize the ways in which language is apprehended.

To embody these propositions, I present a version of Apollinaire's 'Annie' (*Alcools*) (*overleaf*; see Appendix I (iii) for French text), originally called 'Fanny', presumably to deflect critical attention from its occasion, the emigration of the courted Annie Playden to America. In order to make the reading process more fruitfully difficult, I have had recourse not only to *scriptio continua* but also to the ragged column, to a certain centrifugality of layout and to vertical syntagmatic decoys.

The general purpose of installing a halting, tentative reading, which has to find its way through a highly irregular rhythm of ocular fixations and saccades, is to perform the existential predicament explored by the poem, the search for a reconstructed relationship in conditions of disabused wishful thinking, with, more particularly, a discourse which contains the convenient slurrings of context (*scriptio continua*), a vengeful(?) fragmentation of the contentedly unified (the rose-filled garden, the complacent correspondence between house and garden),

F(Ann)ie

OntheTexasseaboard

La mer,

cigarette?

Comme tu tremblais!

Comme tu te serrais contre moi!

On aurait dit que tu me prenais pour un...

Le transistor s'est arrêté.

between

M-O-B-I-L-E and Galvestonthere's

a large garden

brimming with roses

andthere's

a villa, too, itself

a giantrose

Often

a WomanWalks

Quite alone

SATURDAYEVENINGPOST SATURDAYEVENINGPOST SATURDAYEVENINGPOST SATUR

and whenIpassbyon the limetreelinedroad WE

Look at each other

The woman is a Mennonite so

her rosebushes, her clothes have no buds/buttons

There are 2

miss-

ing on my jack-

et

The lady and

I

observe (almost)

the same rites

READER'S DIGEST READER'S DIGEST READER'S DIGEST READER'S DIGEST READER'S DIG the illusory equanimity of the non-tendentious (column of indefinite articles—but how obsessive this is), a language which itself is losing its buttons ('miss-/ing', 'jack-/et') and which typographically prefigures the way in which the 'I' of the poet becomes a button lost by the lady. This loss is presented as a case of wilful abstention (Mennonite), even though the capacity for love seems limitless (plethora of roses, albeit without buds and thus without future growth). If Apollinaire is the poet of mysterious in-between spaces ('Entre Mobile et Galveston', 'Entre l'amour et le dédain' ['Clotilde'], the nameless street 'entre la rue Aumont-Thiéville et l'avenue des Ternes' ['Zone']), then the tabular layout and different kinds of word-spacing help to suspend the speaker in between, to make the text a limbo and the name of the writing nameless, freed of all origins.

But if we find in this text the psycho-erotic narrative of a specific relationship, we find, too, that surpassing of the specific in bodiless, non-human percepts and affects, that point at which objects and subjective feelings become densities, intensities, forces, beyond any personal manifestation. Deleuze and Guattari tell us that: 'Les percepts ne sont plus des perceptions, ils sont indépendants d'un état de ceux qui les éprouvent; les affects ne sont plus des sentiments ou affections, ils débordent la force de ceux qui passent par eux' (1991: 154) [Percepts are no longer perceptions; they are independent of a state of those who experience them. Affects are no longer feelings or affections; they go beyond the strength of those who undergo them (1994: 164)]. Thus, the separation of the column of indefinite articles tells us not only of personal obsession but also of a new 'atmosphere' in which objects are caught in their very becoming, throw off their individual traits and grow into the impersonal, the collective singular; as Deleuze puts it:

> Devenir n'est pas atteindre à une forme (identification, imitation, Mimésis), mais trouver la zone de voisinage, d'indiscernabilité ou d'indifférenciation telle qu'on ne peut plus se distinguer d'*une* femme, d'*un* animal ou d'*une* molécule: non pas imprécis ni généraux, mais imprévus, non-préexistants, d'autant moins déterminés dans une forme qu'ils se singularisent dans une population (1993: 11)

> [To become is not to attain a form (identification, imitation, Mimesis) but to find the zone of proximity, indiscernibility, or indifferentiation where one can no longer be distinguished from *a* woman, *an* animal, or *a* molecule—neither imprecise nor

> general, but unforeseen and nonpreexistent, singularized out of a population rather than determined in a form (1997: 1)].

And equally the titles of newspaper and magazine ('Saturday Evening Post', 'Reader's Digest') are proper nouns which capture not what these media outlets have as specific identities but what they have as symptoms of a readerly condition, or what their readerships have in the way of expectations, curiosities, social attitudes, reading pleasures: a proper name is acquired 'quand il s'ouvre aux multiplicités qui le traversent de part en part, aux intensités qui le parcourent' (Deleuze, 1990: 15–16) [by opening [itself] to the multiplicities everywhere within [it], to the intensities running through [it] (Deleuze, 1995: 6)]. The same might be said of the intertexts—the reference to Butor's *Mobile* in explicit quotation, within which one also hears echoes of Rimbaud's 'Royauté', and the allusions to Dos Passos (*USA*), Proust (lime trees) and John Denver (Galveston)—which, although originating in a specific reader, become the available channels of countless currents of association. And inasmuch as the wresting of impersonality from individuation, and vice versa, might occur in the materials of the text itself, then the adoption of tabular dispositions becomes crucial to the whole enterprise: because it is tabularity which, by maximizing the materiality of language, acts against the single-minded fluency of the linear, in which acoustic and graphemic singularities are absorbed into the discourse of a particular personality.

My incorporation of photography into this translation (Figs 8–9) tries to capture something of this paradoxical release of an unattached and continuing heterogeneity from a particular encounter by resorting to the contact sheet. In her introduction to *Magnum Contact Sheets* (2011: 9) Kristen Lubben points out that contact sheets belong to a practice made obsolete by digital technology: 'the use of the contact sheet as a record of one's shooting, a tool for editing, and an index to an archive of negatives'. In my own application, I want the contact sheet to act as a record of mental activity, I want it to explore the unedited, and I want it not to fall back into archive but instead to track the ongoingness of associative improvisation. In this sense, the contact print has an unwritten, or textually unrealized, genetic function. Most particularly, I do not want my contact prints to seem to pursue the teleology of the chosen shot, the decisive moment of the sequence, the equivalent of a synthesis which allows all other shots to fall away into the not-chosen, the second rate. The teleological view of the contact sheet has two related consequences. First, the selected exposure enters a present of

F(Ann)ie

<No.31>

<No.32>

<No.33>

OntheTexasseaboard

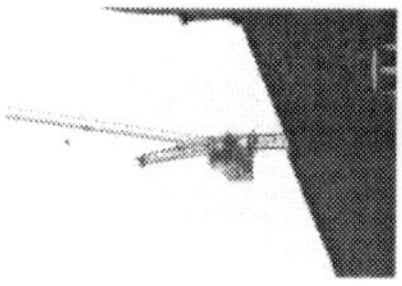
<No.25>

<No.26>

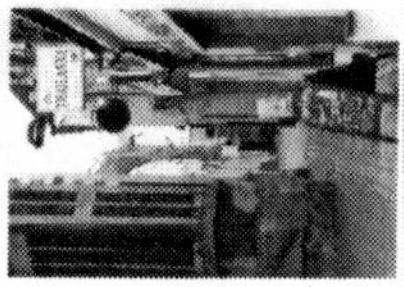
<No.27>

La mer,

cigarette?

Comme tu tremblais!

Comme tu te serrais contre moi!

On aurait dit que tu me prenais pour un...

Le transistor s'est arrêté.

between

M-O-B-I-L-E and Galvestonthere's

<No. >

a large garden

brimming with roses

andthere's

a villa, too, itself

a giantrose

<No.34>

<No.35>

<No.36>

Figure 8: Translation, with photo-collage, of 'Annie'

Often

a WomanWalks

Quite alone

<No 28 >

<No 29 >

SATURDAY EVENING POST SATURDAY EVENING POST SATURDAY EVENING POST SATUR

and whenIpassbyon the limetreelinedroad WE

Look at each other

The woman is a Mennonite

SO

her rosebushes, her clothes

have no buds/buttons

<No 19 >

<No 20 >

<No 21 >

There are 2

miss-

ing on my jack-

et

<No 22 >

<No 23 >

<No 24 >

The lady and

I

observe (almost)

the same rites

<No 30 >

READER'S DIGEST READER'S DIGEST READER'S DIGEST READER'S DIGEST READER'S DIG

Figure 9: Translation, with photo-collage, of 'Annie'

significance, while the others are consigned to a past of remembered circumstantial event, without significance. Analogously, one might say that the ST's 'present of significance' is captured in a 'fairest-of-fair-copies' TT which condemns rejected variants to a purely marginal existence, outside the space of the text's sense. In the 'non-selective' contact sheet, on the other hand, images trace befores and afters, pasts and futures, which may all be presents, and, conversely, a sequence of presents which are bound to be pasts and futures; the contact series promotes an elastic timeline whose elements may also be re-negotiating their temporal location. A contact series remains a series while refusing to depict an unfolding duration or create a teleological narrative.

Secondly, the unedited, genetic nature of the contact sheet means that it never comes fully to consciousness; it embodies a state described by Ferdinando Scianna: 'In effect, a contact sheet reflects the conscious and unconscious mind of the photographer. Often even the photographer cannot interpret it correctly. Nonetheless, it is through the analysis of contact sheets—a form of self-analysis—that a photographer can try to grasp the direction of meaning that lies behind his own images' (Lubben, 2011: 209). 'Directions of meaning' might be equated with the Deleuzean notion of sense, which can never realize its own accomplishment but only enrich itself through proliferation. In a world of sense we are acutely aware that a photograph, by the company it keeps with other photographs, quickly passes beyond anyone's ability to tell us what exactly it depicts.

And Scianna's unconscious includes, of course, Walter Benjamin's optical unconscious, that capacity of the photograph to cling on to what the eye edits out, or to make available to us, through the camera's prosthetic virtuosity, what would remain hidden from us (1977: 371–2; 1999: 510–12). But, with contact sheets, it is not so much the unconscious which lurks in individual photographs, but the unconscious which is an ever-present accompaniment of the conscious, the self-inverting sides of a Möbius strip, whereby every photograph is a question about the motives for its having been taken. Contacts sheets still belong to a private,[2] genetic world, prior to choice and publication; they are still involved in an unpredictable becoming, a line of flight propelled by moods, hesitations, existential bifurcations and diversions.

The translator's discourse with himself about a poem he is translating, equally, may take many forms. Jacques Roubaud tells us that, as a first step towards remembering a poem, he commits the rhyme-words to memory (2000: 41–2). I produce a translation of 'Marizibill' in *bouts-rimés*, a kind of pre-memorization of a version not yet finally written:

hooker
Cologne
forsook her
on loan
shook her

bled dry
compose her
Shanghai
Formosa
wry

weaves
fate
leaves
grate
sleeves

How might I find my way to a 'faithful' translation from this position, left in the desert with only these rhymes as a compass? How many approximate or proximate poems might be engendered by my journey? And in how many other directions might this virtual 'Marizibill' be taken? This structure of lexemes is itself so fragile. What if my 'wry' were 'rye', 'sleeves' were 'reprieves', and so on? In this floating world I begin to think of Paris, of the abstracted woman, sitting idly at the café table in Manet's *La Prune* (1878), an alternative 'Marizibill':

She sat quite still
Neglecting a cigarette

Eyeing from time to time
The saturated plum

The bodice of her pink dress
Crammed with anecdotes

But mostly gazing
At the unseen clientele

Rehearsing Sundays
Improvising weeks

Later she was snapped by Brandt
Lamplit after a quick Chinese

At home the door she closes
Has a faulty catch.

This poem, with a different point of departure, nonetheless sidles alongside the Apollinaire, orientates itself towards it, is informed by an awareness of it. I might then wish to weave these verses into my version of 'Marizibill'. Translation here begins to communicate the kind of life that the ST pursues in the mind of the translator, something fitfully and perhaps imperfectly remembered, something elaborated upon, toyed with, living out its potential permutations. It is not just that the ST is a literary artefact, but that it comes to take up residence in a mind which is itself a literary repository of potential texts and intertexts. A text establishes its literariness partly by the affiliations it creates with the circumambient literary world of discourses, modes of enunciation, genres; and this circumambient world is activated afresh by each new reader/translator:

> Le texte est une productivité. Cela ne veut pas dire qu'il est le *produit* d'un travail [...], mais le théâtre même d'une production où se rejoignent le producteur du texte et son lecteur: le texte 'travaille', à chaque moment et de quelque côté qu'on le prenne; même écrit (fixé), il n'arrête pas de travailler, d'entretenir un processus de production
>
> (Barthes, 1994: 1681)

> [The text is a productivity. That does not mean that it is the *product* of a programme of work (...), but the very theatre of a production in which the producer of the text and his/her reader meet: the text is 'at work', at every moment and from whatever angle one approaches it; even written (fixed), it does not stop working, sustaining a process of production].

The photographic version of this alternative 'Marizibill' (Fig. 10) visually fills out the Manet connection, but does so under a 'banner' photograph which announces that these fragments of Manet paintings are excised from photographs of photographs of the paintings found

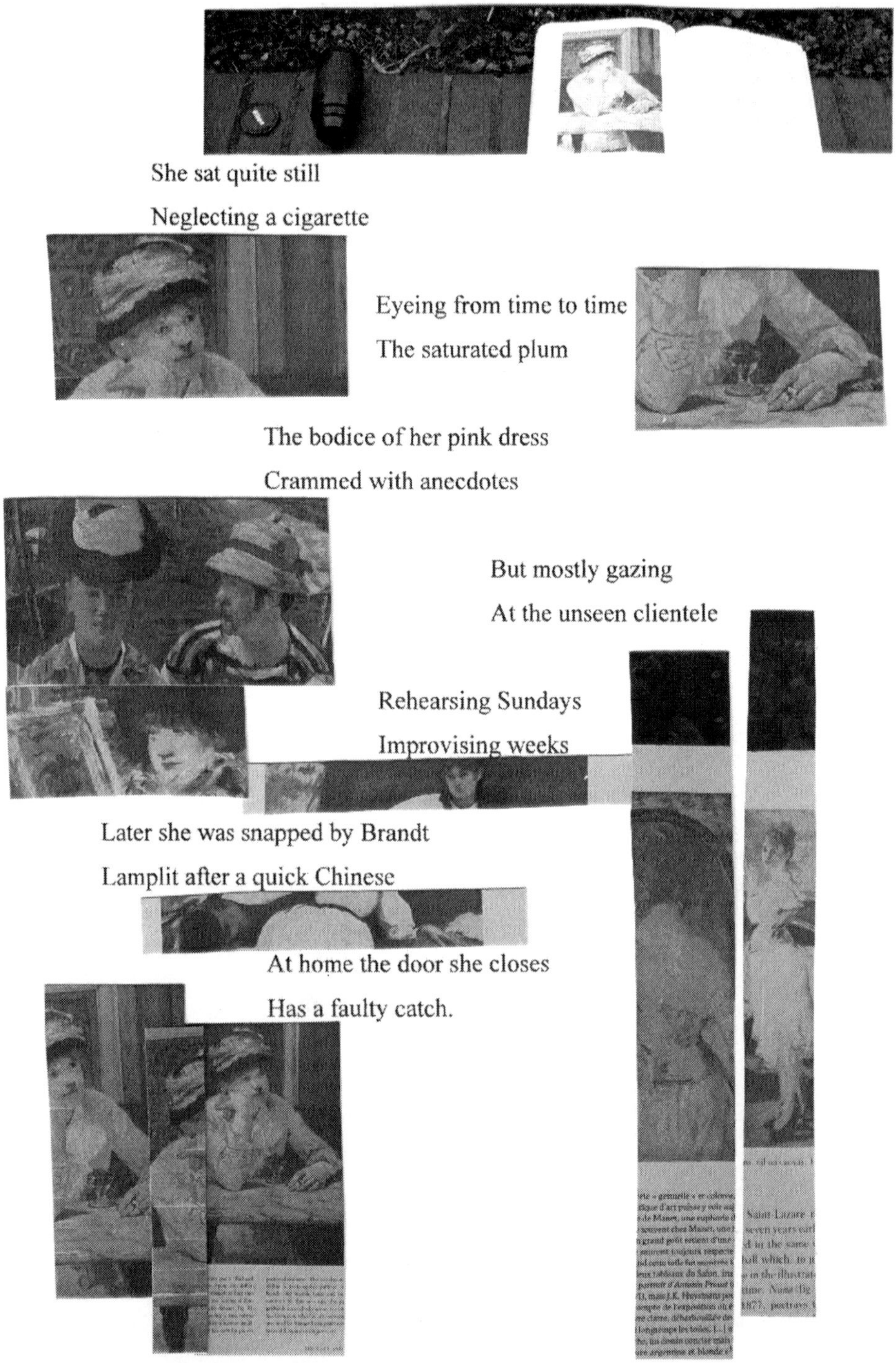

Figure 10: Verse adaptation, with photo-collage (Manet), of 'Marizibill'

in sundry books and catalogues. Marizibill is thus aligned with a work of art in the age of mechanical reproduction/reproducibility, according to the analysis of Walter Benjamin (1974a: 471–508; 2003a: 251–83). This analysis underpins the sense of the photographic commentary as a whole. But, before exploring that derivation in more detail, we need to say three things about the relation of Impressionism—and more particularly Manet's impressionism of the 1870s—to photography.

First, there are many senses in which Impressionism is already in league with photography, in its compositional and spectatorial innovations: cut-off figures, close-ups, plunging views, exploitation of differential focus, blurring of bodies in movement, reassessment of the mechanics of animal and human locomotion, polarization of near and far, replacement of the frame of the support (canvas) by the frame of the eye (viewfinder). Secondly, Impressionism is already concerned with the breaking down of the distance of aura, with the creation of proximity. Some of the features contributing to this shift have already been listed. One should add that the characteristic Impressionist viewing position is thus an involved one: many of the compositional devices implicate the viewer in the events depicted, a participation visually reinforced by the demands of optical mixture (the active reconciliation and blending of painterly 'touches' in the eye of the spectator). Thirdly, Impressionism occupies an ambiguous position in that shift, traced by Benjamin, from spectatorial contemplation [Kontemplation] and concentration [Sammlung] to a more unsettled response which Benjamin, further on, relates to distraction [Ablenkung] or the scattering of attention [Zerstreuung]. Of Atget's photographs, Benjamin writes: 'Ihnen ist die freischwebende Kontemplation nicht mehr angemessen. Sie beunruhigen den Betrachter; er fühlt: zu ihnen muß er einen bestimmten Weg suchen' (1974a: 485) [Free-floating contemplation is no longer appropriate to them. They unsettle the viewer; he feels challenged to find a particular way to approach them (2003a: 258)]. Impressionism sets us uncertainly between the synthesized distance of mood and the turbulent proximity of individual chromatic sensations, between the contemplative figures in landscape to the off-centre and off-balance figures of the urban environment, between the absorbed gaze and the snatched glimpse or glance. In these respects, Impressionist paintings do not have an unequivocal cultic value which photographic reproduction then undermines. Impressionism shares a powerful indexicality with photography; the direct perceptual encounter, 'sur le motif', the spirit of pleinairism even in the studio (see the fragments from Manet's *Devant la glace*,

1876–7, or *Liseuse ou la lecture de l'illustré*, 1879), the swift, tireless painterly gestures, the 'overallness' of its technique which constantly distributes attention across the canvas[3]—these habits help to persuade attitudes away from the reverential towards the voyeuristic.

A first and important aspect of the technological reproducibility of art, an aspect not explicitly referred to by Benjamin, is the production of the cosmopolitan: the uniqueness of the artwork, in its 'home' location, is geographically dispersed as copies are multiplied; gathered before us in Fig. 10 are fragments garnered from books in several formats and languages, and if the pictures as a group all belong to Paris, they are now re-located in Chicago, Washington, Hamburg, New York, Providence, Tournai. Shanghaied. The prostitute is translation, the gravitational and radiational centre of polylingual and polymorphous contact: in the Impressionists' world not only does prostitution touch, by implication at least, the lives of many working women (dancers, artists' models, milliners, laundresses, actresses), but the liberation of women into all forms of social activity (theatre, café, park, horse-racing, department store) and the respectabilization of the street (Haussman) lead to a problematization of social status, behavioural attitudes, sexual availability (see Lipton, 1986). Part of the reason for including a reference to the photograph by Brandt, a photograph depicting a prostitute outside a Chinese restaurant in Hamburg in 1933, is that the part of the prostitute is played by Eva Boros, Brandt's future first wife.

Women in public places in the late nineteenth century are dislodged from the 'authenticity' of their domestic environment and the way we read them has become correspondingly inquisitive; we may be encouraged to disregard origins and to gather all our evidence by repeated glances or one-off glimpses, dislocated pieces of perceptual information. The poem's distichs, with their two- and three-stress rhythms, belong to an hypothesizing mentality embroidering on minimal perceptual data. The photographic fragments are more nervous, stammering, distracted, cursory. For Benjamin, it is the evidential nature of the photograph which invests it with a political instrumentality, with an invitation to be put to use by the masses into whose hands it delivers that evidence as empowerment. The fragmentary photographic reproduction undoes the integrity and thus the authority of the original painting; it compels—Benjamin says 'enables' (2003a: 254) [macht sie ihm möglich (1974a: 476–7)]—'the original to meet the recipient halfway' [dem Aufnehmenden entgegenzukommen] and puts at his/her disposal a 'testing', analytical account of the original. At the same time, 'aura' is undone by the original's having to justify itself in a new perceptual environment.

How is this, then, to be related to translation? Translation, though by no means a reproduction of the ST, insists on its reproducibility (understood in broad terms). Translation politicizes the ST to the degree that it inserts it challengingly into a status quo by performative means: performance in the text (the activation of all the languages of textual presentation, and tabular writing) and performance of the text (translation from language towards paralanguage, and from *langue* towards *langage*). This concentration on the performative brings the ST into proximity; the tabular and performative translator is like Benjamin's surgeon (2003a: 263; 1974a: 495–6), penetrating the patient (ST) by operating, intervening to establish the close-up. Our treatment of 'Marizibill' uses both the tabular and the multilingual to pursue investigative intrusions in a ST already permeated by the cosmopolitan. The photographic accompaniment supports this activity by reinforcing the perceptual shock mechanisms that tabular structure and typographic irregularity already trigger; the shock effect 'seeks to induce heightened attention/ to be buffered by intensified presence of mind' (2003a: 267, 281) [durch gesteigerte Geistesgegenwart aufgefangen sein will (1974a: 503).[4] But my alternative 'Marizibill' is rather more complicated. Here, it is not so much the painted images which need dislodging from their auratic reclusions—we have explored some of the affinities between Impressionism and the photograph—as the poem itself. Not only are its distichs on the road to self-ritualization, but its trajectory wishes a finality in the image of the unclosable door (the privacy that cannot be achieved, the accessibility that must be conceded to) and the pun on 'catch'. Impressionist painting and photographic fragment collude to undermine this urge to frame and formalize, and, instead, reinstate a free multiplicity of blind fields.

Reconfiguations of Marizibill's story grow out of the metamorphic variations which inevitably accompany the activity of translation, as much in its pictorial as in its linguistic guise. Images, fragmented images, like items of language, generate infinities of reconfiguration and otherwise would be inanimate and un-becoming. Such a process can occur only in a polyglot reader and it is only for the polyglot reader, for the reader whose familiarity with the SL/ST is assumed, that the notions of mistake and infelicitous choice cease to weigh, cease to threaten, cease to signify, are nullified. Take the opening line of Apollinaire's 'La Nuit d'avril 1915':

> Le ciel est étoilé par les obus des Boches

which I translate as:

> The sky is starlit by the Boches' shells

Greet (Greet and Lockerbie, 1980: 203) translates 'étoilé' by 'is starred by'. Alternatively, we might say 'is starry with', or 'is spangled with', or 'The Boches' shells light up the sky with stars/festoon the sky with stars/scatter the sky with stars/throw stars about the sky', etc. Is this an exercise in linguistic resourcefulness or a test of getting it right? What would 'right' mean in these circumstances? Rightness has significance only where a reader might be misled by wrongness, or sold short by the less felicitous, in the world of the monoglot reader. For the polyglot reader, for whom choice and variant are absorbed into lines of continuous variation, notions of the wrong and the infelicitous can get no purchase, because they are absorbed into change, because they can never isolate themselves, but are part of an expanding conglomerate. And mistakes themselves have no interest as mistakes (they can be corrected), but only as possible manifestations of (creative, intentional) mishearing, acoustic or graphic hallucination.

Consider:

> The sky is starlit by the abuses of the Boches
>
> (Le ciel est étoilé par les abus des Boches)

or even:

> Rough use of pockets fills the sky with stars
>
> (Le ciel est étoilé par les abus des poches)

or even:

> Ill-use of does festoons the sky with stars.
>
> (Le ciel est étoilé par les abus des biches)

How do we capture the incorporation into the text of a reader's optical or auditory fantasy? None of these distortions of the ST infringes the line's structural principles: an alexandrine with a 2 > 4 > 4 > 2 rhythmic shape, ending with a feminine rhyme. If a literary text is expressly designed, by its very rhythms and acoustic patterns, to release the reader's associative mechanisms, to activate their *imaginaire*, if translation, in one view at least, is meant to be not a translation of a text but a translation of a reader's response to a text, then this is much more like reading than misreading.

We have argued that a ST cannot be treated as definitive if it is to survive, to have a future, and that continuous variation is part of the programme of this future. We have also argued that translation is a second-order creation which transforms itself into a first-order creation in the very process of translation. Part of that transformation is the achievement of a textuality, a TT-specific textual metabolism. Apollinaire's 'La Nuit d'avril 1915' (see Appendix I (iv) for French text), considered overall, is already something of a mirage, an illusion. It is written in alexandrines, observes the rule of the alternation of masculine and feminine rhymes, employs Apollinaire's favoured cinquain, rhyming *ababa*, which, for the purposes of poetic closure, becomes a septain. Where lines are split the division usually falls, as one might expect, at the caesura (ll. 4 and 14). The penultimate line, however, begins to suggest much freer forms of segmentation, and a definitive unravelling of stanzaic structure, into distichs and monostichs, occurs in the final seven lines. This insinuates the suspicion that recourse to classical prosody is not sufficient to keep elements integrated with each other, that thought cannot but move spasmodically, disjointedly. As a result the formal correctness looks not so much like a pledge of organic interwovenness as a ritual nominally acceded to as a way of keeping things going. That further formal disintegrations should visit the process of translation is not to be wondered at:

> The sky is starlit with the Boches' shells
> The magic forest now my home
>   is putting on a ball
> Machine guns play a tune
>   in demisemiquavers
> But you have the word
>   ah, yes, the fateful word
> To the loopholes To the loopholes Drop your picks
>
> Like a desperate planet searching for its seasons
> Heart exploded shell you whistled your romance

And your thousand suns have emptied the caissons
Filled without a sound by the gods of my eyes

We love you life and set your nerves on edge

The shells intoned a love to die of
A dying love is sweeter than the others
Your breath swims in the river
                                        where the blood runs dry
The shells were whining
                                    listen to ours singing
Deep-purple love saluted by those about to die

The humid spring the night light the attack

It's raining omysoul it's raining but it's raining lifeless eyes

Odysseus how long it takes to return to Ithaca

Stretch out on the straw and conjure a fine remorse
Aphrodisiac a pure effect of art

But
        organs
                                in the wisps of straw you sleep in
Paradisiac the hymn of the future

If I now wish to sow this text with the variants (restored to the status of metamorphoses) provided by the text as it appears in *Lettres à Lou* (10 April 1915; 1990: 273–4), by the manuscript sent to *L'Intransigeant*, and by the version which appeared in *L'Élan* (No. 9, March 1916) (1965: 1094–5), and with suggestions for new material, what steps are necessary? Most obviously, I must avoid overstocking the poem, pushing it too far in the direction of exhaustiveness. The effect, indeed, should be the opposite: that I am unwriting the poem, increasing its unfinishedness, re-hypothesizing it. And in order to achieve this I must find ways of animating the page, projecting a restlessness. How does one transform an itemization of alternatives, inertly juxtaposed on the page, into a set of verbal ideas exerting different and changing degrees of pressure on a reader, who is not just reviewing his/her options but wondering how to push the text forward, how it might ramify? We translate towards a genetic inhabitation of the ST; translation is the way in which STs become part of our own creative agenda. I want, therefore, to develop a mode of presentation which acts invitingly, or provocatively. We speak of performance *in* the text as well as *of* the text; but by this we do not merely mean an engaging spectacle, a firework display of typographic ingenuity. We mean a performance not in front of a reader but undertaken by the reader, a performance which involves the reader's becoming a translator, with an appetite for textual extensions and reformulations. My next version of 'La Nuit d'avril 1915', therefore, is in some senses both a retreat from, and an elaboration of, my first version. The text, I hope, looks more ill at ease, less sure of itself, a lame duck in need of remedies and revitalization. Many ask whether a TT might be an improvement on the ST; and, as we have seen, many, including Borges and Bonnefoy, would say 'yes'. But we should also envisage a translational practice which is retrogressive the better to be progressive, which 'recule pour mieux sauter'. And here the translational satisfactions are to be derived from producing a TT which is fruitfully interim, which re-activates the ST in the minds of those who thought they knew it, which is stimulating by virtue of the dissatisfactions and teasings it puts the reader to:

April Night 1915

The sky is starlit with the Boches' shells
The Boches' shells punch out
a starry constellation *constellé*
The magic forest now my home [sole domain]
is putting on a ball
Machine guns play a tune
in (demi)semiquavers in fractioned quavers
fractured
Or grind the coffee. What more's for breakfast?
[But you have] the word
but
ah, yes, the fateful word
To the loopholes To the loopholes Drop your picks
They're sounding the ALERT *Get back indoors*

Like a desperate planet searching for its seasons
HEART exploded SHELL you whistled your romance
{**I'm never alone here are the two caissons**}
And your thousand suns have emptied the caissons
~~Filled without a sound by the gods of my eyes~~
~~Xxxxxxxxxxxxxx~~
The casings, spent, stand easy in the easy vestibules

★

We love you
Life and set your nerves on edge...

★

The shells intoned a love to die ~~of~~ for
The shells went howling for a lovelorn echelon
A dying love is sweeter than the others/ *loves on the wane are sweeter*
My
Your breath swims in the river
and **'ll** **,**
where the blood runs dry

The shells were whining
SING
listen to ours singing
[Deep-]purple love saluted by those about to die
{Vae victis **Lou**}

★

The humid spring the night light the attack

★

The claypipe shooting gas the blind
gesticulate like ants

★

soldier
It's raining omysoul (it's) raining but it's raining lifeless eyes

★

††††† Odysseus how long it takes
to return
to Ithaca

But, tell me, Blaise,
is Montmartre
that far off? Is
Nîmes
so long ago?

★

Stretch out on the straw and conjure a fine remorse ???????
Aphrodisiac ~~a pure effect of art~~ *afrovertigo the mouth of darkness*

★

But
organs
in the wisps of straw you sleep in
Paradisiac the hymn of the future *the rasping reeds*

About this translation I would only wish to add that, in his letter to Lou of 10 April 1915, Apollinaire's 'lettre en vers' is interrupted and the letter is then brought to a conclusion in prose. This closing prose passage describes the morning after. Apollinaire writes: 'On entend la mitrailleuse moudre le café, un avion nous survole' [You can hear the machine gun grinding the coffee, an aircraft is flying over us]. Yes, it is probably breakfast time, or at least time for a cup of coffee, but the word 'moudre' picks up the musical reference in the third line of the poem, through the phrase 'moudre un air' (i.e. play a tune on a musical instrument with a handle, whether barrel organ ['orgues aux fétus de la paille'?] or hurdy-gurdy) (*Le Nouveau Petit Robert*, 1993: 1446). And about the 'forêt merveilleuse' of line 2 we learn that a new cabin is being built in it and that it provides a well, for washing: 'Aujourd'hui, me suis lavé à fond au puits dans la forêt sous la pluie' (1990: 277) [Today, I gave myself a thorough wash, in the rain, at the well in the forest] ['Il pleut mon âme il pleut mais il pleut des yeux']. Finally, I have inserted '*Is Nîmes so long ago?*' partly because Apollinaire refers to Lou as 'mon (pauvre) amour de Nîmes' and partly because he notes: 'Hier soir j'ai enlevé mes souliers pour la première fois depuis mon départ de

Nîmes' (1990: 277) [Yesterday evening I took off my shoes for the first time since leaving Nimes].

'Un avion nous survole' is the first nudge for my photographic treatment of the text (Figs 11–13). We begin with a simple narrative. The three pages present a triptych, the central panel of which presents fragmented images of bombardment by night. On either side are equally fragmented images of aircraft: on the first sheet, a reconnaissance aircraft works out the coordinates of the area to be bombarded, while, on the third, an aircraft, the morning after the bombardment, takes photographs of the extent of the devastation.

This simple narrative is complicated by three factors. First, by the mechanism of metamorphosis. We say that, in metamorphic change, A turns into B, and imply thereby that A turns into something different; in fact we mean that A self-differentiates itself into B; it would perhaps be nearer the truth to say that A turns into A_1. An aircraft overhead becomes a subsequent bombardment which, in its turn, becomes an aircraft overhead: the bombardment is almost an interstitial phantasm ($A > A_1$ (B) $> A_2$ (C)). But this is not a straightforward chiasmus or reversion: an overhead aircraft does not re-become an overhead aircraft since function has changed, since the vision has changed, since the relation of the aircraft to past and future has changed. In metamorphosis there is a changing dosage of past and future, but there is certainly no going back. Apollinaire's own text grasps this fact: while its discourse blends those about to die, dying love, the emptying and re-filling of ammunition chests, Ulysses' return to Ithaca, remorse, its course is set by desire ('Qui pur effet de l'art soit aphrodisiaque') on a future heading ('L'hymne de l'avenir est paradisiaque').

Second, this series is shadowed, in the photographs, by the negative–positive metamorphosis. There are no negatives here, but the photographic fragments of night-time bombardment have that visual effect. The negative is the 'other side' of the positive, a spectral space, a space of virtualities, of embryonic, amorphous and flattened forms, the space of the phantasm. This space lies, to a greater or lesser extent, in any metamorphic series, as an agent of transmutation. The positive of the reconnoitring aircraft carries within itself the negative of a night-time bombardment, which, when, in its turn, printed out into a positive, reveals an aircraft reaping the whirlwind it has sown. Like the self-differentiating elements of the metamorphic series, a return to the negative to reprint another positive will always produce a positive which differs from its predecessor, a positive re-invested with the ongoing activity of the negative.

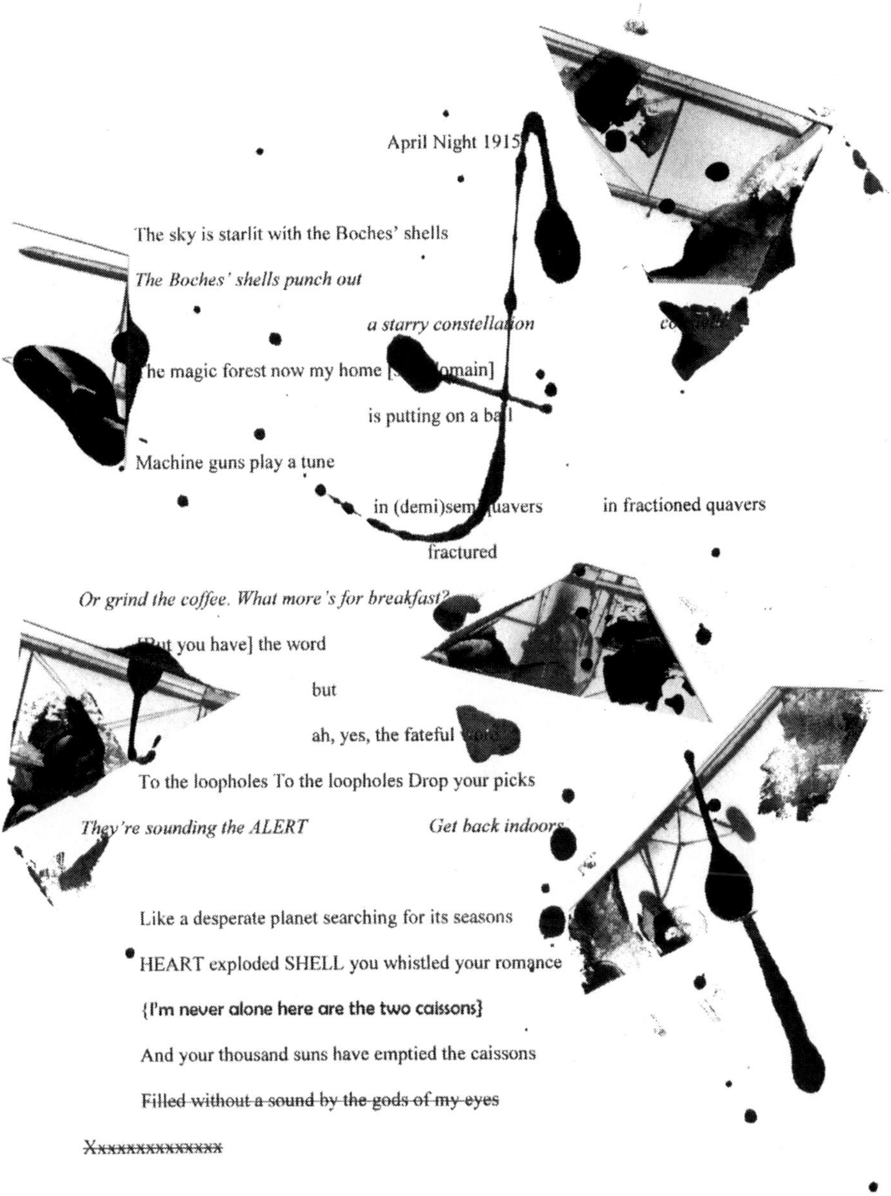

Figure 11: Translation, with photo-collage and enamel-paint doodles, of 'La Nuit d'avril 1915'

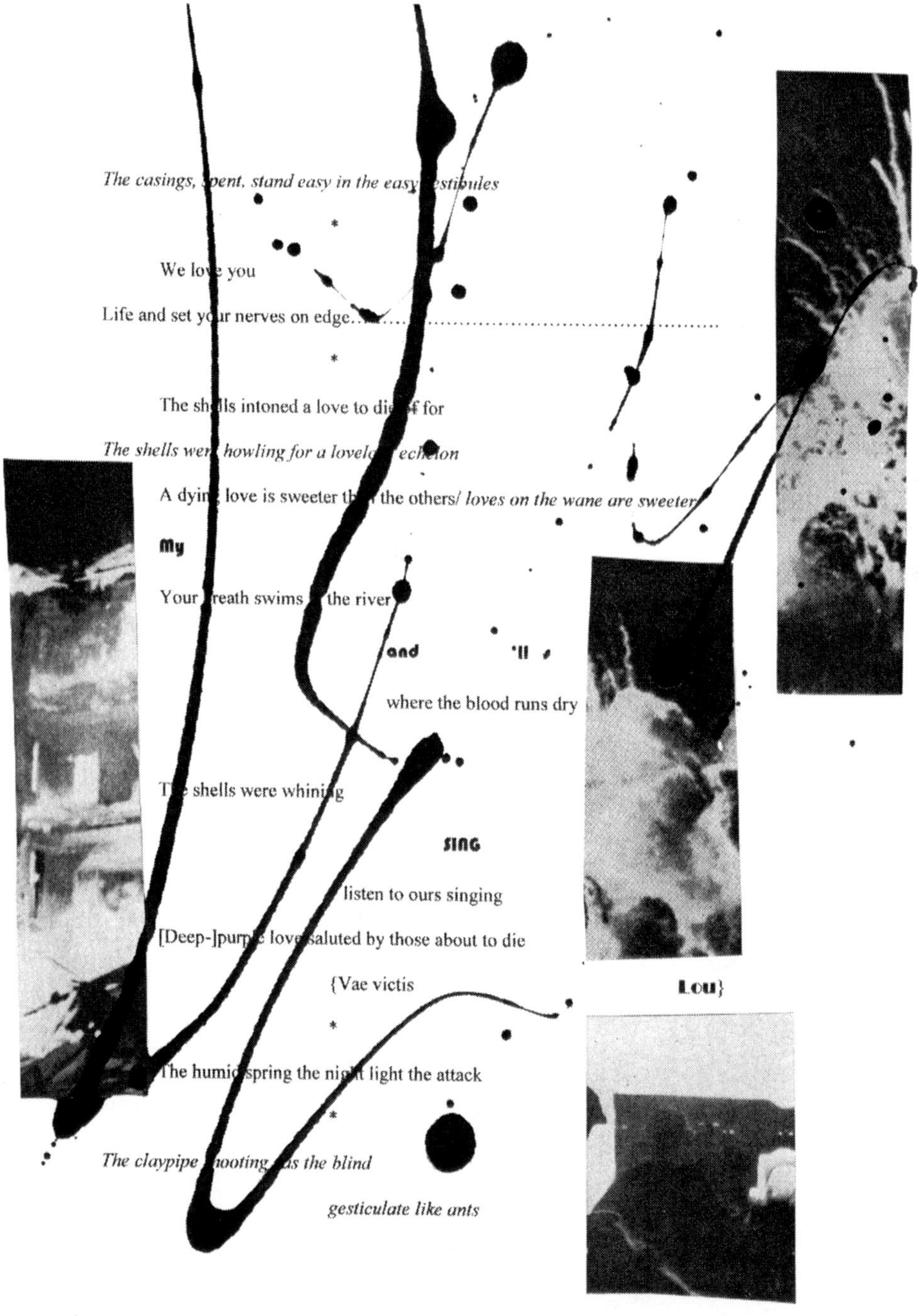

Figure 12: Translation, with photo-collage and enamel-paint doodles, of 'La Nuit d'avril 1915'

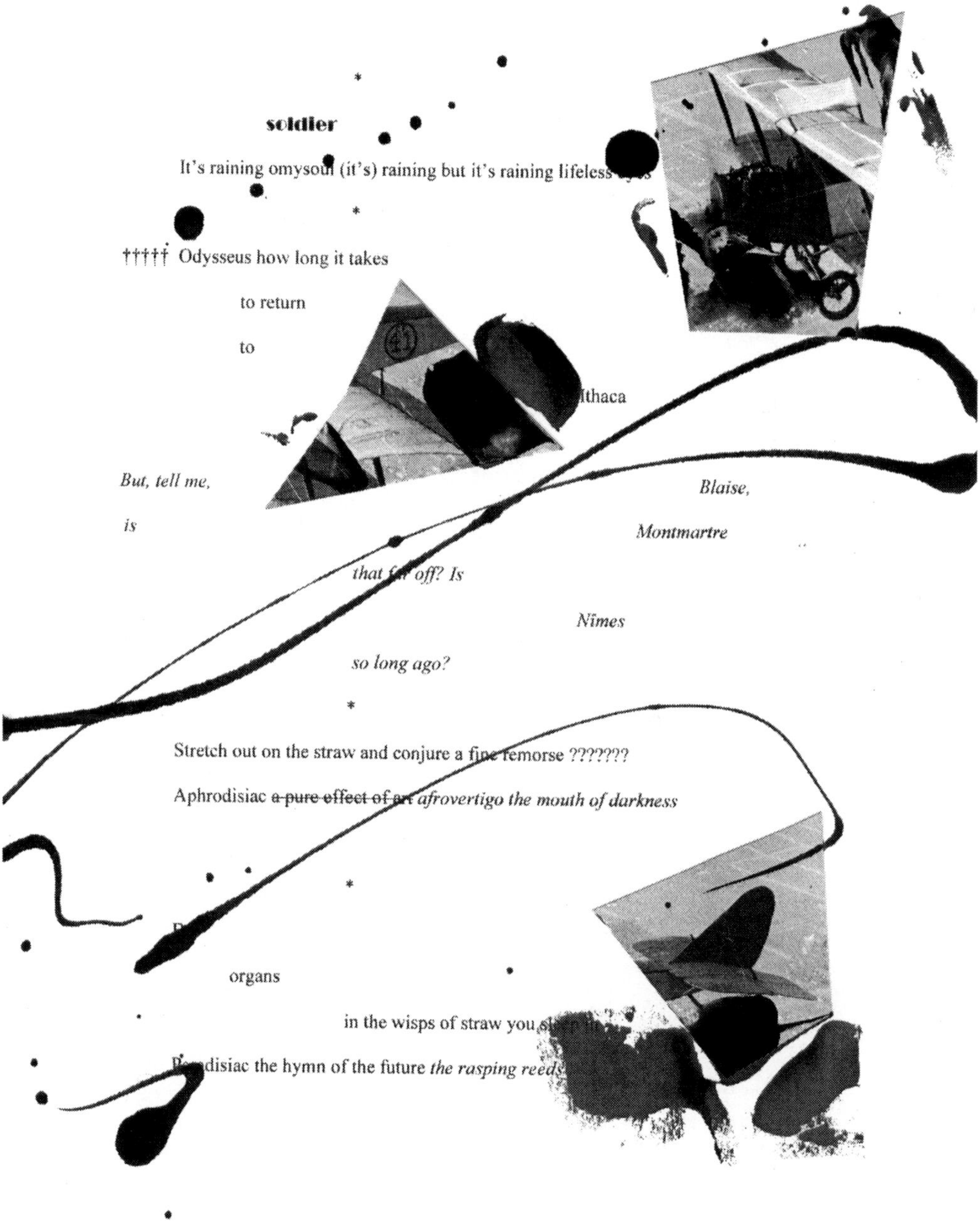

Figure 13: Translation, with photo-collage and enamel-paint doodles, of 'La Nuit d'avril 1915'

Third, we are encouraged to see these photographic fragments as pieces of consciousness or perception overflying the text. The aircraft carries out a reconnaissance of the text; the text is bombarded, done violence to, pulverized, disseminated; the text is retrieved as a new landscape, as something which demands an unfamiliar kind of topographical/typographical reading. Yes, this is an allegory of the blasting of the linear into the tabular, but the devastated state of the tabular is the pretext for new kinds of linguistic nomadism or refugee-ism.

But this is a text also overflown by the photographic. The text belongs to the world of the positive, of daylight. The overpainted traceries and spots and smudges of black are attempts to take text into the kingdom of night, of the negative, or at least to re-inform the positive with the negative; and the images of overflying aircraft are themselves made subject to the incursions of this darkness. Beyond that, these photographic fragments and the metamorphic series they create are expressions of the Event, or of sense, as it hovers over the particular actualizations and actions which take place on the battlefield below; as Deleuze himself puts it:

> Les deux moments du sens, impassibilité et genèse, neutralité et productivité, ne sont pas tels que l'un puisse passer pour l'apparence de l'autre. [...] Si la bataille n'est pas un exemple d'événement parmi d'autres, mais l'Événement dans son essence, c'est sans doute parce qu'elle s'effectue de beaucoup de manières à la fois, et que chaque participant peut la saisir à un niveau d'effectuation différent dans son présent variable [...] Mais c'est surtout parce que la bataille *survole* son propre champ, neutre par rapport à toutes ses effectuations temporelles, neutre et impassible par rapport aux vainqueurs et aux vaincus, [...] tellement au-delà, se tenant là où se tient l'Événement, participant ainsi de sa terrible impassibilité. 'Où' est la bataille?
>
> (1969: 122)

> [The two moments of sense, impassibility and genesis, neutrality and productivity, are not such that one may pass for the appearance of the other. [...] If the battle is not an example of an event among others, but rather the Event in its essence, it is no doubt because it is actualized in diverse manners at once, and because each participant may grasp it at a different level of actualization within its variable present. [...] But it is above all because the battle *hovers over* its own field, being neutral in relation to all its temporal actualizations, neutral and impassive in relation to the victor and

> the vanquished, [...] so much beyond, at the place where the Event is present, participating therefore in its terrible impassibility. 'Where' is the battle? (2004b: 116)].

Translation Studies has invested heavily in a theory and analytic methodology based on the objective of a single-version translation (fairest of fair copies, *corrigé*). If the translator were constrained to produce, say, eight versions, what theory and methodology would Translation Studies then entail? Surprisingly, perhaps, translation would no longer be an exercise in the solution of linguistic difficulties, nor would it primarily be about interpretation. It would look to undermine the assumption that the text (ST) is universally and monoperceptually visible; it would be translation's task to diversify the text's perceptibility. How is the translator to make translation an exploration of the ST, how is he/she to keep the ST travelling away from its point of departure? Translation itself is as constantly drawing STs back into the flow of time as it is redrawing maps and redisposing the territories of language and cultures. Translation is *métissage*, interbreeding, hybridization, grafting, creolization. We can concur with McGann's underlying law: 'The textual condition's only immutable law is the law of change. [...] The law of change declares that these histories [the life histories of different texts] will exhibit a ceaseless process of textual development and mutation [...]' (1991: 1). Translation does not merely register that change, that change's inevitability, but actively works to produce it. And within the work of literature which we may consider, by its very nature, to be subversive, but which by its fame and longevity is likely to be reterritorialized and normalized, translation works a work of deterritorialization and re-subversion. If, one last time, we resume this Deleuze/Guattari terminology, we might say that translation is a minority literature, which takes place in the rhizome, where 'il n'y a pas de langue en soi, ni d'universalité du langage, mais un concours de dialectes, de patois, d'argots, de langues spéciales' (1980:14) [there is no language in itself, nor are there any linguistic universals, only a throng of dialects, patois, slangs, and specialized languages' (1988: 7)].

3

The Linear and the Tabular

The distinction between metaphor and metamorphosis made in the previous chapter highlights a distinction between two models of translation. Metaphor is a form which relates to knowledge. I put target text (TT) against source text (ST) in order to measure a greater or lesser degree of identity. This identity can be arrived at only by processes of interpretation: what does the ST mean? What does the TT mean? What does it mean that the TT is identified with the ST? The relationship between ST and TT is, in this model, essentially spatial: juxtapositional and static. Metamorphosis, on the other hand, is a force which relates to empowerment. I put a TT in the line of flight of the ST in order to create a relationship of 'and'. The 'and' is an 'and' of expanding experience and experiment ('N'interprétez jamais, expérimentez...' (Deleuze, 1990: 120)) [Never interpret; experience, experiment... (Deleuze, 1995: 87)]. What the TT seeks to produce is not an identification with, nor an analogy or equivalent of, the ST; the TT slides out of, morphs out of, the ST, as a process which endows it with a new mode of existence, a new style, as Deleuze defines that term: 'Le style, chez un grand écrivain, c'est toujours aussi un style de vie, non pas du tout quelque chose de personnel, mais l'invention d'une possibilité de vie, d'un mode d'existence' (1990: 138) [Style, in a great writer, is always a style of life too, not anything at all personal, but inventing a possibility of life, a way of existing (1995: 100)]. And, in order to achieve this new mode of existence, tabularity is the crucial, transformative paginal strategy, because tabularity, by the agency of layout, 'dis-assigns' consciousness and allows the reader constantly to reconstruct and redefine the perceptual and affective field and to appropriate and assign consciousness, as desirable, ad libitum.

Over the past few years I have been arguing that translation should entail the translation of the linear into the tabular not only as a physical transformation of text but also as a transformation of readerly mentality. In an article of 2009 entitled 'From Linearity to Tabularity: Translating Modes of Reading', I laid out the case with a table of twenty characteristics of tabular translation, again reminding the reader that I was more interested in the linear and tabular as attitudes of mind, as reading strategies, as approaches to language, than as dispositions of text, although it is the disposition of text which most evidently engenders these attitudes of mind and reading strategies (2009: 42). I have, over the years, revised and added to this table, whose components now number thirty, and present it, as a point of indispensable ongoing reference, as Appendix II. But it is particularly on the relationship between tabularity and dis-assigned consciousness that I wish for the moment to concentrate.

This redistribution of consciousness is what we might regard as the attachment to the principle of metamorphosis of the principle of montage. And we might look upon Apollinaire as being among the first to associate montage with 'l'esprit nouveau', even if the history of montage goes back deep into the nineteenth century (see Phillips, 1992: 22–6). For Apollinaire, montage was a significant strategy for the new lyricism for two closely related reasons. First, it opened poetry to the universe and thus served the democratization of the poetic means. The poem is like a daily newspaper, the poet a receiver and synthesizer of incoming voices, of mixed languages and registers, and their re-transmitter: 'Dans le domaine de l'inspiration, leur liberté [celle des poètes] ne peut pas être moins grande que celle d'un journal quotidien qui traite dans une seule feuille des matières les plus diverses, parcourt des pays les plus éloignés' (1991: 945) [In the area of inspiration, [poets'] liberty cannot be less than that of a daily paper which, in the space of a single sheet, deals with the most varied of materials and covers the most distant countries].[1] Secondly, this availability to the universe is part of the poet's essential dialogue with the natural world:

> Qu'on ne s'étonne point si, avec les seuls moyens dont ils [les poètes] disposent encore, ils s'efforcent de se préparer à cet art nouveau (plus vaste que l'art simple des paroles) où, chefs d'un orchestre d'une étendue inouïe, ils auront à leur disposition: le monde entier, ses rumeurs et ses apparences, la pensée et le langage humain, le chant, la danse, tous les arts et tous les artifices, plus de mirages encore que ceux que pouvait faire surgir

> Morgane sur le mont Gibel pour composer le livre vu et entendu de l'avenir
>
> (1991: 944–5)

> [No surprise, then, if, with the only means they [the poets] as yet have at their disposal, they endeavour to prepare for this new art (vaster than the simple art of words) in which, conductors of an orchestra of unheard-of proportions, they will have available to them: the entire globe, its sounds and appearances, thought and human language, song, dance, all the arts and all the artifices, even more mirages than Morgan le Fay could conjure up on Mount Etna to compose the book of seeing and hearing of the future].

About this vision for a new art we should note four things: (i) we should underline that its objective is the multi-sensory or synaesthetic; (ii) it is a poetic art which will capitalize on the expressive flexibility and directness of communication of the phonograph and the cinema;[2] (iii) it is as available to the microcosmic event as it is to the macrocosmic;[3] (iv) it has an ambiguous attitude to sensory material directly transcribed from the environment (including onomatopoeia). About this last we should make some clarifying remarks.

If we mention ambiguity it is because we find, in Apollinaire's 'Anti-tradition futuriste', under 'Construction 1: Techniques sans cesse renouvelées', 'Description onomatopéïque', and then, under 'Construction 2: Intuition vitesse ubiquité', 'Trémolisme continu ou onomatopées plus inventées qu'imitées' (1991: 938) [Construction 1: Tirelessly renewed techniques or rhythms/Onomatopoeic description/ Construction 2: Intuition speed ubiquity/Continuous vibration and onomatopoeias more invented than imitated]. Where 'Construction 1' seems happy with onomatopoeic description, 'Construction 2' insists that onomatopoeia should be inventive rather than imitative. The latter formulation seems, at first sight, to chime best with Apollinaire's convictions: in 'L'Esprit nouveau et les poètes' he seems to put his case unequivocally:

> On imagine fort bien que l'harmonie imitative puisse jouer un rôle, mais elle ne saurait être la base que d'un art où les machines interviendraient; par exemple, un poème ou une symphonie composés au phonographe pourraient fort bien consister en bruits artistement choisis et lyriquement mêlés ou juxtaposés, tandis que pour ma part, je conçois mal que l'on fasse consister tout

> simplement un poème dans l'imitation d'un bruit auquel aucun sens lyrique, tragique ou pathétique ne peut être attaché
> (1991: 947)
>
> [One can very well imagine that imitative harmony could play a role, but it could be the basis only of an art in which machines would be used; for example, a poem or a symphony composed on the phonograph might very well consist of noises artistically chosen and lyrically mixed or juxtaposed, while for me it is difficult to conceive that one could make a poem consist quite simply in the imitation of a sound to which no lyric or tragic sense, no pathos, can be attached].

Such a view coincides with his general disparagement of 'naturalisme photographique' (1991: 1684) and of the overdescriptive bent of Futurism (1991: 971); with the advent of recording technology, verbal onomatopoeia sounds both anachronistic and redundant. And yet Apollinaire does accept that poetry must find ways of absorbing the new soundworlds, that it must involve itself in acoustic experimentation, that it must find ways of promoting multi-sensory experience. One might recall his own experimentation with the sounds of new shoes, gramophones, buses, and sirens in 'Lettre-Océan', or his programme for a new acoustics in 'La Victoire' (see Chapter Six). But the crux is not onomatopoeia *per se*, but the re-definition of poetry in relation to the real, the embedding of poetry in the ambient. This redefinition must also absorb: the shift of attention in the modern world from the subject/motif perceived to the perceptual mechanisms and the perceiving consciousness themselves;[4] the shift, as already broached, of perceiving consciousness from its place in a circumscribed identity to a position of neutrality, or free transfer, or dispersal;[5] and contemporary, and particularly Cubist, thinking about the fourth dimension.[6] All these elements are intimately interrelated.

Among the benefits that Apollinaire derived from the Futurists, one might guess that their notion of lines of force helped him to think more clearly about the fourth dimension, particularly in terms of a spatial dynamism, as opposed to the configurational geometries of Cubism.[7] Many identified the fourth dimension as time, but this must have seemed rather too uninquisitive a solution to those artists who were attempting to track the deformations of bodies in motion or the redisposition of spatial dimensions in a world no longer bound by the rules of perspective.[8] In a rather dismissive remark made in an unfinished draft letter of 1917, addressee unknown, Apollinaire connects the fourth dimension with the representation of movement:

> Cela ne veut pas dire que les cubistes qui les [les futuristes] ont précédés n'ont pas tenté de résoudre ces problèmes et celui de la représentation du mouvement par exemple n'a pas moins sollicité l'attention des cubistes que des futuristes. Dans le langage des ateliers cubistes on l'appelait problème de la quatrième dimension (1991: 870)
>
> [That does not mean that the Cubists who preceded the Futurists did not try to solve these problems, and that of the representation of movement, for example, as much preoccupied the Cubists as it did the Futurists. In the language of the Cubist studios it was called the problem of the fourth dimension, that's all].

But if this draft letter indicates some loss of interest in the term, that does not necessarily entail a loss of interest in the concept.[9] In the view of the Futurists, '[e]very object reveals by its lines [i.e. force-lines] how it would resolve itself were it to follow the tendencies of its forces' (Apollonio, 1973: 48); a few paragraphs further on, in the same manifesto ('The Exhibitors to the Public 1912'), the signatories—Boccioni, Carrà, Russolo, Balla, Severini—add: 'All objects, in accordance with what the painter Boccioni happily terms *physical transcendentalism*, tend to the infinite by their *force-lines*, the continuity of which is measured by our intuition' (Apollonio, 1973: 48). If we think of the fourth dimension in terms of force-lines, therefore, we identify it with the virtual extendability of objects towards infinity, or with the extension outwards, towards infinity, of the energies produced by motion, light and colour. Elsewhere ('The Plastic Analogies of Dynamism—Futurist Manifesto 1913', Apollonio, 1973: 118–25), Severini speaks of 'spherical expansion in space', but this notion evidently includes other geometries: lines, planes, volumes (Apollonio, 1973: 123).

Apollinaire attributes fourth-dimensional thinking partly to the encounter with Egyptian, African and Oceanic sculpture (1991: 12), presumably on the basis not only of its unapologetic formal distortions and free manipulation of proportions to achieve a new truth to the figure but also of its multi-planarity and the complex spatial geometries those planes project. But, most fundamentally, Apollinaire's own fourth-dimensional thinking revolves round the space of extension itself, its enveloping multi-directionality, its infinitely expandable dimensions:

> Telle qu'elle s'offre à l'esprit, du point de vue plastique, la quatrième dimension serait engendrée par les trois mesures connues: elle figure l'immensité de l'espace s'éternisant dans toutes les directions à un moment déterminé. Elle est l'espace même, la dimension de l'infini; c'est elle qui doue de plasticité les objets. Elle leur donne les proportions qu'ils méritent dans l'œuvre [...]
>
> (1991: 11)

> [Such as it offers itself to the mind, from the plastic point of view, the fourth dimension is engendered by the three known dimensions: it figures the immensity of space extending infinitely in all directions at a given moment. It is space itself, the dimension of infinity; it is what endows objects with plasticity. It gives them the proportions appropriate to them in the work [...]].

The suggestion here that the fourth dimension is the multi-directional projection into infinity of the known three dimensions seems to run counter to those for whom a non-Euclidean geometry is the sine qua non of the fourth dimension ('Or, aujourd'hui, les savants ne s'en tiennent plus aux trois dimensions de la géométrie euclidienne' (1991: 11) [Now, today, scientists no longer hold to the three dimensions of Euclidian geometry]). But Apollinaire is more interested in the way in which spatial extension makes proportions and volume more malleable, more relative. It is a vision that is anti-perspectival and belongs either to a reversed and widening perspective, or to a soft, planar space, changing, curved, adapting itself to the viewer's or the object's mobility: 'Encore un petit effort pour se débarrasser de la perspective, du truc misérable de la perspective, de cette quatrième dimension à rebours, la perspective, de ce moyen de tout rapetisser inévitablement' (1991: 44) [Just one more small push to rid ourselves of perspective, of the miserable trick of perspective, of this back-to-front fourth dimension, perspective, of this means of inevitably diminishing everything].

But lines of force, like the fourth dimension, have other characteristics which we should consider. Force-lines, the Futurist painters tell us, are what involve the spectator in the picture, are what put the spectator at the centre of the picture's action, at the centre of the ambient. This is very much the effect of the concentric circles, the 'spherical expansions' of Apollinaire's 'Lettre-Océan' and, one might argue, of all calligrammatic enterprises: because immediately it ceases to be linear and becomes tabular, we have to think of writing itself as the creation of lines of force and the page as that which allows their self-development, their radiation, their infinite extension. While the linear continues to pursue the perspectival, to set its sights on a teleology, the full-stop, the horizon of its ambitions, while it aims to keep everything within a hierarchy of scale (main clause and subordinate clauses, clauses and phrases) with its elements syntagmatically related, the tabular develops non-syntagmatic relationships, undoes hierarchy, plays with parataxis or ataxia, lets text re-imagine its relative proportions, lets its elements create new ties both with each other and with items beyond the text, or with associations, memories and fantasies passing through the text. In this sense, the tabular page has both infinite depth and infinite extension into its blind field.

What is clear from the foregoing is that the notions of simultaneity and ubiquity also play a part in this vision of fourth-dimensional extendability. Both of them depend on the active participation of montage which helps establish the principle of synchronic polymorphous readability. Metamorphosis, as has been clear throughout, is more to be found in readerly processes than in text, and it is a paramount purpose of tabularity to translate textual being into readerly being, to embody and dramatize the readerly interrogation of language and improvisation with language and to create a free heterogeneity of tempo and spatial disposition which allows the readerly to re-imagine the writerly.

It is not always easy to make sense of Apollinaire's declarations about the fourth dimension, grandiose as they are in their claims. But while the Greeks, like the perspectivalists, seek scalar consistency and thus 'destroy' proportions—that is, nullify proportion as a free-expressive device, as a variable and active agent of plasticity—a multi-dimensional universe allows infinite scalar modulation, enables the artist freely to adapt proportion, planar complexity, volumetric relationships, to suit the object's plastic needs. It is this escape from human scale (the Greek art) into a world without scale, or in which scale is always to be re-defined, that Apollinaire prizes above all in the fourth dimension: 'L'art des peintres nouveaux prend l'univers infini comme idéal et c'est à cet idéal que l'on doit une nouvelle mesure de la perfection qui permet à l'artiste-peintre de donner à l'objet des proportions conformes au degré de plasticité où il souhaite l'amener' (1991: 11) [The art of the new painters takes the infinite universe as its ideal and it is to this ideal that is owed a new measure of perfection which allows the artist-painter to give the object proportions appropriate to the degree of plasticity he wishes to achieve for it]. And when Apollinaire shifts his enthusiasms from the relatively monochromatic vision of the Cubists to Delaunay's Orphism, then colour finds itself doing the same service as force-lines or planes, as an element of infinite extendability and multi-dimensional possibility. Of Francis Picabia's work Apollinaire writes: 'Il abordait ainsi un art où comme dans celui de Robert Delaunay, la dimension idéale, c'est la couleur. Elle a par conséquent toutes les autres dimensions. [...] La couleur dans cet art est saturée d'énergie et ses extrémités se continuent dans l'espace. [...] La couleur ne dépend plus des trois dimensions connues, c'est elle qui les crée' (1991: 45) [He thus engaged with an art in which, as in the art of Robert Delaunay, the dimension of the ideal is colour. Consequently it contains all the other dimensions. [...] Colour in this art is saturated with energy and its extremities continue out into space. [...] Colour no longer depends on the three known dimensions, rather, colour creates them itself] (see Chapter Five).

Crudely put, then, our conclusions about the fourth dimension might be these: three dimensions are established in perception by a fixed point of view (perspective) and by what Henri Poincaré calls 'l'effort d'accommodation et [...] la convergence des yeux' (1968: 79) [the effort of accommodation and [...] the convergence of the eyes]. Fourth-dimensional experience becomes possible: (a) if the disjunction of convergence and accommodation produces a new, isotropic version of 'complete visual space'; (b) if a mobile spectator gathers multiple points of view in a space which is constantly re-configuring itself, and thus reconstitutes space as multi-dimensional; (c) if one resorts to conceptual rather than perceptual notions of form; (d) if one imagines the infinite extension or projection of matter/energy in all directions, such that notions of scale, proportion, shape, lose their fixity and become malleable, variable; (e) if one assents to notions of a hyperspace of the spirit, or of heightened consciousness (the influence of Theosophy). The fourth dimension grows out of a pluralistic view of geometry; Poincaré reminds us: 'Une géométrie ne peut pas être plus vraie qu'une autre; elle peut seulement être *plus commode*' (1968: 76) [One geometry cannot be truer than another; it can only be *more convenient*]. But Poincaré also reminds us to distinguish between the space of geometries and the space of human experience, or what he calls 'espace représentatif' ('espace visuel', 'espace tactile', 'espace moteur')—that is to say, not a pre-given space within which we operate (continuous, infinite, three-dimensional, homogeneous, isotropic) but a lived space, generated by our own sensory and muscular involvement with it.[10] This 'espace représentatif'—'Nos représentations ne sont que la reproduction de nos sensations' (1968: 82) [Our representations are no more than the reproduction of our sensations]—is neither three-dimensional, nor homogeneous, nor isotropic: in fact, Poincaré declares: '[. . .] *l'espace moteur aurait autant de dimensions que nous avons de muscles*' (1968: 81) [*motor space would have as many dimensions as we have muscles*]. But whether our fourth-dimensional hypotheses favour the temporal or the spatial, the physical or the mystical, we should understand the fourth dimension as a set of conjectures by which modernist thinking looked to open up new perceptual/conceptual possibilities and to achieve new complexities of perceptual consciousness.

As we speak of opening up new perceptual/conceptual possibilities, we must add one further facet to fourth-dimensional explorations: Apollinaire's championing of the phonograph and cinema as the future vehicles of poetic production. These facilities will provide poets with 'une liberté inconnue jusqu'à présent' (1991: 944) [a freedom hitherto unknown], not least because they allow experimentation with the simultaneous and polyphonic: '([. . .] Comme si le poète ne pouvait pas faire enregistrer directement un poème par le phonographe et faire enregistrer en même temps des rumeurs naturelles ou d'autres voix, dans une foule ou parmi ses amis?)' (1991: 976–7) [([. . .] As if the poet could not record a poem directly on to the phonograph and at the same time record natural noises or other voices in a crowd or among his friends?)]. We shall have more to say about the cinema and its fourth-dimensional possibilities in due course, in our translation of Apollinaire's 'Lundi rue Christine' (see below), where we shall borrow from the cinematographic thinking of Dziga Vertov, partly because of the centrality of montage, both aural and visual, to his revolutionary enterprise, partly because of his theory of the interval. The phonograph, for its part and along with its capacity to graft an ambient soundscape on to the individual voice, as, simultaneously, part of its own constitution and the field of its potential effects, acts as the auditory equivalent of the newsreel camera, collecting acousmatic[11] sounds and voices and making them transportable, re-locatable, re-combinable. And if, as Apollinaire envisages, poetry might be recorded directly to disc, without the mediation of paper, then text would be its performance, and 'liveness' would be the dimension in which it made its sense. Not, then, the deciphering and interpreting of script, but the auditory and psycho-physiological response to an uttering voice in a particular acoustic. Recording is a process of activating different dimensions of aural receptivity.

Bearing all these factors in mind, I present a tabular translation of Apollinaire's linear 'La Porte' (*Alcools*, 1913) (see Appendix I (v) for French text):

2 + 4 The O

D oo R f the **hotEL**

2 + 4 smi ch ing my
iles ill **blood** A

5 + 3+4 whatmydearmothercanitmeanformeemrof A
1 TO
+ 5 be this employEE
3 for m al[one]
3 **who** *no[thing]* **exists B**
~~3~~ 4 *coupled PI-*
MUS
~~3~~ 2 swimming
in
4+ the **listless**
2(!) … DEPTHS B
3 Fresh Angels **b**
r
o
3 **ught to land**
3 in Marseille(s)
3 yesterday [a.m.] c
4 I hear die once
4 and die again
1+5(!) humble as I am which
4 a distant air who am C
4 **nothing**
2 has worth D
2 MY CHILD
4 I have giv'n you 4 all that I had

2 **now WORK d**

As I take the ST away from its linearity, I want to keep that ST as an originating shape in the reader's mind. So I have indicated its rhyme-scheme in the right-hand margin (couplets) and also its metrico-rhythmic structure—predominantly in the left-hand margin, although it begins to stray into the main field of the text, chasing errant elements. I have tried to adhere to this metrico-rhythmic structure, albeit in fragmented form; but I have had to change a 3 > 3 hemistich to a 4 > 2, I have given 'smiles' two syllables, I have stretched one syllable ('DEPTHS') to two, by introducing a syllable's worth of suspension points, and I have created a 5 by borrowing a word ('which') from an unrelated clause. The shift from one language to the other is thus experienced as some monstrous metamorphosis, monstrous in the sense that it necessitates linguistic distortions. The linear formality of the ST survives as a set of spectral hieroglyphs which the new writing acknowledges and partly incorporates while installing its own re-territorialisation of the text. How many lines does this poem have? Unfortunately, the left-hand margin has relinquished its role as the initiator of enunciatory beginnings and takes its place among a multitude of margins which scatter the voice into an overallness which requires the constant re-initiation of language without any guarantees of vocal continuity. I will not comment on the possible meanings of the variations in letter-size, typeface and disposition, other than, by way of example, to say that the employment of *scriptio continua* in the address to the mother expresses an impulse of fusion with the mother, thwarted by the mirroring of 'for me' at the end of the utterance; when the mother comes to speak, she operates with a speech mechanism which is separative, and the injunction to work is an act of ousting, an order to the poet to constitute himself as an independent entity. The play of notions of solitude and dependency is clearly important to the poem's activity. These variations in letter-size, typeface and disposition also alert us to the fact that paralinguistic features, vocal colourings, play an extremely significant role in the performance of the poem or in the performance that the poem is, but they do not indicate exactly what those vocal colourings are. More important still than the significances of individual features is the way in which these features engage the freedoms and responsibilities of the reader, publicly activating and exhibiting both, increasing both, compelling a spiritual investment in text, and a participation in its making, that the reader can fulfil only if he/she makes the same kind of journey from the ST that the translator has.

My further, second-stage tinkerings (Fig. 14) add two further protagonists to the mix, handwriting and photography, the one predominantly

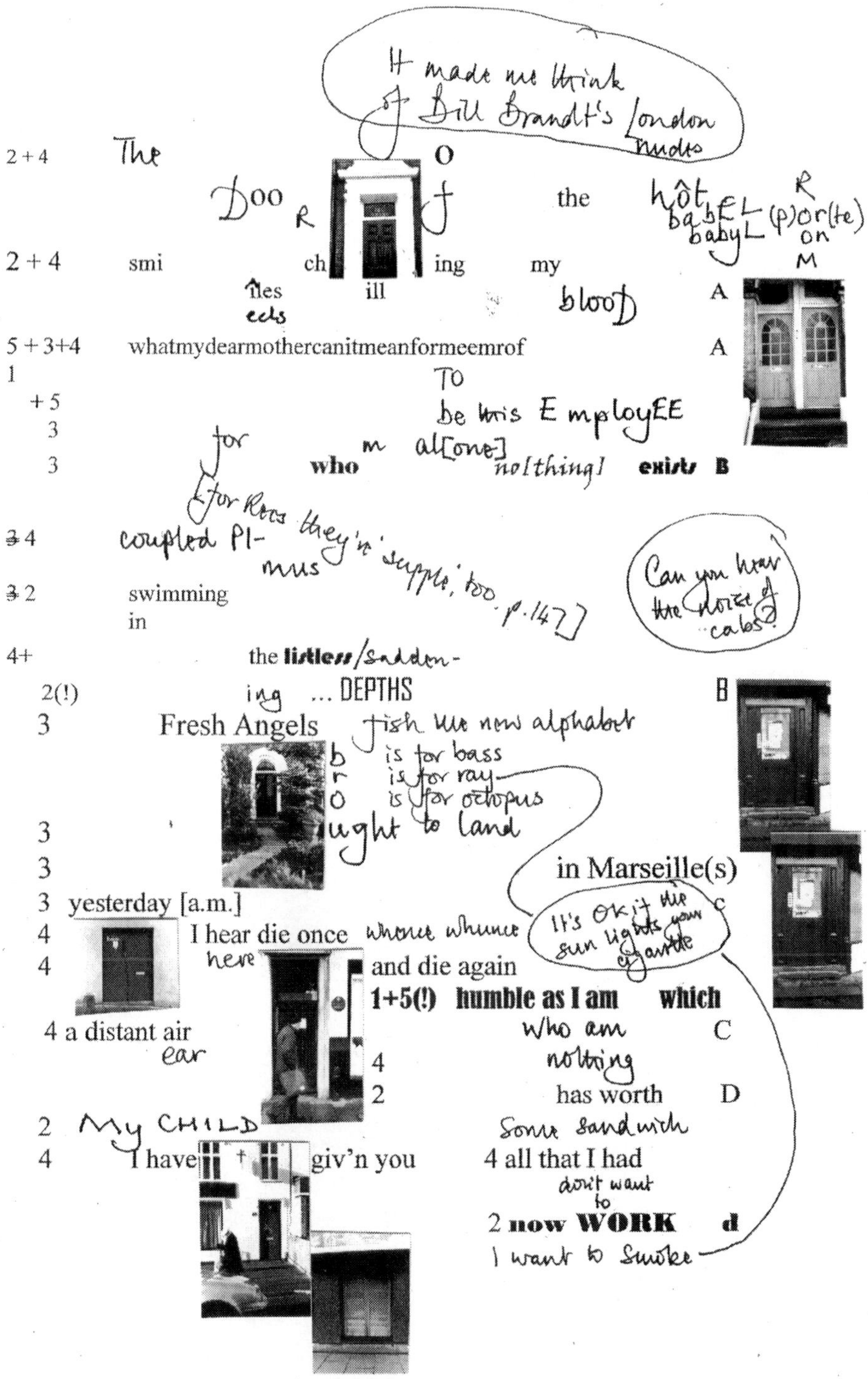

Figure 14: Translation, with photo-collage and handwritten interventions, of 'La Porte"

serving metamorphosis, the other montage. My use of handwriting has several functions: I count graphology as the art of discovering in styles of handwriting the timbres and intonations of a voice; handwriting is the graphic equivalent of the voice. Handwriting introduces into text the activity of time, the pressure of time, the ongoingness of response. These handwritten marginalia and annotations are the very quick of reading. But, above all, handwriting is the agent of metamorphosis: in its very cursivity it declares its desire to pursue joined-up change, a graphic choreography of lexical shape-shifting. This desire, this capability, traces the modulations of the text in the reader's imaginary, the kinds of things that 'thicken out' the experience of text: variations on the sounds of words, homophones, homonyms, paronomasia, the signifying impulses of morphemes, real and false, the impulse of phonemes or graphemes to summon up related words and ideas, all kinds of involuntary association. These further workings incorporate, for example, materials from, and allusions to, Apollinaire's two poems dedicated to hotels: 'Hôtels' (*Alcools*) and 'Hôtel' (*Le Guetteur mélancolique*, 1952, originally *Banalités*, seven poems published in *Lacerba*, 15 April 1914). To the former we owe the noise of the cabs and the image of the hotel as a modern Babel, which through the shared etymology of the Hebrew *Bābhel* (< Akkadian *Bāb-ilu*, ironically 'gate of God') begets Babylon, which, in turn, recalls, perhaps, Arnold Bennett's *The Grand Babylon Hotel* (1902) (*A Fantasy on Modern Themes*). The poem 'Hôtel' has a final line which, as in 'La Porte', treats of the topic of work but sounds like a defiant rejoinder to his mother's injunction 'Now work', namely: 'I don't want to work I want to smoke' ('Je ne veux pas travailler je veux fumer'). And the desire to smoke—'pour faire des mirages'—accompanies an image of the sun reaching through the window to light the poet's cigarette. This re-working also generates further moves which consolidate or justify previous 'decisions': Apollinaire's 'anges' are at once angels and angel-sharks, but also angel-fish, and the '-iles' of 'smiles', under the forward influence of the circumflex on 'hôtel'—the importation of a French accent into the speaking of the line—and the backward influence of 'ill', shifts to 'îles' ('eels'). With Babel, Douglas Adams's (*Hitch-Hiker's Guide to the Galaxy*) babel-fish emerges. At the same time, the angel-fish triggers a fish alphabet, like the one we find in Greenaway's *A Zed & Two Noughts*, and the part-vertical writing of 'brought' turns itself into a horizontal set, a list. The ambiguity of 'ray' then allows a connection with the sun as cigarette-lighter. Additionally, I have begun to include the accidents of my own researches as I undertook the translation: Garnet Rees's edition of *Alcools* for the Athlone French

Poets (1975) contains, in its 'Commentaries', the misprint 'pi-mus souples' (147), a Freudian slip, something that spontaneously suggests itself, one of those examples, perhaps, of voluntary or creative misreading, or mis-remembering, so integral to the reading experience.

The photographs, on the other hand, speak a radically different language: they are an infiltration of the text by a documentary mentality, an infiltration of things seen—here doors—an infiltration of visual data from the outside, instead of being, as with the handwritten, an expansion from within. These photographic fragments are glances or gazes without a point of view, or with a disembodied point of view, alternative spaces and consciousnesses; anyone might have taken these photographs because the camera took them. Put another way, they are an acousmatics of the eye. What designs do these photographs have on us, what re-configurations of our understanding do they entail? They are the products of a prosthesis of the eye, a kind of machine for disjunctive experience, from anywhere at any time. And through this prosthetic aid we multiply the existential sense of the door as, variably, an access to an invisible other space, an unpredictable opportunity, a fatal temptation, a derision of one's confinement, a figure of enigma, and of potential, fatal disobedience; the images further conjure up for me the doors in Brandt's nudes of Campden Hill, Hampstead, or Belgravia; but they might equally trigger Eliot's Fräulein von Kulp 'Who turned in the hall, one hand on the door' ('Gerontion'), or any of countless other such instances. And, in the right-hand margin, two sets of paired doors imitate the activity of rhyme.

This combination of the handwritten and the photographic, the metamorphic and the montaged, the within and without, the associative and documentary, in a tabular disposition, argues that, through the combination of media, but more especially through the tabular itself, reading can create its own fourth dimension, its own multi-dimensionality. Tabular space engineers, dramatizes, the searching restlessness of the eye, encourages patterns of fixation and saccade, plays with foveal and peripheral contrasts, insinuates itineraries of the eye, like those traced on paintings, drawings, photographs and texts by A.L. Yarbus and others (Gandelman, 1991: 6–13), eliciting now an optic, now a haptic, strategy. The linear text seems designed for an eye which, as it were, obediently follows the text—though this may not, of course, be the case—falling into the rhythm of the lines' back-and-forth; and this in turn establishes assumptions about the consistency of the eye's speed, the steady purposefulnesss of its trajectory, the evenness of its assimilation of text. In the tabular text, eye movement necessarily becomes heterogeneous, qualitatively variable, distractable, improvised. What we find difficult to imagine or understand is that tabular reading turns text from something which exists and is waiting to be read, by any number of readers, in more or less the same way (the isotropic version of reading and reading-space, the version of linear reading) into something which exists only in its very being read, by a particular individual, in its eye-activated movement, where the very rests and distractions of the eye are part of that movement and not a momentary opting out; reading, as this engaged and endlessly provoked activity, deepens, diversifies and singularizes itself. Linear reading is the reading of decipherment and construal; tabular reading is an exacerbation of the phenomenology of reading.

And, as the eye engages with paginal space, so it must negotiate between the real and the virtual. The page is real space as a support of print in the environment of reading, an object among others, handled, looked at, finding its place in the circumstances of a day, of a life, competing with other kinds of sensory experience, coloured by all the particularities of both reader and reading ambience. But this awareness constantly crosses back and forth with the virtual space of the text, with fictional, and fictions of, space. Fictional space is any one of those spatial metaphors that the reading mind might generate from text: territorial, social, geometric, galactic—desert, room, cube, cosmos, city, precipice. The fictions of space are underlying modes of apprehension. In rejecting perspective, we tend to reject notions of space as an empty container, pre-formatted, waiting to receive its consignment of objects and features, and favour instead space generated by mobility, projected by moving bodies, constructed by moving bodies, constantly re-configuring itself. But when we come to the page, and particularly to the space of the tabular page, we may as much envisage it as a receptive space, a gravity-free, non-dimensional, nebulous space, without top or bottom, left or right, the kind of space in which writing cannot rationally conduct itself, cannot establish its normal coordinates, as a cinematic space in which the reading eye constantly adjusts its focus, its depth of field, its film-speed, and treats language as a screen protagonist rather than as a medium, a protagonist with motives and feelings made manifest by and in its performative activity. In the tabular, the text/page cannot be mapped by any convenient Euclidean triangulation; the tabular is a hyperspace in which the wandering eye gathers verbal particles of different proportions, proximities, velocities, at odd angles to each other, and weaves them into polymorphous, *n*-dimensional figures.

The fourth dimension grows out of the adoption of new underlying conceptual and perceptual positions. Much of our reality is made up of what we are accustomed to, what seems to demonstrate itself by experimental fact or by perceptual convenience. But nothing prevents us *a priori* from assuming the contrary to this position. In the case of Apollinaire's *poèmes-conversations*, for example, we assume that snippets of dialogue come to a central auditory mechanism (the poet) from a space that is isotropic (having uniform physical properties in all directions). But what if we thought of the space of the *poème-conversation* as non-isotropic? How would we relate the overheard snippets to each other, that is, how would we *hear* them in relation to each other? Would we hear them cubistically, since when we say of Cubism that it multiplies points of view, or shifts perception from the perceptual to the conceptual, we are as good as saying that it enters fourth-dimensionality? This is a question we might ask in relation to 'Lundi rue Christine'.

'Lundi rue Christine' (see Appendix I (vi) for French text) may seem to offer few problems: a *poème-conversation* composed of stray snatches of conversation which confront us with the ever-renewed marvel of how much heterogeneous and unpredictable human activity takes place within every circumscribed human space, how varied are the social backgrounds and expectations. Society lives for ever on the brink, or in the midst, of theft, sexual abuse, all kinds of illicit behaviour, all kinds of project and memory. And the problem of writing it is a problem of segmentation and grouping, of what stanzaic structure does what kind of justice to embryonic narratives and thematic connections. But clearly such a gathering and 'composing' is necessarily random and can respond to a wide range of compositional strategies. In my first translation I have re-arranged Apollinaire's lines using an out-of-the-hat method, and have incorporated along the way observations (the italicized lines) culled from a holiday in Spain (10–18 April 2012), visiting Segovia, Avila, Salamanca, Zamora, Leon, Burgos and Alcalà de Henares. My principal task was then, once again, one of line-grouping/stanzaic formation:

MONDAY

RUE CHRISTINE

When you've finished we'll play backgammon
Plim plam plim
You're a dead loss
You walk so slow my back aches
Chugchugchug

Translating Apollinaire

When you come to Tunis I'll see you smoke some hashish
The fountain flows

Six mirrors never take their eyes off each other
Someone looking after the *porte cochère* while the other goes up
And the Retrochoir in Avila's cathedral in limestone

A little maid is all I've got
Or the well-drilled contingent of gas-heaters
These crêpes were delicious
The patronne is consumptive
In Smyrna in Naples in Tunisia
Soaps picked up in hotels were his olfactory bank
I owe my landlady bugger it 300 francs
I almost forgot the Virgin with her scissors and generous thimble
I think we're going to get even deeper into this mess
Piles of saucers flowers a calendar
Should do the trick

Once there he introduces me to a chunky chap
The Dane smokes his cigarette as he consults the timetable
Seda natural bordada con hilos dorados y plateados eighteenth century
The concierge's mother and the concierge will let anything in
The red-headed waitress has been carried off by a bookseller
Wait you've taken the glue
That's eight or nine years ago
A conductor with a sore throat
It's absolutely impossible
But where is it for God's sake

Listen Jacques what I'm going to tell you is very serious
I'd rather cut off my exactly so than give them to her

The number of places he revisited just by washing his hands

Louise has forgotten her fur
The floor is sprinkled with sawdust
If you've got the bottle you'll come with me tonight

Honour often hangs on the time on the clock
On the road to Salamanca storks follow the plough like seagulls

Sir he says to me would you care to see what I can do in the way of
etchings and paintings

That seems to make some sense
Three gas lamps lit
Prohibido tocar los objetos
The major fifth
Or the guerrilla snipings of ill-clad graffiti 1832
I'm leaving at 8.27 pm
A journalist who what's more is only a passing acquaintance

That woman's got a nose like a tapeworm
I'd been puzzling over the strangely skirted Cristo 'de Burgos' anonymous
The last time I was in China
Here we are sir
Who says to me
That flock of sheep on an island of dull grass
Was the dog also grazing
Dress as dark as her fingernails
Listen it's delightful
The malachite ring
My dear sir

Multi-purpose shipping company

The black cat slinks across the brasserie
After lunch café du Luxembourg
So it's true
Those sleeping or grieving squires half the size of their supine knights
I haven't got a fur-coat but I'm not cold

The *poème-conversation* is a poem in process, never more than a draft, infinitely to be added to or subtracted from, thriving on its own polymorphousness. In this sense it is the radio-ear equivalent of Dziga Vertov's 'kino-eye':

> Kino-eye uses every possible means in montage, comparing and linking all points of the universe in any temporal order, breaking, when necessary, all the laws and conventions of film [poetic] construction (1984: 88)

But however flexible and accommodating the *poème-conversation* is, its central significance remains constant: the problematic nature of urban consciousness. Briefly put, urban consciousness is a consciousness made non-unified and self-disseminating by the very variety of heteroclite phenomena by which it is assaulted. Montage is as much the predicament as the solution to, the mode of management of, the predicament. The ability to write is overtaken by the need to edit. The locatedness of each utterance is countervailed by its acousmatic nature and by the ubiquity of the receptor-mechanism, the poet, who can be anywhere and everywhere. Is he an integrated or merely a virtual part of the situation? If the truth be known, it is not just that a presiding consciousness has been dispersed; it has been actively multiplied.

In suggesting that the modern urban consciousness is a cinematic consciousness we are suggesting not only that we have to envisage a camera-ear, which does not eavesdrop so much as hear in non-human ways, but also that consciousness itself has achieved a disembodied, objective status, one which can see/hear 'without limits or distances' (Vertov, 1984: 41), one whose very mobility, like that of the cine-camera, 'a beau nous approcher ou nous éloigner des choses, et tourner autour d'elles, il supprime l'ancrage du sujet autant que l'horizon du monde, si bien qu'il substitute un savoir implicite et une intentionnalité seconde aux conditions de la perception naturelle' (Deleuze, 1983: 84) [however much it brings us close to things or distances us from them, and revolves around them, it suppresses the anchorage of the subject as much as the horizon of the world, such that it substitutes an implicit knowledge and a secondary intentionality for the conditions of natural perception]. But the unanchored subject is not entirely obliterated, remains always a potential and intermittent actor, by proxy, as vicarious participant. And, indeed, we may feel that many of these conversational snippets are attributed utterances, on the basis of writerly involvement or empathy, like free indirect speech. But, again, the camera's ability to move freely and invisibly within the community generates a related cinematic experience of participatory co-existence, of a Romains-style unanimism, as though café habitués or their like could, through speech, create the equivalent of the swirling orchestrations of starlings' 'murmurings':

> C'est en fonction de ces données que Mitry proposait la notion d'*image mi-subjective* généralisée pour désigner cet 'être-avec' de la caméra: elle ne se confond pas avec le personnage, elle n'est pas non plus en dehors, elle est avec lui. C'est une sorte de Mitsein proprement cinématographique
>
> (Deleuze, 1983: 106)

> [It is in line with these features that Mitry proposed the notion of a generalised *semi-subjective image* to designate the camera's 'being-with': it does not blend with the character, nor is it outside,

> it is, rather, with him/her. It is a kind of *Mitsein* peculiar to cinematography].

Given this multi-dimensionality of disembodied consciousness, little is to be gained, in relation to 'Lundi rue Christine', in trying to separate out conversational material from recorded events or authorial observations. Much is said about Apollinaire's abandonment of punctuation in terms of rhythmic effects and syntactic ambiguation, but little attention is given to the consequences of the omission of inverted commas or other speech indicators in these *poèmes-conversations*. In our analysis, their omission leads to the scumbling of objective and semi-subjective perceptual states, and doubts about the factual or fictional nature of the directly transcribed/indexical. What, then, is the task of the reader? If we think of each utterance as a shot, then each shot is on the brink of narrative/perceptual/affective expansion, but is nipped in the bud, so that there is a repeated pressure but no outlet. Glimpses of autobiography might be the clips of a newsreel, reported direct speech might be first-hand, but might be second-hand, third-hand, the emergent personal or protagonistic might already have been absorbed into the patchwork of the collective. As this set of indecisions unfolds, so our attention shifts from the shots themselves to the cuts or intervals between them, to the interactions of the lines and the 'field' of experience they trigger. Vertov's first formulation of his theory of intervals ('WE: Variant of a Manifesto', 1922) does not give much away:

> *Intervals* (the transitions from one movement to another) are the material, the elements of the art of movement, and by no means the movements themselves. It is they (the intervals) which draw the movement to a kinetic resolution.
>
> The organization of movement is the organization of its elements, or its intervals, into phrases (1984: 8–9).[12]

In our application of this 'theory' to the *poème-conversation* we understand 'phrases' as 'stanzas' or 'line-groups', and 'kinetic' as 'kinaesthetic'—that is, as the psycho-physiological tensions (and their resolution?) generated in the reader/listener by the sequencing of shots. Michelson's evasive 1992 article points us in the direction of mathematics (as opposed to Eisenstein's *musical* conception of the interval) and of the fourth dimension and Einsteinian relativity. In what is for me an infinitely permutable text, a theory of intervals must be based on the changing patterns of reciprocal influence that lines can exert on each other, the different rhythmic, semantic, tonal and associational pressures they can apply to each other. The modern urban consciousness constantly re-sifts the phenomena by which it is surrounded, re-aligns them, re-adapts them to changing additions and deletions. These phenomena are frequently unsourced (acousmatic) and cannot easily be apprehended in themselves: consciousness continually re-inhabits their interactive field, momentarily disengaging now one phenomenon, now another, in a complicated weave of variable sensation. This is poetry not as an intended text, to be deciphered and interpreted on the strength of its formal closure, but as a play of language harvested from an environment whose value is experiential and sense-producing, but on the strength of open-ended variation.

What, then, was my next task as translator (see Fig. 15, for first page of new version)? Most obviously it was necessary to redistribute the lines, to make sense-productive their relationship with the page. If the page is the café, then the talk, even if drawn from sources beyond the café, must find its appointed places there, since its space is also the ear of the poet. The lines must be arranged in such a way that the positions of enunciation (margins) provide a complicating counterpoint for the line-groupings. And the margins can develop their own dynamic, expressed either in stepped diagonals, moving in both directions, or in groups of lines set over against each other, or in single observations more or less floating free. A text aligned on only one margin is neither orchestrated nor improvised, does not challenge the reader to listen differentially, does not demand special accommodations, is expressively and projectively inert.

I then handwrote the lines which I had not myself supplied, trying to create different calligraphic styles for each utterance. The purpose of this procedure was twofold. First, as the text stands, the uniformity of typeface implies a uniformity of vocal timbre. In the absence of speech-signs I wanted to invest these lines with a spokenness, a spokenness in real time; handwriting is both an act of immediate transcription and the affirmation of the speaker's voice, his/her continuing and pressing presence. These lines may be acousmatic (unidentified), but they have identity. Secondly, I wanted to imply that the lines could be repeatedly handwritten, in ever-modified calligraphic styles, depending on how they related to each other, on what order they appeared in. I wanted a way of giving each line a temporary singularity, which would inevitably be vulnerable to relativisation. A changeable handwriting dramatises the activity of the interval. Handwriting helps us to understand the sense in which the process of editing (ordering or re-ordering of shots)

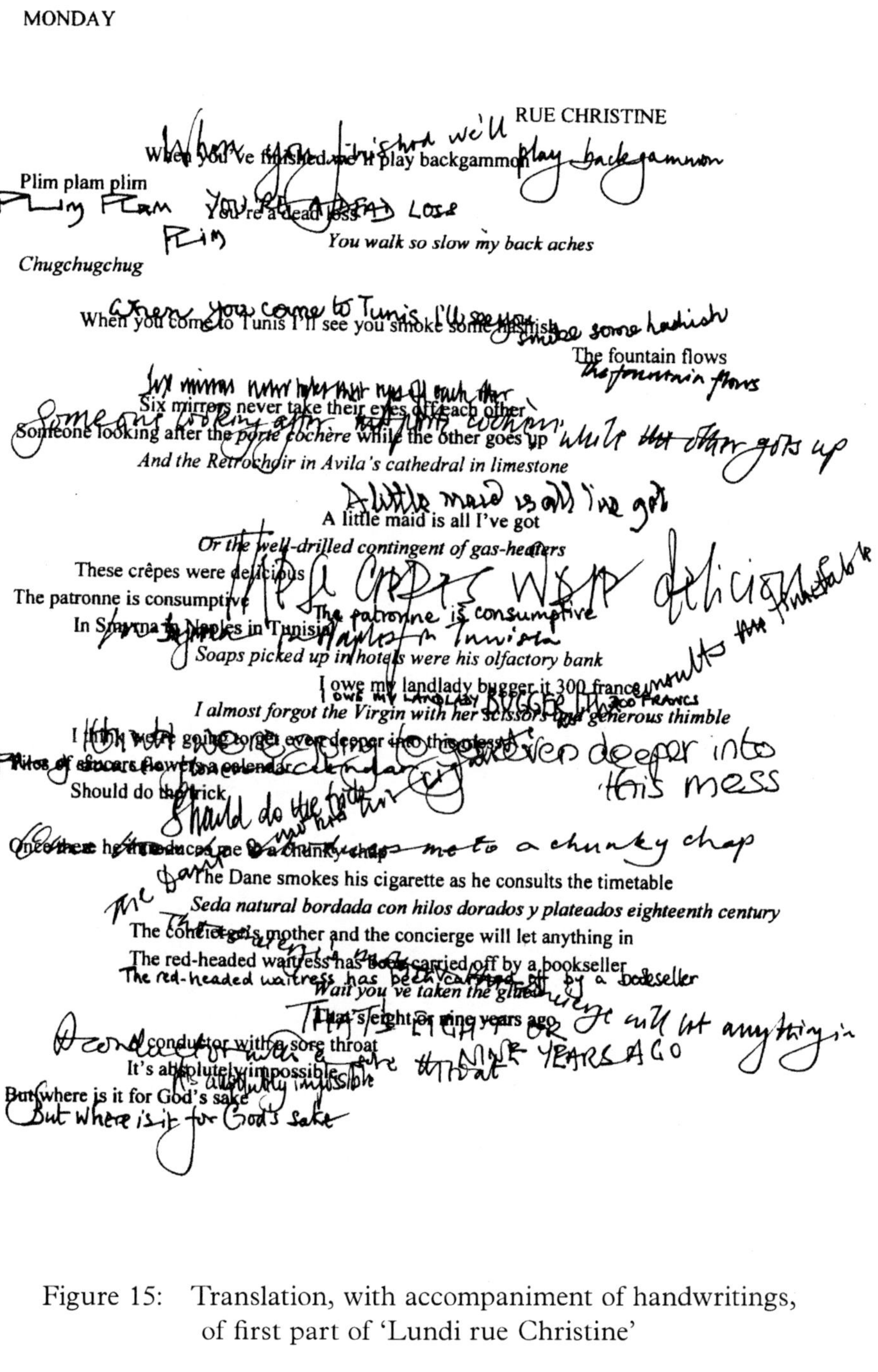

Figure 15: Translation, with accompaniment of handwritings, of first part of 'Lundi rue Christine'

is a maieutic operation, a midwifery of collision, collusion, transition, the metamorphic series.

Here we have not quite finished with the fourth dimension. If the page is the café, then the successive and simultaneous, the vocally isolated and the polyphonic, intermingle; and at the same time we hear differentially, with different clarities, with different amplitudes, with different tempi. Here handwriting makes a third contribution: because it has a wayward, shape-shifting, size-varying way of occupying the page, it implies different degrees and kinds of resonance. There is a natural equation to be made between legibility and audibility, so that different calligraphic styles suggest different modes of hearing, and perhaps listening, different auditory perspectives. The handwritten text is not a substitute for the printed text. It folds out of the printed text as the printed text's invisibility or virtuality, providing another set of auditory dimensions. And we might make these observations rather more detailed. Handwriting can serve the same purposes as Vertov's experimental camera: where Vertov draws on slow motion, superimpositions, freeze-frames, split-screen, dissolves, the whole panoply, to take the eye into dimensions of seeing that redefine human relationships and human activity in a techno-machinic environment, the handwriting of text might invite the ear to hear in close-up, indistinctly, in accelerated mode, superimpositionally, recedingly, and so on. While the printed text tends to promote an isotropic view of space and a uniform, unproblematic audibility, a varied and variable handwriting animates and diversifies space as a chamber of multi-dimensional resonance. While the printed text gravitates towards studio sound, handwritten text gravitates towards locational sound.

The final step is a photographic one (Figs 16–17). These photographic fragments derive not from the lines in roman that beget the handwritten but from the lines in italics, my trip to the cities of Spain. Like the lines of the printed text, the photographs are permutable arrangements, momentarily finding their own architectures or sculptural forms, but without insisting. They are photographs about encounters in foreign places, conversations, leisure activities, sites awaiting occupation; but there are darker tones: funerary inscriptions, and 'the well-drilled contingent of gas-heaters', which, along with the Virgin, act as tutelary spirits, bringing warmth in intemperate circumstances.

The presence of handwriting reminds us that a printed text *precedes* reading and follows speaking and listening; the handwritten text tries to compress that process, to make more coincident speaking and listening

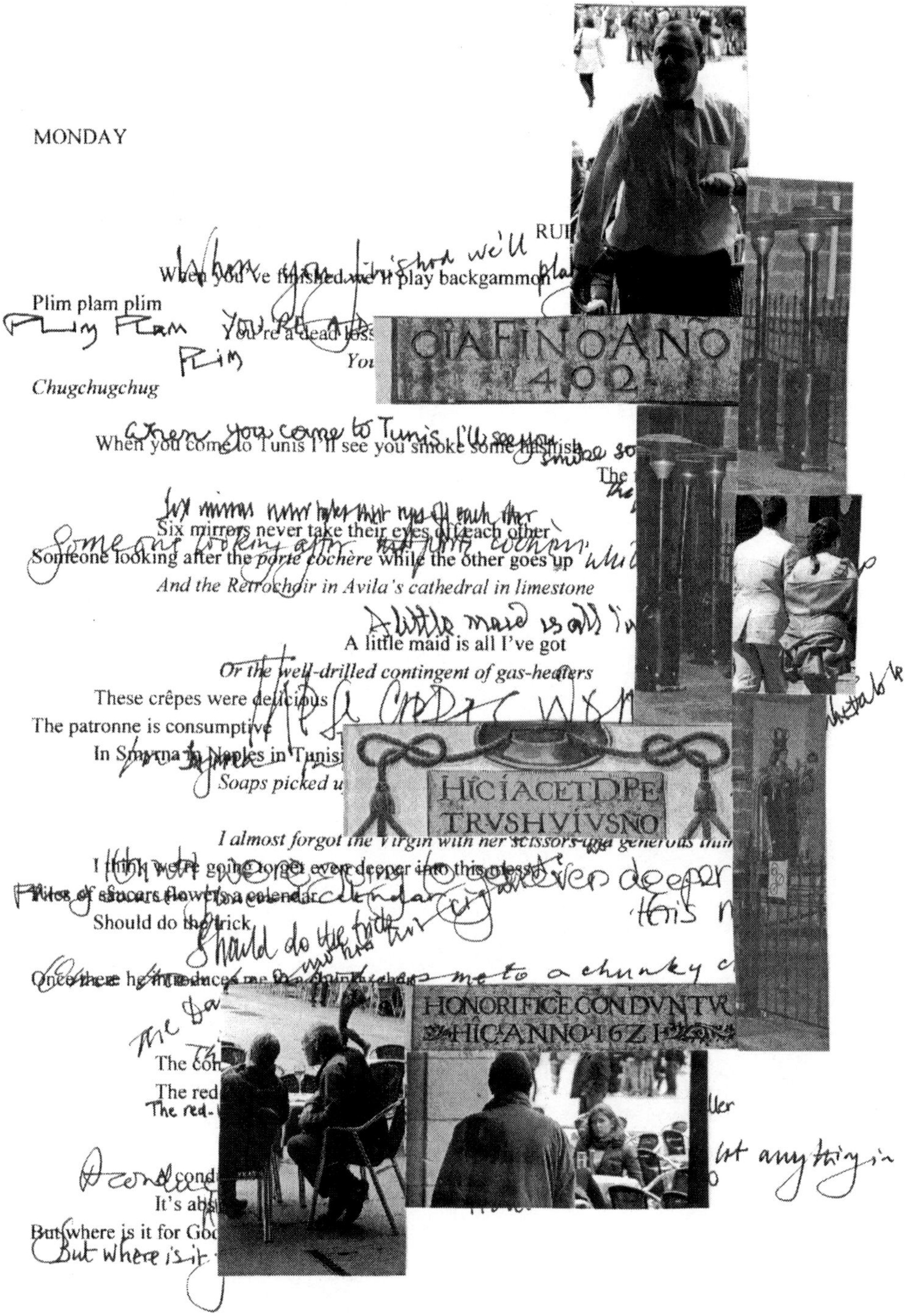

Figure 16: Translation, with accompaniment of handwritings and photo-collage, of 'Lundi rue Christine'

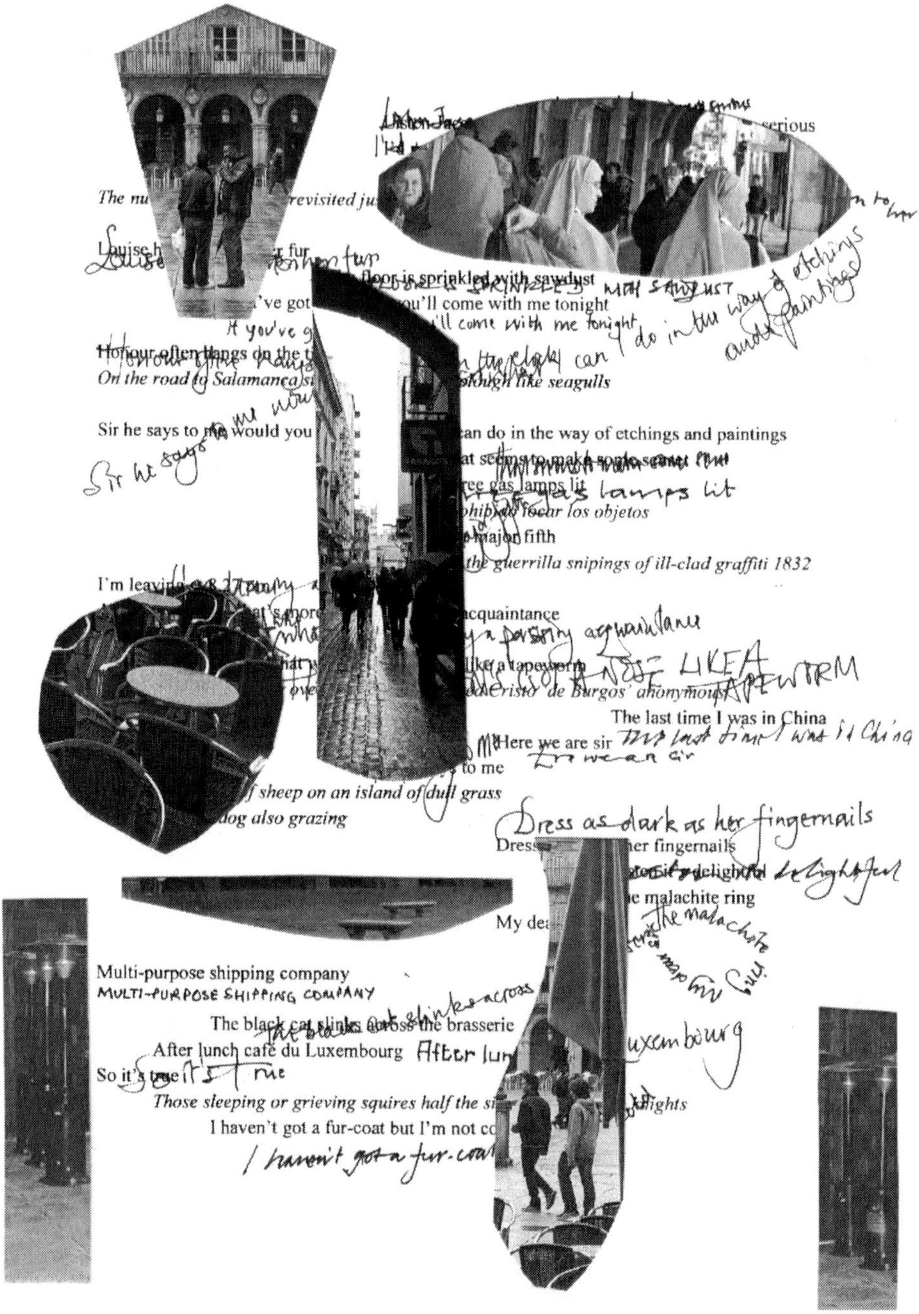

Figure 17: Translation, with accompaniment of handwritings and photo-collage, of 'Lundi rue Christine'

and reading. Indeed, we might say that the handwritten is more listened to than read, has less the durability of text than the evanescence of speech-flow. The *poème-conversation* itself is less a written text than the moment of listening, a moment of transcription. With a photograph, we might make a similar distinction: between 'the taking of' (*generating* an image of) and 'the image of' (an image created from the taking, of the taken). That is to say, the moment of taking is the moment of looking-at, not of being-looked-at, with the benefit of a lens which is a visual prosthetic, which sees the invisible or the visually passed over. The very shapes of the photographic fragments are not shapes projected by the eye. They are cut out of the field of vision. And the process of cutting exacerbates the looking; these are not the comfortable, conventional, endlessly repeated 6″ × 4″ rectangles. These, in their very variety, promise a variety of looking, or a problematic of looking. And to deprive them of their frame (rectangularity) is to discourage interpretative approaches and to re-install the paramountness of the moment of espying. This is to reaffirm that photographs 'develop', that they have no single quiddity, but shift along the scale from the indexical to the iconic, or from the iconic to the symbolic, as they are put to different uses with the passage of time (Scott, 1999: 27–45).

The question, then, is how to find one's way back, from the symbolic to the indexical, from interpretation to pure sensory experience, from a moment of being to a moment of looking. What is here enacted is twofold: the supercession of the text's textuality and the re-installation of the pre-textual (speaking and listening, looking, *not* reading); and the concomitant shift from the organizational to the aggregational, from ordered phenomena to competing stimuli. We read in order gradually to dispense with reading. Let us remember that the attraction of the phonograph lies in its being able to dispense with text and to put the listener/poet, like the *poème-conversation*, at the centre of life, recording 'le lyrisme ambiant', that lyricism lying in its very polyphony, in the very simultaneity of its constituents (1991: 976). For Apollinaire, the magic lies in a spatial eternity (infinite extension in all directions, ubiquity) made lyrical and fourth-dimensional by being caught 'à un moment déterminé' (1991: 11). Because it seems to compress time, photographic fragmentation changes the intensity and nature of the look: it gravitates towards micro-focusing and the glance or glimpse, the non-arrested look, the caught-sight-of, in a mobile and busy environment. And, accordingly, the progressive superimpositions are a direct result of the hubbub of the urban scene, of the as-if-simultaneous interventions of ever-changing points of attention. It is right that we should lose our bearings in the modern world, that we should experience the world as parataxis, enumeration, montage, photographic fragment; our very disorientation makes more vivid our sensory participation, our experiential availability, which, in Apollinaire, gravitates towards the unanimistic, a unanimism paradoxically intensified by heterogeneity, constructibility, permutability. Apollinaire may note, apropos of Gris, that the social function of art is much diminished (1991: 41), but with an artist 'aussi dégagé de préoccupations esthétiques, aussi préoccupé d'énergie que Marcel Duchamp' [and Apollinaire], art and the people might be reconciled (1991: 48).

Earlier in the chapter we spoke of the redistribution of consciousness as the attachment to the principle of metamorphosis of the principle of montage. The negotiated settlement between the continuous and the discontinuous, the metamorphic and the multi-dimensional, the consecutively generated and the patched together, between transition and interval, finds its full textual expression in the tabular. As my coda, I would like to address a final translation of the linear into the tabular, a final negotiation between metamorphosis and montage, in a rendering of the epitome of the line, Apollinaire's single-line 'Chantre' (*Alcools*):

> Et l'unique cordeau des trompettes marines   3 > 3 > 3 > 3

In the previous chapter we concerned ourselves with continuous variation as a key to the alternative texts, or texts alongside, which reading releases, voluntarily or involuntarily, in its intertextual, associative, acoustic and visual embroideries. Among these supplements we singled out those creative acoustic deformations of text produced by aural hallucination or mishearing:

> Le ciel est étoilé par les abus des biches/poches

There is nothing whimsical or artificial about this practice. As users of language, we are all aware how much one word is nearly another, how every particle of language is prone to slippage: we have figures and tropes at our elbow constantly to remind us of this fact: paronomasia, rhyme, homophony, punning. Freud's *The Psychopathology of Everyday Life* (2002/1901) provides a comprehensive account of the kinds of slip, and complicity between forgetting and remembering, that life is full of, and implies that, just as we might assert that normality is controlled or diluted neurosis, so normal speech is the avoidance of slips of the tongue, the successful suppression of interruptive material.

Who is not familiar with the act of will required to resist the solicitations of the scatological? Tourette's syndrome is never far away. While Freud is, on the whole, more concerned with slips of production rather than of reception (although he does deal with slips in reading); while he is more interested in *correcting*, by analysis, those slips which are the eruptions of half-suppressed materials; while he is concerned with 'texts alongside' which are the *involuntary* surfacings of material from *outside* the intended context, my subject is the ear's creative acoustic transformation of text. It remains nonetheless important to allow that creative morphing and the pathological are coextensive and equally deeply embedded in human processing mechanisms.

Apollinaire's single alexandrine has, on the face of it, a rich structural self-sufficiency: the second hemistich rhythmically parallels the first, each hemistich has a *coupe enjambante* at its secondary accent ('uni/que', 'trompe/ttes'), the noun groups are chiastically arranged (adjective + noun > noun + adjective) and their syllabic values correspond to each other, the introductory particles in each hemistich assonate ('Et', 'des'), and the /i/ of 'unique' is answered by the /i/ of 'marines'. Many have commented on the mutually echoing puns to be found in the line—'cordeau' says 'string' but reveals a marine brass instrument, 'cor d'eau' (as well as 'corps d'eau'), which harmonises with the 'trompettes marines'; the trouble is that 'trompettes marines' says brass instruments but means roughly made, single-stringed ones. Jonathan Culler's comment on this punning and its implications is as elegantly persuasive now as it was back in 1975:

> Reading this punning activity and creation of equivalences as synecdoche for poetic activity generally, and calling upon the basic convention which allows us to relate what the poem says to its status as a poem, we can produce an unified interpretation: that the poem has a single line because the marine trumpet has only a single string, but that the fundamental ambiguity of language allows the poet to make music with a single line of verse (1975: 177).

The music we want to make is the music of creative mishearing, of multi-dimensional acoustics, so as to break open the poem's apparent self-enclosure.

Let us begin by exacerbating our sense of the line as acoustic metamorphosis:

> Etluniquecordeaudestrompettesmarines

Scriptio continua is the glossolalia of writing. But it is also a more accurate transcription of speech-flow than a spaced version, which is like a frame-by-frame Muybridgean analysis of lingual locomotion. But immediately we adopt *scriptio continua* we transform lexis and phonology into the linguistic noise of a language we are unfamiliar with. We hear our own language in a state of regression toward an inchoate, pre-symbolic state, a state of pre-lapsarian fusion, which listening does its best to counter as it tries to hold language in the realm of the differentiable and unambiguous. Writing is clearly an instrument of the symbolic, of the articulate, of the discursive, but *scriptio continua* reminds us how close the oral is, and the force of the oral lies in its ability to take language back to the body and to all those interferences that the body might supply. This pre-articulate, or fusional, oral world is governed by an anamorphic perception in which solutions multiply, vie with each other, turn into each other, like the visual figure of the duck and rabbit. But literary hearing would not be literary if these 'texts alongside' were not activated by the text we have in front of us; and these 'texts alongside' are as much a matter of the text's consumption as of its genesis (variants, revisions). One might want to claim that one of translation's particular characteristics, not to say obligations, is to bring those 'texts alongside' to the surface.

We might then begin to imagine a situation in which the ST is not a finished piece which the TT tries to emulate or reproduce; the ST is the *prima materia* of the TT, the *matériau sonore*, which, like *musique concrète*, cannot generate an abstract score (i.e. the preplanned translation), cannot be notated (as meaning), but must be reworked as a material, experimentally, by processes of montage, re-arrangement, mixing. Literary translation actually (re)constructs the matter of language (with its psychic, affective envelope). And this has a further implication: it means that, vocally, translation will hold open the road to that reading of language which engages Barthes's 'grain of the voice' (1982a), the pronunciatory function, which links the matter of body and the matter of language, as opposed to the articulatory function, which gives expressivity to meanings already arrived at. As I shift from French to English, I in effect change bodies. I am not looking at the source language (SL) and the target language (TL) as at a pair of objects, as a mute spectator; I am not performing tasks which are essentially visual tasks: consulting a dictionary, running my eyes over the alternatives provided by a thesaurus. I am shifting from one manifestation of my voice's physiology and temperament, of its habits and variables, to another, a task made complex by the cross-interferences—translation is a dialectical process both in terms of uttering and listening—the palimpsestic audibilities, the linguistic memories.

As one drifts into acoustic metamorphosis, acoustic hallucination, one begins to hear every sound trail as intertextual summoning, as processes of acoustic sedimentation. And we begin to undo lexical and syntactic boundaries, flexibilize them, so that grammatical and syntactical categories themselves drift and shape-shift. Presented as a phonetic string—

> /elynikəkɔRdodetRɔ̃pɛtəmaRin(ə)/

—this segment of speech-stream might be heard, in a homophonic translation, as

> Eh! Lunatic chord, o day trumpet, marine / / x x / x / / x x / (11)

But it requires only four substitutions and one omission to become:

> Et l'inique corbeau des tempêtes, ma reine 3 > 3 > 4' > 2
>
> And the iniquitous crow of the tempests, my queen x x x / x x /
> x x / x x /
> (13)

The 'reine' at the rhyme, and the aquatic connection, might encourage us to hear, prompted by Nerval:

> Et l'inique corbeau des tempêtes, sirène (Sirène, syrène)

which in turn leads me to shift the English to:

> And the single string of the water strumpets x x / x / x x / x / x (11)

where the 'single string' is now the G string of sirens turned lap-dancers. Orpheus and the sirens have long been part of the interpretative weave of 'Chantre', so much so that we might imagine this line as Madeleine Boisson does (see Gullentops, 1996: 72):

> Et l'unique chœur d'eau des Sirènes marines

Meanwhile, the crow turns in the mouth, is prized apart by the gravitation of the voiced /d/ of 'des' to its unvoiced /t/; /y/ recovers its place from /i/; 'tempêtes' recovers its /R/:

Et l'unique cor, beauté, trempette marine

And the single horn, beauty, sea-dip   x x / x / / x / x (9)

This is now an alexandrine with a very different shape—a trimetric 5 > 2 > 5, where the 5s are chiastic: 3 > 2 → 2 > 3. In the English, we hear another kind of horn:

And the unicorn, beauty, sea-dip   x x / x x / x / x (9)

This sorting through what is to be heard and imagined is no game of pure inventiveness, but a recognition that the signified does not inhere, singly, univocally, as it might seem from a dictionary, but plays around the signifier, as a nebula of further signifiers, as a field of potentialities, of sense, which the reader hears his/her way into, through this fantasizing or hallucinatory process.

Of course, none of this acoustic morphing would be possible without the continuity of the speech stream, the potential lexical shapes, the suggestiveness of the metrico-rhythmic collocations. Here, linearity acts as a cue, or a mnemonic, or a word-constructional template, seeking to establish the tabularity that is as if concealed within it. The single line begets a multidimensionality of music which one might think of as overtones, or harmonics—that is, tones over and above the fundamental which contribute to the constitution of a sound and to its singular quality. Or one might think of these texts alongside as enharmonic, as the microtonal continuum within which the line takes place. In normal circumstances, text asks us to hear language and its acoustics *as printed*, in the scale, as it were, of the tempered system; it is, as Russolo points out, as if the infinite gradations of the seven colours of the spectrum had been abolished and there was only one yellow, one green, one red, and so on (1986: 62). Only by this reduction can meaning be kept stable. In enharmonics we hear the discrepancies between this 'convenient' tempered scale and the natural one. Russolo argues that if musical reality is to re-engage with life sounds and noises, enharmonicism must be adopted and the tyranny of the semitone put aside. Where in nature/life there are changes in pitch, they are enharmonic—that is to say, morphs rather than jumps. And if we have applied Deleuze's notion of 'continuous variation' to translation, to generate a 'translation-by-metamorphosis', then clearly enharmonics are the principle of variational infinity in linguistic acousticity. If the tempered system is the musical equivalent of Euclidean geometry,

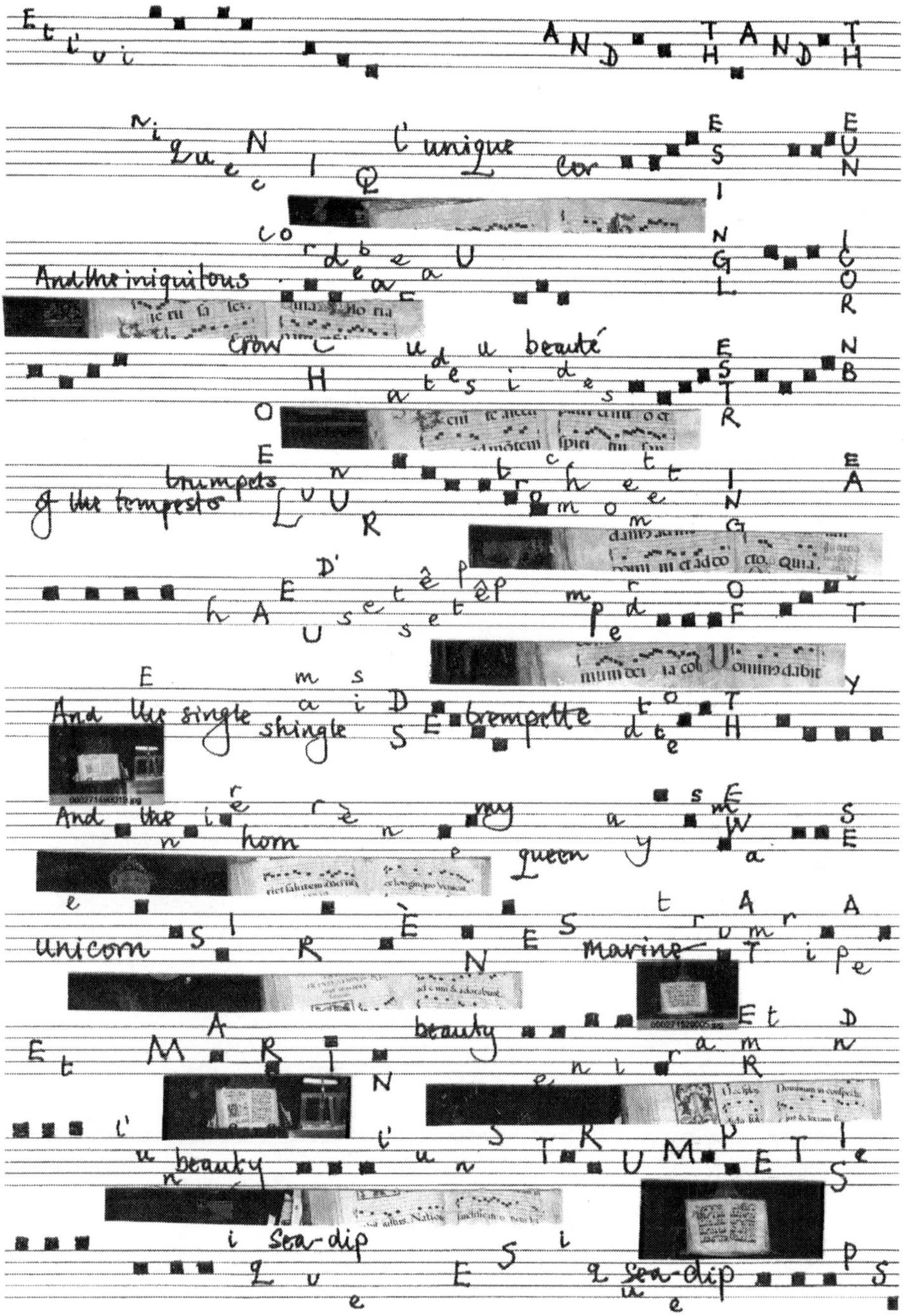

Figure 18: Handwritten translation on music paper, with notation and photo-collage, of 'Chantre'

then enharmonics produce the infinite expansion of musical space and subject the 'duodecimal octave' to new perceptual tunings.

But, paradoxically, what this enharmonic, metamorphic listening produces is a set of alternatives which, in respects other than the acoustic, are far removed from each other, which occupy different worlds, different geographies and topographies, different image-fields, different literary resonances. These alternative texts are as much a montage as a metamorphosis. And this dual being is something that I can capture in a tabular account of the poem (Fig. 18).

But why have I chosen this particular photographic 'setting' for my translation? Most obviously because 'chantre', first attested c. 1260, denotes the cantor, the one whose function is to sing in religious services; only in the fifteenth century does it expand to encompass the poet; its archaic flavour clings tenaciously to it. But it is also chosen because Russolo observes that the musical system so direly in need of rejuvenation 'is basically the same one that was handed down from the Middle Ages' (1986: 63). Because laying the TT out on staves dramatizes the morph/jump conflict: enharmonics sets it own dynamic continuity against what Russolo calls the 'fragmentary [or 'intermittent'] dynamicism' of the diatonic–chromatic system (1986: 68). For us, in this translation, language is the instrument of that enharmonics, while the notated music persists with intervals. These strung-out words and graphemes are not the *result* of the line, not *manifestations* of that line; they are the materials of a new construction, of the phonemic–graphemic continuum within which the line falls; and that continuum is a tabular construction. And the photographic strips are themselves short, interspersed staves, with lines of script looking for their music, not integrated into the music, not themselves music, in the way that Apollinaire's line is (has become). But at least the musical notes in the medieval manuscripts are short draws of the scribe's quill, so that the music is, as it were, written in the strokes of the pen, in the pen's very writing. We have then the sense of the pen/quill as a listening instrument, of a composing communicated to the movements of a hand. The diminutive contact prints of the manuscript choirbooks are designed to remind us that the tabular works always to reduce the presence of the photographer (author) in favour of the montagiste (agent, engineer), that the full photograph, with the guarantees and credentials that its frame provides, must give way to the fragment and to the uncertainties and incorporative flexibilities which its unframedness makes available.

4

Frames and Blind Fields

In their account of the work of art in *Qu'est-ce que la philosophie* (1991), Deleuze and Guattari describe it as a territory, a habitat, which maps out its topographies and their interactivity (1991: 175/1994: 185). The dynamic of this habitat is, in the first instance, defined, indeed generated, by its frame, which may take one or several of many forms. But frames are not the geographic limits of ready-mapped outlines; they are, rather, an integral part of the work's constituents: 'Les cadres ou les pans ne sont pas des coordonnées, ils appartiennent aux composés de sensations dont ils constituent les faces, les interfaces' (1991: 177) [Frames or sections are not coordinates; they belong to compounds of sensations whose faces, whose interfaces, they constitute (1994: 187)]. However, the work is also constantly traversed by forces and dimensions larger than its own; it is solicited by deterritorializing lines of flight which look to open it out onto other force-fields. So the work is equally and oppositely subject to a process of *décadrage*: 'Le cadre ou le bord du tableau est en premier lieu l'enveloppe extérieure d'une série de cadres ou de pans qui se joignent, en opérant des contrepoints de lignes et de couleurs, en déterminant des composés de sensations. Mais le tableau est traversé aussi par une puissance de décadrage qui l'ouvre sur un plan de composition ou un champ de forces infini' (1991: 178) [The frame or the picture's edge is, in the first place, the external envelope of a series of frames or sections that join up by carrying out counterpoints of lines and colors, by determining compounds of sensations. But the picture is also traversed by a deframing power that opens it onto a plane of composition or an infinite field of forces (1994: 187–8)]. This tension between *cadrage* and *décadrage* is at the centre of Apollinaire's poetry and has much in common with framing as we find it in cinema and photography.

When one thinks of the frame, one thinks of a multiplicity of perceptual modes attached to it. In André Bazin's comparison of painting and the cinema, he proposes that the frame in paintings exerts a centripetal force, creating a space oriented inwards, in which the work can establish its counter-reality and enact its suspension of disbelief. The space of the screen, on the other hand, is centrifugal; the screen is a '*cache*' that positively masks what falls outside it, and 'tout ce que l'écran nous montre est [...] censé se prolonger indéfiniment dans l'univers' (2002: 188) [and everything that the screen shows us is reckoned to extend indefinitely out into the universe]. One thinks of the cinematic frame as a mobile, inquisitive eye, exploring scenes, following moving bodies, and the optical suspense of the spectator is built on the expectation that the film-frame will constantly move into its own blind field, will constantly explain itself by metonymic expansion. The photographic frame, for its part, shares with the cinematic frame the masking and the blind field. But we do not expect to move into the photograph's blind field, however much we may desire to. Language becomes the necessary key to that blind field and, in this sense, photography and text are symbiotically related. Unless, of course, the photograph has an aesthetic justification for withdrawing into its own centre. One might think of the photographic frame as being, like the cinematic frame, a moving eye, searching for its subject, selecting the best angle, the optimal framing. But when the search is complete (subject, angle, composition), the frame seems to change its role and becomes that which immobilizes its subject in order to endow it with significance, whether that significance is evidential, aesthetic or to do with the revelation of the optical unconscious. The frame-as-eye becomes the frame-as-window or frame-as-mirror. What I want to suggest is that Apollinaire, with his sense that the future lies with the cinema, has a strong sense of the masking rather than the enclosing frame; that the forces at work in a text are less centripetal than they are transversal or centrifugal, or at least that the balance between these directions is always a hotly contested one.

The need to break the frame is part of the politics of the translation from the linear to the tabular. But in this chapter I want to address various halfway houses between the linear and the tabular, where the frame is not simply removed but is converted into an edge, converted from the sign of completion into the wound of interruption or abbreviation, from the formally achieved into the formally arbitrary. And I want to do this by first of all considering the line of verse, then the line-group, then the poem as a whole, through the translation of passages from 'Zone' (*Alcools*) and translations of '1909' (*Alcools*). In this particular enterprise the photograph's contribution derives not only from its deframing of itself (fragmentation) but also from its ability to counteract the gravity-pull of language towards its own temporal sedimentation.

What, then, for translation, are the crimes of the frame? In the standard presentations of linear printing, the source text (ST) comes to us pre-packed, defined by the space in which it is set, anchored to its margins. The target text (TT) will usually consolidate this frame and in so doing endorse it as a guarantor of significance. Consequently, the TT will justify itself as an interpretative practice. Consequently, too, the TT will consolidate the ST's being *as a text*, something whose very transferability seems to depend on the maintenance of its textual integrity. The frame thus installs the museum mentality as outlined by Merleau-Ponty. The frame makes the work more intensely visible, not unprejudicially, but as part of a particular order, and endows it with 'une conscience d'elle-même qui est toujours rétrospective …' (2008: 95–6) [a consciousness of itself which is always retrospective (1993: 96)]. But all works have a future perspective, are 'un champ ouvert' or 'un nouvel organe de la culture humaine' (2008: 96) [an open field/a new organ of human culture (1993: 96)]. The museum mentality threatens, therefore, to remove the work from a living historicity and place it in 'l'historicité de mort' (2008: 101) [historicity of death (1993: 100)][1]—that is, a historicity, or history, which is competitive, canon-forming, external and which takes us out of painting or literature as an 'entreprise entière' (2008: 97) [entire undertaking (1993: 97)], ongoing and enveloping, into the exemplary, the representative, the dismembered. The mentality of the museum, 'ce recueillement de nécropole' (2008: 100) [this meditativeness befitting a necropolis], engenders 'une révérence qui n'est pas tout à fait de bon aloi' (2008: 100) [a somewhat spurious reverence (1993: 99)]; the museum visit is a payment of respects to works no longer believed to be involved in the *making* of art (a belief which translation, if too complacent, may help to consolidate). In this sense, then, the museum has a politics, an ideology, which is institutional, and it as much enframes the spectator as it does the work:

> Thus museums work to enframe not only artifacts, but also beholders. The museum serves to define our expectations, discipline our desires, and produce both a past and a future dominated by our eternal presentness (Duro, 1996: 6).

Inasmuch, therefore, as translation acts 'deframingly', either by leaping directly to the tabular or, as in the present chapter, by structurally undoing the linear, so both text and reader are liberated into a space where all knowledge and decisions about texts have still to be made, in which texts rejoin the multifariousnesss of language, where desires and associations are undisciplined, where the dailiness and historicity of the real world invade the eternal present of the text and where, above all, the ST is re-involved by the agency of the TT in the tireless making of literature. All that lies outside the text, the infinite expanse of the blind field, which is also the text's fourth dimension, extending in all directions, *n*-dimensionally packed with other texts, other soundworlds, other associative applications, and with all manner of reading environment and reading habit, must be made available to the text.

In these circumstances we might understand the blind field as outlined, in cinematic terms, by Deleuze: 'Et qu'il y a toujours à la fois les deux aspects du hors-champ, le rapport actualisable avec d'autres ensembles, le rapport virtuel avec le tout' (1983: 31) [And that there are always simultaneously the two aspects of the out-of-field: the actualisable relation with other sets, and the virtual relation with the whole (1992: 18)]. As Deleuze points out, these two aspects are not to be separated from each other, inasmuch as the second ('the virtual relation with the whole') is the result of the infinite extension of the first ('the actualisable relation with other sets'), the first constituting a direct contact with the blind field, the second being reached indirectly, through the infinite multiplication of the first. In our own perception, translation *is* the blind field of the ST, and each TT is the ST's actualized relation with another set, the multiplication of TTs projecting a virtual whole. But we would add two riders: the ST can, at any time, make direct contact with the virtual whole of *langage*, or the multilinguisticity of the language medium; and within any TT, as we will see below, frames can be multiplied so that even *within* the frame of the ST countless blind fields are already being indicated. The blind field is that re-imagining of the ST which the ST can neither (fore)see nor understand (since the re-imagining takes place beyond its time and space), but which the act of translation makes virtually present within it.[2] But this is not all: the blind field of translation introduces the ST into a new spatio-temporal context, a new reality, not just the reality of readers of framed texts but the reality of a total environment. The text is already in this environment by virtue of being on the library shelf; but it is translation which opens the text up to that environment, makes the text permeable to that environment. While the blind field is occupied by all the graphemic, acoustic, intertextual, experiential associations generated by the text in the reader, it is also occupied by all that may have filtered into the text of ambient realia. Translation is not just about what a ST is translated into but also and equally about what is translated into the ST.

Apollinaire first published 'Zone' in December 1912 and then collected it in *Alcools* (1913). In the proofs it was entitled 'Cri' [Cry], but Apollinaire adopted 'Zone' apparently in reference to the customs zone on the Franco-Swiss border in the Jura, where he was staying with friends in October 1912, itself an ambiguous frame. The area enjoyed a certain relaxation of customs restrictions. Additional to this sense of relaxations of disciplines and rigours, to be seen in the verse-form itself, there is also a sense of freedom created by the in-between, by being on borders, now one thing, now another, undefined, among options, also to be seen in the verse-form. But the word 'zone' also refers to the no-man's land beyond the city's old fortifications, between the city and country, city and suburbs, not the in-between of either/or, but the in-between of neither/nor, an area usually colonized by the poorer populace, the down-and-outs, ragpickers, travellers. 'Zone' is both a frame of opportunity, of unframing, and a frame of potential imprisonment, Apollinaire's inability to shake off a past, his own remorses, guilt-feelings, lost opportunities.

I have elsewhere related metre to perspectival thinking (2012a: 38–40), in the sense that metre is a stabilization and measured quantification of rhythm, a framing of rhythm. Metre compels us to listen to verse in a particular conventionalizing, transfixative way; it regularizes the perceptual mechanisms of the ear. Rhythm, on the other hand, restores qualitative factors to verse-acoustics, multi-dimensionalizes the acoustic fabric, situates verse in the unfolding of real, experiential time, encourages improvised responses. In a syllabic verse such as French, metrical regularity can only be maintained by the strictness of number: 12 absolutely cannot be 11 or 13. A particular verse-line can express its metrical particularity only by remaining in its hermetically sealed numerical stratum. In the latter half of the nineteenth century this situation changed, for two reasons. First, the more systematic use of the *impair* (a line with an uneven number of syllables) set up potential auditory slippages between lines, where the exclusive use of even-syllabled lines had provided a clear two-syllable safety zone between them (12, 10, 8, 6); and within the *impair* it is inevitable that adjacent measures could also have only one-syllable differences: 3 > 4, 5 > 4, 2 > 3. If the *impair* allows us to imagine a continuum of categories of verse-lines between 1 and, say, 15, then free verse will go on to encourage free passage between these categories and therefore a re-definition of the categories themselves, since their ontology no longer necessarily lies in their 12-ness or their 10-ness, but precisely in their power to morph into other shapes. I say 'necessarily' because a line of 12 syllables may indeed continue to allude to the alexandrine, but it will be an allusion to an alexandrine and not in itself one; this is to say that free-verse lines like these have formal characteristics which operate only allusively, intertextually, never as properly constituted. One of free verse's great attractions is its fantomatic nature. Second, the alexandrine was undone from within: the two-hemistich (6 > 6), four-measure norm was broken down by the accentual dilution or erasure of the medial caesura and by increasing recourse to heterometric three-measure alexandrines. The caesura is of huge structural significance in the classical line in that it constitutes a firm and expected expressive/discursive articulation and accentuation at the sixth syllable to match that on the twelfth.

I want to explore these issues in a brief examination of lines 71–6 of 'Zone'.[3] In the *brouillon* (Décaudin, 1996: 78), line 71 runs:

> Je marche dans Paris tout seul parmi la foule   2 > 4 > 2 > 4

an alexandrine, 'spoiled' in the final version by the addition of an initial adverb:

> Maintenant tu marches dans Paris tout seul parmi la foule
> 3>2>4>2>4 (9//6)

This 'maintenant' is a paradox : a *cheville* which destroys, rather than ensures, metricity, whose only justification is, seemingly, a structural one: it recurs, 'stanza-initially' again, at line 89, but here, contrarily, it establishes a 7//7 equilibrium, in a line which otherwise would be a 4//7 hendecasyllable:

> Maintenant tu es au bord de la Méditerranée   3 > 4 > 7

In l. 72 the *brouillon* is, apart from the pronominal revision (moi > toi), unchanged in the final version:

> Des troupeaux d'autobus mugissants près de toi roulent

As Gouvard (1996: 197 n. 10) points out, this looks like an alexandrine with 'roulent' tacked on as an awkward extra monosyllabic measure: 3 > 3 > 3 > 3 > 1. Line 73, not in the *brouillon*, is a regular alexandrine:

> L'angoisse de l'amour te serre le gosier   2 > 4 > 2 > 4

Line 74, also not in the *brouillon*, is a peculiarly clumsy, slack line of thirteen syllables:

> Comme si tu ne devais jamais plus être aimé

unless we practise an apocope on 'Comm(e)'. But that would still leave an inarticulate alexandrine (2 > 4 > 3 > 3??; 2 > 7 > 3??). The final version of line 75—

> Si tu vivais dans l'ancien temps tu entrerais dans un monastère   8//9

—feels rather like a *trimètre* (4 > 4 > 4) with 'dans un monastère' (5) tacked on (I am counting 'ancien' as a dissyllable; if I counted it as a trisyllable, as is allowable, I would create a more balanced 9//9 (4 > 5 > 4 > 5) line). But, whatever my solution, the result would be an improvement on the *brouillon*'s

> Si je vivais dans l'ancien temps je me retirerais dans un monastère
> 4 > 4(5) > 6 > 5 (8(9)//11)

Finally, line 76—

> Vous avez honte quand vous vous surprenez à dire une prière
> 4 > 7 > 6 (2 > 4) (17)

—is not a line that appears in the *brouillon*; but in the version in *Les Soirées de Paris*, it has an initial 'Et':

> Et vous avez honte quand vous vous surprenez à dire une priére.

Given the metrico-rhythmic structure of the line, it is doubtful whether a syllable here or there would have mattered to Apollinaire. It is more likely that his removal of 'Et' was motivated by the desire to extend the relational possibilities of the line: instead of being coordinated with line 75 it can now either stand on its own or relate either backwards or forwards. But this leaves us with a sequence of lines which runs: 9//6 (15); 6//7 (13); 6//6 (12); 7//6(?) (13); 8//9 (17); 4/7/6 (17).

The response that Gouvard seeks to establish when confronted by this kind of metrical waywardness is a redemptive one: he sets out to show that those poems in free verse ('Zone', 'Cortège', 'Le Voyageur', 'Vendémiaire') 'obéissent à un ensemble de contraintes spécifiques et possèdent leurs propres caractéristiques formelles' (1996: 194) [obey a set of specific constraints and possess their own formal characteristics]. One drawback of Gouvard's method is that it deals with lines singly, as individually problematic, when, as we have already indicated, the problem lies in relationships, in a constant sense of slippage, of outlines which will not hold still. This condition is naturally exacerbated by the reader's inability to make any consistent decision about synaeresis/diaresis and the counting or not of the *e atone*.

Jean-Pierre Bobillot's approach (1993) is more unequivocally dedicated to optionality: Apollinairian prosody, non-determined and non-determining, is a set of virtualities, open to constant re-negotiation (across metricity, pseudo-metricity, non-metricity, as across different structural configurations—'included' alexandrines, *vers démontés, vers emboîtés*), 'selon un perpétuel mouvement d'*oscillation de la lecture*' (1993: 312) [according to a perpetual movement of *readerly oscillation*]. Accordingly, the syllable slips in and out of a prosodic function; that is, it shifts between a situation in which it means everything, is indispensable to a certain metrico-rhythmic pattern, and a situation in which it means nothing.

But, whatever one's attitude or approach, we are here confronted with the alexandrine as a breakable or extendable form, opening itself to intrusions or expansions by refusing to maintain its poise, by consenting to slip into the prosaic. Indeed, it is almost as if poetic language, usually rendered sufficient to itself by metre and thus integrated into the alternative reality of the work, agreed to resume its garrulous everdayness, its commerce with the streets outside, by letting the twelve-syllable frame go soft and thus reconnect with the blind field of its lowly origins.

My version of these lines runs as follows:

now you're walking in Paris	/ x / x x / x (7)
alone in the milling crowds	x / x x / x / (7)
Herds of lowing omnibus drive by	(x) / x / x / x / x / (10)
close to you	/ x x (3)

Love's pains contract around your throat as if	x / x / x / x / x / (10)
you were bound	x x / (3)
never to be loved again	/ x x x / x / (7)
If these were days gone by you'd join the bro-	x / x / x / x / x / (10)
therhood of monks	x / x / (4)
shame takes a grip when you	/ x x / x x (6)
catch yourself in prayer	/ x / x / (5)

This sequence has within it three iambic pentameters, the first of which is headless. They are identified with 'steady' enunciation by their initial capital and their alignment on the left-most margin. But they are glimpses of an order which is being constantly undone, or are themselves already part of a fantomatic mechanism in which they are allusions, citations, intertexts, without authorization, the detritus of a past order. Or, again, they are accidents, not justified by their belonging to a repertoire anterior to this verse instance, but by a perceptual consciousness in the very process of coming into being, creating a pattern that is utterly contingent, utterly determined by experiential impulse or psychic drive. In this latter sense, their capitals are undeserved: an opportunistic appropriation of enunciatory authority. They are accompanied by lines whose margins shift, in an unassuming lower-case mode, and which find their rhythmic movements each according to its particular needs, without reference to some line-transcendent template. If there are syllabic kinships between some of the lines, it is as if to underline that each brings with it a very different rhythmic realization of that number, or rather, that the number is a chance result of a certain rhythmic behaviour which had no particular number in view. Besides, the metrico-rhythmic account of these lines is by no means stable. As we have said, a rhythmic view is a multi-dimensional view (not restricted to accent/stress and syllable-number) and admits paralinguistic features, features of vocalization, such as pausing, amplitude, tempo, pitch-variation, tonal outline, as rhythm-giving. I only have to slacken my voice, decrease its intensity, lower pitch, decrease speed, to create a sequence like: x x / x x / x; x / x x x x /; / x x x / x x x /; / x x; x / x / x x x / x x; x x /; / x x x / x x; x x x / x / x / x /; x x x /; / x x / x x; / x x x /.

But, in another version, I wanted to capture the rhythmic regularities and meanderings of the French lines in photographic form and have thus 'written' a photopoem (Fig. 19) in an attempt to convey the lines' varying movements and expressive qualities. It will be clear from

Figure 19: Photopoem translation of lines 71–76 of 'Zone'

my initial prosodic analysis why some of these lines have the shape they have. The intrusive 'Maintenant' of line 71, for example, is, in terms of its figures, different in scale and addresses a different street-scene from the rest of the line, which is carefully parcelled out in proportions 2 > 4 > 2 > 4; we begin the line in a here and now of animated conversation before drifting into a more homogeneous, middle-distance relationship with the street. Line 72, devoted to buses, has a segmentation created by the regular triangular incisions and culminates in the singular note of bus on road-surface ('roulent'), almost an exclamation mark. The following lines, the couplet on love, are much differentiated, both prosodically and photographically: line 73 comprises two close-moulded hemistichs, tight-fitting parallelograms, details of a classical statue, while line 74 is a curvilinear design of ill-assortedness, of what has failed to come together; this is the line of a ragged thirteen syllables. Finally, the 'religious' lines are equally differentiated: line 75 is 17 or 18 syllables in length and requires us to practise a system of overlapping measures if we are to contain it within manageable margins; in so doing, we create misalignments of the cloister pillars. Line 76, on the other hand, also 17 syllables long, is the four-image narrative of a trimetric rhythm: 'Vous avez honte' (a play of hands, awkwardly restless)—'quand vous vous surprenez' (a shifty look of acknowledgement or admission)—'à dire une prière' (the hand masks the mouth in its uncertain mumbling).

While, for the whole photograph, the frame offers an opportunity for untroubled individual contemplation, these fragments propose a collective (shared spectatorship) and restlessly mobile experience. Without the frame and its regularity, it is no longer the subjects of individual photographs and their inherent value which arrest the eye; it is, on the contrary, the dynamic interaction of glancing contacts with images which compel and puzzle the eye. This is a more thoroughly paratactic world than that of the text, a world without conjunctions, without causality or concession or condition or hypothesis, in which the eye indulges in a whole range of behaviours—ocular fetishism,[4] voyeurism, glancing, glimpsing, gazing, scanning[5]—insinuating its own conjunctions or enjoying pure, inconsequential, optical heterogeneity. The photopoem is then also a *poem* of modes of seeing, or the very mechanism which releases multiple modes of seeing. It is thus that someone else's desire to express themselves (the ST) becomes most completely, perhaps, the viewer's enquiry into him/herself. Since photographs are such a global lingua franca, since we all seem drawn towards the same photographic repertoire, so our ability to assimilate photographs to our own vision, to act as if they were our own reflections, to make 'shifters' of them, correspondingly increases.

The second passage from 'Zone' that I wish to consider, this time from a formal, rather than metrico-rhythmic, point of view, occupies lines 121–34 (see Appendix I (viii) for French and Beckett's translation) and is a description of emigrants. In this passage the demonstrative adjectives—'*ces* émigrants' (twice) and '*cet* édredon'—neither of which appear in the translations of Beckett (1986: 149) and Revell (1995: 9–11)—are precisely demonstrative gestures, gestures of showing and framing, gestures of placing over against the observer, although we cannot really tell whether they are being pulled towards us or thrust away ('these/this' or 'those/that'). The frame is always shifting. In 'Zone' more generally Apollinaire constantly changes point of view; but in the emigrant passage this has a peculiar poignancy, as we shift between the poet addressing himself as a second-person singular reacting to the sight of the emigrants with tears—'Tu regardes les yeux pleins de larmes...'—through the second-person plural of 'comme vous transportez votre cœur', which may be addressed to readers or to himself as an almost out-of-body experience, to the compassionately encompassing first-person plural of 'nos rêves', to the neutral observer of 'Je les ai vus souvent'. In these shifts of position we perhaps capture some of the poet's existential turbulence, a complex play of varied impulses, of varied degrees and kinds of involvement with the subject, which the frame cannot properly contain.

In a previous treatment of this passage (2012a: 161–2) I looked for a verse-form which would enact the repetitive cycles of aspiration and resignation, which would capture the mirage of change that masks debilitating routine, but which, at the same time, would distil a predicament and block further metamorphosis. I chose the terza rima sonnet. I wanted the mindless reiteration of the terza rima as it is found in Hugo von Hofmannsthal's 'Ballade des äusseren Lebens'. And I wanted the final couplet to act not as a moment of invocation, stock-taking, exhortation, as it does in Shelley's 'Ode to the West Wind', but as an entropic congealment. This is what emerged:

> Believer-emigrants; you watch them; tears well
> Up. They pray. The women suckle their young. At Saint-Lazare,
> The station hall is seasoned with their smell.
>
> They, like the Magi, are following their star,
> Looking to earn some silver in the Argentine
> And then come back to where they are.

You transport your heart, a family transports its eiderdown,
Bright red. Our dreams, that eiderdown, are all untruths.
Some stay, in shabby digs in town,

The rue des Rosiers or des Écouffes.
Often, at evening, I've seen them in the street.
Like chess pieces they seldom move.

They're mostly Jews. Their wives wear wigs.
And, pallid, in the backs of shops, they sit.

Terza rima, in its 'pure' state, is framed at the sides by its concatenated rhymes (aba, bcb, cdc, etc.), but is unframed at top and bottom. In this sense it is like an indefinitely extendable scroll, an accompaniment of the very passage of time, a present continuous (imperfective). In the form used here, however, the terza rima sonnet, the poem has a bottom frame (the final couplet), but its side-frame has been loosened by its heterosyllabicity and by recourse to half-rhyme. The emigrants go away, but do not go away, or come back. Their lives are ghetto-ized (rue des Rosiers, rue des Écouffes, chess pieces, shops). But if these features of their lives point to the constraints of framing—that is to say, point to the failure of a form to achieve its inherent forward momentum, to get its seeds (the middle lines) properly to germinate—the corresponding loosening of the structure, the partial opening of a blind field, through heterosyllabicity and half-rhyme, adds to the portrait's complexity in two principal ways. While the gravitation towards half-rhyme and the heterosyllabicity suggest the deterioration of an existential condition, out of tune with itself, they also invite that complexity of response which we find in the modulating personal pronouns; the unframing creates a fuller participatory space for the onlooker. Second, this gesture towards unframing multiplies the portrait's temporality; the consistency of the progressive present, implied by terza rima, gives way to the difficulty of distinguishing between state and event, between the durative and the iterative, the iterative and the punctual, the punctual and the omnitemporal.

The potential equation between the multiplication of temporal possibilities and the diversification of subjectivities, or kinds of perceptual consciousness, gives the contemplation of the emigrants a peculiar poignancy which I wished further to develop (Figs 20–21). First, I selected an Extra Condensed font of Gill Sans MT. I wanted the sense of existential constriction conveyed by the Extra Condensed, and the Gill Sans Serif was important, not only as a modern urban design but also because it installs a rhetoric of the unembellished, of the guileless, of the fundamental. In Fig. 20 I added to the redisposed stanzas a set of three enamel-paint doodles in three colours (black, grey, blue) (terza rima), and then a scattering of photographic fragments, all in rectangular shapes. The different media were kept separate from each other. Fig. 21 retains the same typeface and disposition of the poem as Fig. 20; it also retains three colours in its enamel-paint doodles, but now red, black and grey. But the photographic fragments are more variously shaped and, by and large, more closely integrated into the painted designs.

If we feel an increasing ambivalence in the tense-aspects of the text, thanks to the loosening of the formal frame, we might say the same about the photographic fragments. About the *whole* photograph we might propose the following: the significance of its *taking* relates, at least in the Barthesian account, to tense ('that-has-been', 'he is going to die', 'he will have died'). As the photograph gravitates from the indexical to the iconic, from the situated image to the contextless image, so tense gravitates towards aspect (see Wollen, 1989) and mood, towards aspectual and modal *possibility* (durative or iterative or punctual or omnitemporal; infinitive or subjunctive (optative, hypothetical, concessive, etc.) or imperative). The shift from index to icon, from framed whole to fragment, also marks a shift from the documentary to that which has options on the fictional and speculative. Photographic fragments and texts with unframing/deframing devices thus begin to speak the same temporal language. The painted doodles, for their part, are not so much another set of (third-person) subjects/representations as the traces of the reader-spectator's gestural involvement. These are indeed figures in enamel paint, but they are inhabited by first-person time, impulsive, dynamic, a rewriting of terza rima in the mode of readerly consciousness. And as this consciousness itself becomes part of text, lying among its objects (text and photographs), so it becomes itself a paginal event, something already beyond a *particular* subjectivity.[6] This, then, is translation that also performs translation, a translation which embeds its translator in its becoming.

If Fig. 20 keeps the various media apart, it is in order to pose questions about relationships and the dynamics of interaction. Fig. 21's greater fusion of photographic fragment and painted design creates cross-overs between the non-figurative and the figurative, as if abstract shapes suggested images (and vice-versa), as if, conversely, reality felt it necessary to yield to psychic encryptions, or as if the stray impulses of the hand caught images in their movement. At the same time, the

Figure 20: 1st version of lines 121–134 of 'Zone', with photo-collage and enamel-paint doodles

Figure 21: 2nd version of lines 121–134 of 'Zone',
with photo-collage and enamel-paint doodles

temporality of the photographic images, to the extent that they might be considered eruptions from the unconscious, participates in the instantaneity of the associating mind, short-lived and barely registered. Thus, where Fig. 20 diversifies modes of consciousness and leaves in question their linkages, so that the emigrants' condition is a source prior to the page, producing a set of self-differentiating implications and effects, of which the poem is one, Fig. 21 presents the poem as the prime cause, the experiential origin, and the photographic fragments/painted doodles as the playing out of readerly response in different yet interdependent modes of visual imagination. The blind field of Fig. 20 is generated by the continuation of repercussions into the social and communally owned, a development urged and facilitated by the photographic fragment as common property. The blind field of Fig. 21 remains *within the reader*, whose further responses lie beyond the horizon of the present page, unpredictable, part of an ongoing life.

The emigrants are a social group in which the sensory-motor mechanism has stalled or is only envisaged (the Argentinian enterprise, for example), and in which, therefore, sights and sounds are peculiarly dissociated and dreamlike: 'Like chess-pieces they seldom move'. In order to capture this motor-helpless and radically dissociated state, I present an alternative version of the emigrant passage, whose first step runs as follows:

You watch,	**They come from Russia**
Eyes pricked with tears,	**from Rumania**
Those pitiable emigrants.	**from Poland**
	[illegible word]
They believe in God. They pray.	**They're already**
The women suckle their young.	**afraid of where**
The station concourse,	**they're going. I saw among**
At Saint-Lazare,	**them an old 'pope' at**
Is seasoned with: their smell.	**prayer in Slavish**
They, like the Magi,	**in Slavonic**
Have faith in their star.	**He stopped to scold his sons**
They're looking to earn some silver.	**his daughters**
In Argentina.	*laide marmaille*; **a pregnant**
And then, come home, again,	**woman was laid**
Having struck it rich.	**out on some straw.**

A family transports a red **Poland today is no**
Eiderdown**,** as **you** transport **more than a vague**
Your heart**.** **hope. Poor Polish women,**
That eiderdown**, our** dreams**,** **poor country girls, are**
Are equally unreal**.** **herded off to Germany,**
Some of them stay**,** **packed off from Hamburg,**
At shabby addresses in**,** **to brothels in the States,**
The rue des Rosiers or the rue des Écouffes**.** **or in**
I've often seen them in the street**;** **Chinese ports.**
Taking the air**;** **[to the Indies, to Ceylon].**
At evening**.** **[to the Transvaal].**
Like chess-pieces**;** **Pitiful prostitutes,**
They rarely move**.** **and when they're past it,**
They're mostly Jews**;** their wives wear wigs**;** **suicide's**
And sit anaemically**;** **the only**
In the backs of shops**.** **road to go.**

Here, I have introduced as a second poem, running alongside, as a second voice, more personally involved, lines from a manuscript version of the poem which were ultimately jettisoned, probably because the confessional note was too strong. Other textual suppressions produced similar attenuations of the over-direct, of the sordid and the brutal (Décaudin, 1996: 83). These lines, specifically about Polish emigrants and about their sexual exploitation, relate directly to Apollinaire's own Polish origins—his mother, Angelica/Olga de Kostrowitzky, was of a Polish family—and to judge by the reference in the final version to the red eiderdown—a Polish symbol of family life, according to Décaudin (1996: 89)—Apollinaire wished to give his emigrants a Polish colouring even after he had removed any explicit reference to Poland. I have printed this second voice in bold, partly to make clear its separate origin, but principally to pick up the bold font of the personal pronouns and the punctuation in the left-hand text and thereby to suggest that this second, subtextual voice erupts into the final text, in its inconspicuous corners, in its moments of subjective involvement; or, put conversely, that the final text is not able to eradicate the traces of this draft, which clings on tenaciously, however much pushed to the margins. My reintroduction of punctuation into this non-punctuated text is designed to subject it to the impatience of ongoing time and to the editing of vocal respiration, as if respiration were the vocal equivalent of a movie camera, picking its cuts and shots. The left-hand text is in fact over-punctuated, so that impetus is constantly frustrated, checked, reduced to an almost robotic staccato.

My next task is to discover what expressive possibilities another form of *mise-en-page* might release from the text I have arrived at, remembering that every *mise-en-page* is a particular modal projection of the text. My first version is left-hand justified, so that the presiding consciousness, the margin with its capital letters, belongs to the poem's final version, while the second voice, the voice of a suppressed or repressed *Urtext*, is pushed to the right, both adapting itself to the left-hand voice and also separated from it. In my next version I have adopted a three-column disposition to ensure a thorough interwovenness of my two voices, my two levels of consciousness and response, between which the text continually cuts, *shown overleaf.*

This dispositional decision has, in a sense, been made by the computer; as I press the three-column option, I do not know what distribution of the text will result. I look upon this as a surrealistic engagement with the creative, revelatory power of chance, which will confront me with my own language and my own translation, in segmentations, groupings and expressive guises I could not have suspected. Conventional translation is perhaps over-determined by an intentionalist ethos: it supposes that we must be able to rationalize every choice we make. But, just as the kind of translation we are canvassing proposes that the source text (ST) has a poor comprehension of itself, of its own formal and expressive potentialities, that it is translation's business to draw out hidden texts within the ST, so equally the target text (TT) itself must submit to similar and corresponding mechanisms of linguistic exploration. Reading becomes as richly problematic as language itself, and each entry into the text is likely to produce new configurations of the text's space and time. The tabular leaves the reader with a text which is insoluble, which lies outside the progressions of cause and effect, beginning and end, top left to bottom right. In this sense the text cannot be recuperated as an order of meaning; it can only be inhabited as a landscape or stage which allows any number of assimilative itineraries and trajectories.

In my final version I look to develop the potential cinematic connection and thus gravitate towards a film-strip layout (Fig. 22). In order to accommodate the text in this format I must sacrifice the effect of textual unravelling and accept a greater pressure to make sense of a left-to-right, top-to-bottom, column-by-column reading.

You watch,
They come from Russia
Eyes pricked with tears,

from Rumania
Those pitiable emigrants.

from Poland

[illegible word]
They believe in God. They pray.
They're already
The women suckle their young.
afraid of where
The station concourse,
they're going. I saw among
At Saint-Lazare,
them an old 'pope' at
Is seasoned with: their smell. **prayer in Slavish**
They, like the Magi,
in Slavonic
Have faith in their star. **He stopped to scold his sons**
They're looking to earn some silver. **his daughters**
In Argentina.
laide marmaille;
a pregnant
And then, come home, again,
woman was laid
Having struck it rich.
out on some straw.
A family transports a red
Poland today is no
Eiderdown, as **you** transport
more than a vague
Your heart.
hope. Poor Polish women,
That eiderdown,
our dreams, **poor country girls, are**
Are equally unreal.
herded off to Germany,
Some of them stay,
packed off from Hamburg,
At shabby addresses in,
to brothels in the States,
The rue des Rosiers or the rue des Écouffes. **or in**
I've often seen them in the street; **Chinese ports.**
Taking the air;
[to the Indies, to Ceylon].
At evening.
[to the Transvaal].
Like chess-pieces;
Pitiful prostitutes,
They rarely move.
and when they're past it,
They're mostly Jews; their wives wear wigs; **suicide's**
And sit anaemically;
the only
In the backs of shops.
road to go.

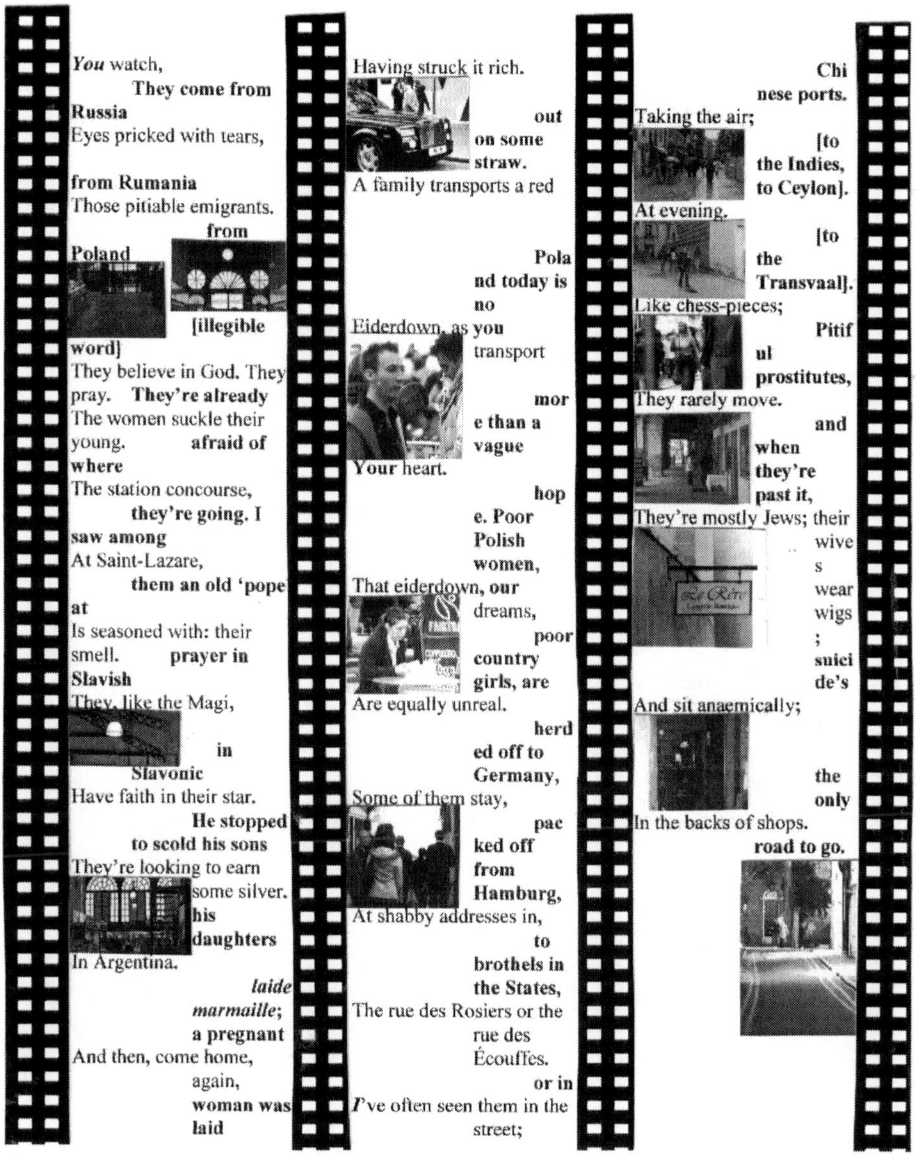

Figure 22: Cinematic translation of lines 121–134 of 'Zone', with photo-collage

But this does not interfere with the columnar's capacity to create a floating and disintegrating texture, and at the same time to suggest *both* individual destinies and sets of perceptions in free fall, *and* a certain drivenness of text. The latter quality is endorsed by the gathering momentum of photographs as we shift from left to right. There is here something that runs away, that cannot be grasped, that cannot orientate action or act as a dam, as a holding formality, and thus a control. In this sense, the film-strip layout intensifies the vanity of the attempts of the punctuation and of the cross-cutting to stem the cinematic drive of 24 frames a second; indeed, it is now the junctures created by punctuation and cross-cutting which endorse the frame-by-frame acceleration. But that frame-by-frame impetus is not impelled by sensory-motor purposefulness; it installs a dispersal, a halting logorrhoea, or logorrhoea of the halting. Rather like terza rima, the film strip implies a lateral framing, set against an unframed top and bottom. But if the filmic analogy and the cinematic motion convince, then the text constantly moves into its own blind field as each of the two textual strands opens into the other, into the elsewhere of the other. The two strands are not, as it were, visible to each other, but they imply each other, and the reader crosses and recrosses that threshold as reading proceeds. But that is not quite all. The photographic fragments scatter visual interest across the whole paginal space. While the lateral frames push the two strands of text towards each other, into each other's path, the photographic fragments themselves keep the whole field open and ensure that linearity does not suppress the free wandering eye of the tabular.

My final subject is the question of framing and blind field in the whole poem, here Apollinaire's '1909' (see Appendix I (ix) for French text). When I first wrote about '1909' (1990: 282–7), I proposed that while 'Annie' traced the transformation of 'femme' into 'dame', '1909' seemed to do the reverse. I was left uneasy by the interpretation offered by Pilkington:

> The poem is built around the contrast between the fashionable elegance and beauty evoked in ll. 1–20 and the 'femmes atroces' of the industrial areas whom the poet prefers since they are born of the modern machine age. The poem is inspired by the desire to grasp the 'real' world as opposed to the transient modes of beauty which merely exist like evanescent bubbles on its surface (l. 27) (1993: 154–5).

This interpretation is shared by Rees (1975: 173) and is apparently borne out by Décaudin's observation (1996: 210) that ll. 24–6 are borrowed from a rough draft of 'Vendémiaire', 'dont la rédaction, plus explicite, montre le poète découvrant cette beauté inconnue [...]. *1909* est ainsi une définition allusive de l'inspiration poétique' [whose more explicit wording shows the poet discovering this unknown beauty [...]. *1909* is thus an allusive definition of poetic inspiration].[7]

My uneasiness about these interpretations stemmed from a sequence of questions. Why are the lines relating to the 'femmes atroces' in the same imperfect tense as those relating to the 'dame'? If the 'femmes atroces' are the source of a new poetry, why are lines 23–7 metrically so regular? What does line 14, with its future tense, mean? Why does the 'dame' become 'femme' like the women of the industrial city, and why are lines 28–9 not separated from lines 23–7? Why is the 'dame' so insistently associated with France? It may be true that the eyes, teeth and lips of the lady are contrasted with the more essential sources of being of the industrial populace ('sang', 'cerveau'), but her poetic reality is greater than that of the 'femmes atroces': the poet's preoccupation with her dress and appearance make her the generator of refrain and of rhythmic configurations rich in variety and modulation. But to endow the lady with the spirit of novelty is to betray the 'femmes atroces'. This is a reason, I suggested, for line 14, which casts the 'dame' as Cendrillon, the 'princess' who would cease to haunt him should midnight strike. But she is in no hurry to leave:

> Et traînait ses petits souliers à boucles

My conclusion was, then, that the 'dame' is something of France's past which projects a future, a past which is moving forward and encompassing the present. Not only does the poet's experience of her span the past ('ottoman violine', 'coiffure à la Récamier') and the future (l. 14), but she also absorbs the present of the industrial city, is in fact created by it; the lines of the 'femmes atroces' and the 'peuple habile des machines' are as it were enveloped by the beauty of the woman (ll. 21–2, 28–9), and her transformation from 'dame' to 'femme' is dependent upon her coming into contact with her industrial counterparts. Armed with these readerly persuasions, my 'grounding' translation emerges as:

1909

The lady wore a dress
Of darkly purple ottoman
And her gold-embroidered tunic
Had two panels
Fastened at the shoulder

Eyes dancing like angels
She laughed and laughed
She had a face in France's colours
Blue eyes white teeth and lips deep red
She had a face in France's colours

A rounded neckline
Hair styled à la Récamier
Arms beautiful and bare

Will midnight never strike

The lady in the darkly purple
Ottoman dress
And gold-embroidered tunic
With rounded neckline
Paraded her curls
Her golden headband
And let trail behind her
Her small and buckled shoes

She was so beautiful
You wouldn't have dared to think of love

I loved the appalling women
In the sprawling neighbourhoods
Where every day new beings came into the world
Iron their blood and fire their brain
I loved I loved the skilled machine-workers
Luxury and beauty are but the foam on their wave
This woman was so beautiful
She made me feel afraid

Then, as the readerly imagination enters into dialogue with the poem, letting itself be persuaded by haphazard elements from the blind field, which, as it were, knock impatiently at the poem's frame, or provide an alternative frame, the translational process sets out on its infinite modulations:

1909 **Oh**

Neuf Ô **neuf** **zero**
oneneinzeronine
Nought neufteenhundredoneuf
if AUGHT

<table>
<tr><td>a street her skill</td><td>The lady wore a dress</td></tr>
<tr><td>lottomane</td><td>Of darkly purple ottoman</td></tr>
<tr><td>ohotto art ill</td><td>And her gold-embroidered tunic</td></tr>
<tr><td>Judith has you</td><td>Had two panels</td></tr>
<tr><td>By the hair</td><td>Fastened at the shoulder</td></tr>
<tr><td>She did wear John</td><td>But you don't just wear a Patek Philippe</td></tr>
<tr><td></td><td></td></tr>
<tr><td>Macabre that</td><td>Eyes dancing like angels</td></tr>
<tr><td>Thedevil's violin</td><td>She laughed, and laughed</td></tr>
<tr><td>Violon viol et</td><td>She had a face in France's colours</td></tr>
<tr><td>Sifting colours</td><td>Blue eyes white teeth and lips deep red</td></tr>
<tr><td></td><td>We all love a multi-tasking product – especially one</td></tr>
<tr><td>That's John again</td><td>That fits into even the slimmest of clutch bags</td></tr>
<tr><td></td><td>She had a face in France's colours</td></tr>
<tr><td></td><td></td></tr>
<tr><td>Shawldancebare</td><td>A rounded neckline</td></tr>
<tr><td>Foot forGérard</td><td>Hair styled à la Récamier</td></tr>
<tr><td>Nippled bolsters</td><td>I let the braids fall out used tecni.art</td></tr>
<tr><td>For Louis David</td><td>Gloss wax to give it texture and hold</td></tr>
<tr><td></td><td>And then slipped on a headband</td></tr>
<tr><td></td><td>Arms beautiful and bare</td></tr>
<tr><td></td><td>O Derma-Genesis, the dewy, tautening glow</td></tr>
<tr><td></td><td></td></tr>
<tr><td></td><td>Will midnight never strike</td></tr>
<tr><td></td><td></td></tr>
<tr><td></td><td>The lady in the darkly purple</td></tr>
<tr><td></td><td>Ottoman dress</td></tr>
<tr><td></td><td>And gold-embroidered tunic</td></tr>
</table>

With rounded neckline
Paraded her curls
Her golden headband
And let trail behind her
Her small and buckled shoes

She was so beautiful
You wouldn't have dared to think of love

I loved the appalling women
In the sprawling neighbourhoods
Where every day new beings came into the world
Iron their blood and fire their brain
I loved I loved the skilled machine-workers
Dressed in poor black shifts of cotton imperfectly
Mordant imperfectly dyed
Luxury and beauty are but the foam on their
wave
This woman was **so beautiful**
She made me feel afraid.

We begin to see some of the ways in which acoustic metamorphosis might insinuate itself, in the treatment of the title, for instance, or of the ottoman. Such metamorphosis also affects 'violine', but here it becomes more appropriate to speak of lexical embroidery. What is curious about the viol- family is its gathering together of musical instruments, violence (including rape and figurative violation), flowers and a colour bespeaking nobility, death, shyness. How rich French is in this colour—violet, violine, violacé, violâtre—as against English (violet, violaceous). And how odd it is that the difference between French 'violon' and English 'violin' disappears in 'violoncello/e', which most English people pronounce as if the second 'i' were still there. And 'ottoman' is no less curious. As furniture, the English piece is a long padded seat usually without back or arms, often used as a chest ('coffre'); but it is also a padded footstool, a 'repose-pied'. In French, where it has a feminine form, 'ottomane', it is described by Robert as a 'canapé à dossier arrondi en corbeille'; it does not double as a footstool. Petit Larousse gives no meaning relating to furniture. And as a textile, ottoman is, for the French, silk with a cotton weft; the English call it, simply, 'a corded fabric'. The examples provided for both 'violine' and 'ottoman' in Robert are, as it happens, taken from Apollinaire's poem. This lady in darkly purple ottoman is as elusive as the words themselves, caught in a network of meanings, metamorphoses and associations which make her a kaleidoscope of moods, personality traits, intentions; about her the dictionaries disagree.

Creative mishearing and lexical embroidery are generated both text-internally and by ambient interference, input from the immediately external world. I am translating Apollinaire's '1909'; I am reading *Vogue* (July 2008) in the doctor's waiting room; there is a Klimt exhibition at the Tate in Liverpool; at home I am reading Cormac McCarthy's *The Crossing* and re-visiting the paintings of Louis David, because my son is working on the French Revolution. Apollinaire's lady acts as a magnet for phrases from *Vogue*; I stumble across a sentence in McCarthy which seems to give the industrial women of the latter part of the poem a fashionspeak they lack. The ottoman and the gold-embroidered tunic take me to Klimt, to his Judith and Holofernes, where Holofernes's head is held like an accessory, a handbag; this picture is also known as 'Salome', so I re-imagine the pairing as Judith and John. David's portrait (1800) of Juliette Récamier, severe, distant, in bare surroundings, reclining not on an ottoman but on what has been variously described as a daybed or a chaise-longue, has little in common with François Gérard's warmly coloured, knowingly seductive and be-shawled 1805 portrait, or Jean-Baptiste Augustin's more brazen, even saucy, 1801 miniature. The reference to the 'nippled bolsters' in David's portrait relates to an observation made by the art critic Ewa Lajer-Burcharth (1999: 272). My final version (Figs 23–4) incorporates photographic fragments, to get closer to Klimtian textures and to act out the poem's dramatic shift in modality as it settles for a moment on the appalling women, the machine-workers, reassuringly present, full-face or full-figure, anchorages for the figments and fetishes that the fashion world throws at us.

I had several reasons for choosing Broadway—which in fact has several variants—as my principal typeface. It was designed by Morris Fuller Benton in 1925 (or 1927; sources disagree), its lower case version, designed by Sol Hess, appearing in 1929. It is a typeface with an unmistakable period style (Art Deco), which casts our 'dame/femme' as an 'It' girl, a girl with sex appeal—Elinor Glyn's *It* was published in 1927—and gives her Frenchness a transatlantic irradiation, as one might hope an Anglophone translation would do. Broadway is variously described as a display or decorative typeface—that is, a typeface not

1909 Oh
Neuf Ô neuf zero
onenseinzeronine
Nought neufteenhundredoneuf
If AUGHT

a street her skill The lady wore a dress
lottomane Of darkly purple ottoman
ohotto art ill And her gold-embroidered tunic
Judith has you Had two panels
By the hair Fastened at the shoulder
She did wear John *But you don't just wear a Patek Philippe*

Macabre that Eyes dancing like angels
Thedevil's violinShe laughed, and laughed
Violon viol et She had a face in France's colours
Sifting colours Blue eyes white teeth and lips deep red
We all love a multi-tasking product – especially one
That's John again *That fits into even the slimmest of clutch bags*
She had a face in France's colours

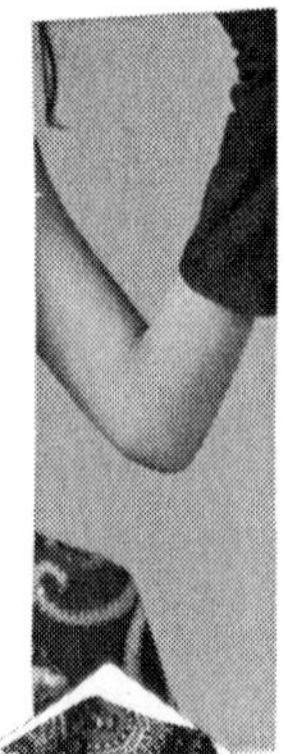

ShawldancebareA rounded neckline
Foot forGerard Hair styled à la Récamier
Nippled bolsters *I let the braids fall out used tecni.art*
For Louis David *Gloss wax to give it texture and hold*
And then slipped on a headband
Arms beautiful and bare
O Derma-Genesis, the dewy, tautening glow

Will midnight never strike

The lady in the darkly purple
Ottoman dress
And gold-embroidered tunic
With rounded neckline
Paraded her curls
Her golden headband
And let trail behind her
Her small and buckled shoes

She was so beautiful
You wouldn't have dared to think of love

I loved the appalling women
In the sprawling neighbourhoods
Where every day new beings came into the world

Figure 23: Translation, with photo-collage, of '1909'

Iron their blood and fire their brain
I loved I loved the skilled machine-workers
Dressed in poor black shifts of cotton imperfectly
Mordant imperfectly dyed
Luxury and beauty are but the foam on their
wave
This woman was **so beautiful**
She made me feel afraid.

Figure 24: Translation, with photo-collage, of '1909'

intended for small-sized and continuous text; Gordon (2009: 402) places it among Billboard and Poster fonts.[8] Against Broadway is set the Tahoma typeface of the industrial women. Tahoma, the Native American name for Mount Rainier, is a humanist sans serif, designed by Matthew Carter in 1994 specifically for computer use, to address problems connected with onscreen legibility. As a humanist typeface, Tahoma harks back to classical—Roman and Renaissance—letter-shapes, with uniform stroke width, prized for unfussy lucidity, a rebuttal of the self-consciously ornate. These elements—the modern technological, the native/indigenous, the humanist—are what Broadway must assimilate, and that process is acted out by the translation, as the two typefaces come into contact and co-existence; but Broadway, also sans serif, already has something of the uncompromising nature of Tahoma: the strictness of its baseline abbreviates the descenders of p and y and produces a strange terminal on g which Garfield describes as 'the solid underlining slap of a Broadway g' (2010: 176). Thus one temporal frame (1909) contains another which postdates it (1925–9), which in turn contains and is post-dated by another (1994). The fact that this post-dating occurs within the bounds of the poem means that the frames are, as it were, both inside and outside each other, both container and contained.

But this is by no means all. If by 'the bounds of the poem' we understand the left-hand margin created by the ST, then several elements break those bounds. The title, written out in various forms, gathers to itself several typefaces—Broadway, Wide Latin (Stephenson Blake, 1992), Castellar (John Peters, 1957), Bauhaus 93 (based on the Herbert Bayer design of 1925), Lucida Console (released 1994 and derived from other Lucida fonts, designed by Charles Bigelow and Kris Holmes, 1985)—as if asking itself what 1909 might mean stylistically, as if asking, too, how many temporal frames might be appropriate, how many temporal frames this material might be passed through, how many contexts in real time it might have; even in the photographic fragments we pick up other potential temporal indicators: 1975, 2031, something ending in 6 . But the title occupies an intermediate ground, sprawling across both a column of readerly associations and speculations to the left of the poem proper, and the poetic text itself. We then slide down into the column of associations which is in the typeface of the 'dame', and which stands outside the poem as the voice of the translator; in fact the 'dame' becomes the poet of her own poem, and its translator. The extratextual space, already ceded on the right to photographic fragments, is then fully occupied by such fragments.

And this extratextual space, the space of photos of fashion and reportage, has already seeped into the poetic text through the channel of the Times New Roman Italic inserts, which themselves attract two brief comments, in the same font, in the left-hand column that runs alongside the poem's first twelve lines. Times New Roman, as a default typeface, has no specific protagonistic role, but rather acts as an aside, or as something overheard from another world.

If the photographic fragments are the text's blind field in this poem, the world of the everyday, of tireless media surfeit and intrusion, then that blind field is ultimately what the poem, on its second page, surrenders to. This blind field is one in which images literally overlap, or echo each other, or stand at odd angles to each other, or shift from colour to black and white, or adopt different shapes, and leave us to ask a question which is posed by more or less all the examples of photographic translation we have presented: what constitutes the experience of *looking among* photographic fragments? Perhaps we can begin to formulate an answer, an answer that will help us to understand the activity of the blind field.

First, the ease with which one passes between photos flattens out time. It is not that one does not recognize temporal differences between the photos, but their power to be decisive, or to vary vividness, disappears—they merely create a temporal and spatial indeterminacy. It is for this reason that narrative(s) while always a possibility, to be played with, never really manage to resolve themselves. Instead, then, of the *sequence of images*, we find what Burgin identifies as the *sequence-image*:

> The 'concatenation' [of images] does not take a linear form. It is more like a rapidly arpeggiated musical chord, the individual notes of which, although sounded successively, vibrate simultaneously (2006: 170).

Photographs presented like this fail to make spectators of us. With the single, whole photograph, a choice is made (framing), and the photo then establishes itself in its own 'Sehenswürdigkeit', its worthiness of being seen (frame), and the responsibility that goes with it. When we look *among*, that choice is as if still not made and the 'Sehenswürdigkeit' not yet established. It is as if we were still looking for the telling photograph and it is this that creates that ambivalence peculiar to *looking among* fragmentary images: the impossibility of telling whether these photographic fragments are a kind of looking (for a subject), or a kind of subject of the look (though not quite yet chosen). The image oscillates between mirror and window.

Thus our spray of photographic fragments draws no necessary benefit from commentary; they do not need to be 'told' in order to acquire their significance. There is no sense in which 'witnesses' can be either reliable or unreliable about these photos, for two reasons: (i) in becoming fragments, these photos have lost their dependency on their whole selves; (ii) what we see continues to have an indexical value, but it is now an index without a referent: 'The smile is arrested yet no longer refers to the life from which it has been taken' (Kracauer, 1995: 48). These fragments await all kinds of reclamation by viewers, reclamations which are entirely unpredictable.

Another factor of ambivalence in looking among is proxemics. There is an implicit assumption in cinematic photography, which, in a sense, looking among photographic fragments is, that *spectatorial* seeing (i.e. seeing as pure witness without psychological pressure and in optimal circumstances) depends on the establishment and maintenance of a certain distance. Close-ups are threatening, or involving, can convert the realist into the expressionist, are at all events disturbances of the contract of distance. But with photographic fragments, distances become difficult to judge, scale difficult to measure: a crowd, for example, may be some way off, but if cropped close and in an unusual shape, may press in on vision with unexpected urgency. Conversely, the close-up, as fragment, may have the pathos of distance, of diminutiveness. Scale, proportion, proximity are all likely to become difficult to read in the world of multiple photographic fragments; but for that reason, the power of these images is more anarchic, their range of expressivity wider and more variable, their interactivity more multiform. But as we have had occasion to mention before, such fragments continually flirt with a negative, value-denying alternative identity: as an arbitrary collection of media detritus. It is the ability of text to act as guarantor and motivation that makes the experience of looking among both necessary and enriching. One enters a blind field because the frame is projected only as 'a provisional limit' (Kracauer, 1965: 19–20) for a text whose fulfilment lies in its being assimilated into, and amplifying the vicissitudes of, readerly existence.

5

The Chromatic and the Acoustic

In the December of the year in which 'Zone' was first published, 1912, Apollinaire also wrote his poem for Robert Delaunay's *Fenêtres simultanées* series of paintings (1912), 'Les Fenêtres' (see Appendix I (x) for French text). It is not a poem that would have sat comfortably in *Alcools* (1913), and diverges from 'Zone' in the way that Delaunay's *Fenêtres simultanées* diverge from his *La Ville de Paris* (1912), marking a shift from his so-called 'destructive' period to his 'constructive' one,[1] from light as an energy which breaks objects apart to light as a generator of endlessly and simultaneously interactive colours (see Godard, 2009: 213–14, 215), or, for Apollinaire, from 'Soleil cou coupé' to 'multiples Soleils', from burdensome subjectivity to multiplied and mobile consciousness. In 'Les Fenêtres' one looks almost in vain for a first person: one might sense an expressive subject concealed behind the apostrophe 'O Paris', but otherwise we encounter 'tu' (once), 'nous' (twice) and 'on' (three times). All these things and the poem's potential source in a *poème-conversation*, rather than in lyric utterance, radically change the position of the translator in relation to the text; the *poème-conversation* is an important instrument in engineering that multiplication of potential subjectivities without presiding identities, and in that dispersal of consciousness, which we identified in Chapter Three.[2]

'Les Fenêtres', which, on at least two occasions, in letters to Madeleine Pagès, Apollinaire mentioned as being a favourite of his,[3] appeared as a 'poème-préface' for the catalogue of Delaunay's work exhibited at the Der Sturm gallery in Berlin in January 1913. The poem's sources are contradictorily described, although commentators have been quick to account for the contradiction. André Billy (1923: 54–5) tells us that he, Apollinaire and René Dupuy (René Dalize), ensconced in the café Crucifix, rue Daunou, more or less took it in turns to supply lines for the poem, a *poème-conversation* put together over glasses of vermouth by a group of friends. Robert and Sonia Delaunay, on the other hand, relate that the poem was composed in Robert's studio, hence the references to the curtain, the window, the sea-urchins and an old pair of yellow (tan) shoes. The conciliatory view suggests that, having run up a draft in the café, Apolliniare proceeded to polish and finalize it in the painter's studio (Steegmuller, 1973: 204; Apollinaire, 1965: 1079).

While, for the literary critic, these conflicting accounts of the poem's genesis, and the proposed explanation, are matters of historical interest which pale into insignificance beside the interpretative problems posed by the finished product, they present the translator with real existential difficulties. On the one hand, this is a poem without an author, dedicated to a painter whose work explores the dynamics of optical physiology rather than personal visual symbolism, and requires the poet to find an equivalent in the psycho-physiological dynamic set in motion by the constituents of language themselves (phonemes, morphemes, lexemes). On the other hand, it is a poem with a multiple but self-impersonalizing authorship, assimilating the givens of an ever-expanding environment; the *poème-conversation* offers the translator the resource of a verbal collage, whereby he/she becomes another client seated at the café-table, recording the comments of fellow-drinkers, and able at any moment to interpose his/her own collaborative contribution. I want to begin with the former of these options and suppose that the source text (ST) is an occasion, an invitation, a provocation, for the target text (TT) to reflect on language, but less on its efficacy as a translational medium, and more on its properties as a psycho-physiological material. It may be that the self of the translator is principally a capacity for linguistic perception out for hire, which uses a native language to unpack and communicate the psycho-physiological forces at work in a foreign-language text, rather as Delaunay uses the screen of the window to unpack the colours in the light reflected from the buildings of the Paris cityscape. And Apollinaire is the window through which we look at Delaunay.

In order to understand the homology that Apollinaire sets out to establish between his text and Delaunay's canvases, we need to understand the senses in which *Fenêtres simultanées* are a critique of analytic Cubism.[4] In seeming to embrace the planar at the expense of the perspectival, Cubism had not in fact abandoned what is descriptive, linear, and immobilizing in the perspectival; nor had it abandoned the notion of point of view, however multiplied.[5] And the will to immobility to be found in Cubism was further intensified (a) by Cubism's dedication to the analysis of the object rather than to the synthesis of light, and (b) by its banishment of colour, which for Delaunay is the very agent of dynamism (vibration, interaction). The Cubists continue to employ a right-angled geometry of line and chiaroscuro—even if the light-source has become problematic—where Delaunay favoured circles and helices. Line for Delaunay is a limit, colour a limitless depth.[6]

Colours come to us from the depths of space, as chromatic waves, different combinations of wavelengths appearing to us as different colours. We would normally expect the breadth in waveband, or range of wavelengths, to depend on how much reflected light we see, and colour would depend on what of the light the object absorbs and what it reflects. In the Delaunayan world, in which objects (the Eiffel Tower, the Great Wheel, the *quais*, buildings) are no more than last vestiges, sources of vision that are constantly being superseded by the demands of colour itself, light has become an independent creative force: '[Delaunay] veut instaurer un système artistique à travers lequel il communiquera l'éblouissement que lui procure la vue de la lumière, douée à ses yeux de qualités et de formes indépendamment de la constitution des objets à travers lesquels elle circule' (Francastel, 1957: 26) [[Delaunay] wishes to establish an artistic system through which he will communicate the dazzling experience generated for him by the vision of light, light which, in his eyes, is endowed with qualities and forms independent of the constitution of the objects among which it circulates]. To think about colours as Delaunay presents them to us in his *Fenêtres simultanées* is to mark their relative vibratory speeds (complementaries—slow; dissonances—fast) and the kinds of dynamism this creates between them, is to experience the intervals between colours, the collisions of the warm and cold, the variations in opacity and transparency, the different axial momentums—horizontal, vertical, diagonal. Delaunay would want us to think of this as a musical arrangement of perceptual impulses and responses. There is a sense, then, in which the Delaunayan window reinvokes Mallarmé's view of the paginal layout of *Un coup de dés* as a record of the 'subdivisions prismatiques de l'Idée', reorganizing linguistic/visual perceptual consciousness.

But what we should also insist upon, as Delaunay insists upon it, is the *depth* of colour, a depth which sound also perhaps has, coming to us as vibrations through the air, frequencies with the power to awaken feelings and responses. Delaunay asks us to associate depth not with the invention of perspective, a vanishing point, calibrated space, but with potentially infinite planar recession through which the eye passes, into the colour's ever-receding heart.

How, then, does the Delaunayan window act? A Paris cityscape, seen through a window, dissolves and leaves behind a purely sensorial experience of colours. The cityscape has been decomposed, dispersed, by the dynamic activity of light, prismatized by the window. This might be an image of the translator's consciousness confronting the ST: one might think of the translator's account of Apollinaire's poem as a further prismatic decomposition of a café scene, the splintering of an already splintered discourse into a stream of lexemes, morphemes, graphemes, phonemes, by a shift of perception from discourse cohesion to psycho-phonetic cohesion. A process of 'abstraction' takes place, in which the physiological is increasingly purified of the semantic, and language is restored to its primitive psycho-physiological drives and values.

The colours that the cityscape becomes, in the window, the viewing consciousness, are both to be looked through, as reflected light, and to be looked at, as pigment; the window is simultaneously our lens and our field of vision. In other words, these colours are both consciousness and the subject of consciousness. Transferring to the realm of the linguistic, we may say that the sounds and rhythms of language are a prismatic experience of words, of discourse. These sounds may derive much of their expressive colour from the words in which they appear, but once prismatized they achieve a certain autonomy, so that when they serve as a 'primary' consciousness of language, their own 'physiology' (buccal being) is a source of sense-associative dynamism. Thus it is that the ST generates a particular kind of proliferative perceptual consciousness in the translator even as that consciousness equally becomes his/her subject.

But before we too quickly espouse this attractive analogy between looking and translating, we should stop to consider Delaunay's doubts about the literary as it might be associated with hearing. These are perhaps most fully expressed in an article written in the summer of 1912 entitled 'La Lumière', subsequently translated into German by Paul Klee and published in *Der Sturm* (No. 144–5) in February 1913. Briefly put, Delaunay's argument, with remarks made by Leonardo as one of its inspirations (see Francastel, 1957: 167–8, 174–5), runs: light, born in the work of the Impressionists, creates movement; movement is generated by inequalities of colour ('mesures impaires')—contrasts, dissonances—which also generate depth. This all adds up to 'simultanéité rythmique' or 'le mouvement synchrome', which, in turn, adds up to human vision. But hearing, on the other hand, is insufficient for such a knowledge of the universe; it lacks depth, its movement is successive and mechanical, and has no relation to the time of perception (*durée*), the perception of visual movement, but is governed by clock-time. Hearing is connected with equality/parity and the geometric, and by the 'geometric', Delaunay seems to mean the object caught in its immobility, in its outline, in its subjection to gravity. The world of the object is the world of the imitative and the descriptive. Delaunay's very elliptical account indicates his impatience with justificatory argument:[7] he seems to align all those notions that, for him, have a negative charge—the evanescent, the successive, the linear, parity, the geometrical, the chronometric, objectness—and to impute to them inevitable causal connections. His beatification of the eye runs against a modern Western view that the optical has led us astray, that the reinstatement of the claims of sound, with its 'engulfing multi-directionality' (Bull and Back, 2003: 5) is an urgent priority. In fact, we might argue that Delaunay reverses the values usually attributed to vision and hearing in the Western debate: for him, vision, not hearing, is 'intuitive, engaged, synthetic and holistic', while hearing, not vision, is 'rational, detached, analytical and atomistic' (Ingold, 2000: 245).

Delaunay's arguments against sounds and language, however, often give way under his desire to do justice both to the work of his friends and to the other arts (for Delaunay's 'artistic network', see Bière-Chauvel, 2005). Often he sees colour as the universal language which assimilates words as much as musical notes. And when he speaks of 'les phrases de couleur', or 'les phrases en couleur', one feels that he includes musical phrases as much as the phrases produced by 'le verbe couleur' (Francastel, 1957: 63). His fondness for describing the arrangement of colours as orchestration or as 'un ensemble de rythmes' (Francastel, 1957: 63) takes us deeper into the world of music, and the latter phrase, equally a literary analogy, takes painting into the realm of time and challenges Lessing's distinction between the spatial and temporal arts. In fact, Delaunay sees his *Fenêtres simultanées* as a synthesis of simultaneity and temporal unfolding:

> *À ce moment, vers* 1912–13, j'eus l'idée d'une peinture qui ne tiendrait techniquement que de la couleur, des contrastes de couleur, mais se développant dans le temps et se percevant simultanément, d'un seul coup
>
> (Francastel, 1957: 81)

> [*At that time, around* 1912–13, I had the idea of a kind of painting which would technically owe its existence only to colour, to contrasts of colour, but developing in time and being simultaneously perceptible, at a single glance].[8]

Simultaneity, then, is not an instantaneous, first-glance experience, but the outcome of an accumulation, an encompassing perception which the play of colours leads us into. Consequently, the objection that simultaneity is not available to literature, given the unavoidable sequentiality of reading, falls by the wayside. Reading, likewise, is a process of gathering, storing, which produces an overall textual display, perceived simultaneously.

And, indeed, Delaunay gave passing thought to literary simultaneity. In notes made in October 1913, he dismisses Henri-Martin Barzun's multivocal writing—different groups of speakers speaking at the same time—as 'literary counterpoint', and goes on: 'Le simultanisme littéraire peut être donné par l'emploi des contrastes des mots' (Francastel, 1957: 112) [Literary simultanism can be produced by the use of the contrasts of words]. This remark is as suggestive as it is condensed. It suggests that lexical differences—that is to say, phonetic and morphological differences—and differences of verbal weight, rather than semantic differences, create the dynamic of language and the simultaneity of its interactions. And let us remember that simultaneity derives from the principle that a colour, its activity, cannot exist without the presence of another colour; colours *naturally* generate simultaneity, as indeed do the sounds of language, in the instantaneous triggering of self-differentiation from other phonemes, reverberating across the totality of the language-field. In this respect, and in relation to verbal weight, we might also recall Mallarmé's phrase describing words taking the initiative, 'par le heurt de leurs inégalités mobilisés' (2003: 211) [mobilized by the collision of their inequalities].[9] This will, in turn, make us think again of Delaunay's pursuit of imparity, of 'mesures impaires', another phrase with profoundly literary associations. But as the discussion proceeds, and Delaunay refers us to Cendrars's *Prose du Transsibérien et de la petite Jeanne de France* (1913), with its decorations by Sonia Delaunay and its subtitle '*Premier livre simultané*', he seems to lose confidence in the case: the *Prose* is constructed on simple contrast which cannot build up depth. And yet the observation following allows that the poem invites a process of verbal substitution or association, of paradigmatic replacement, which multiplies text and dynamizes form:

> Transsibérien-Jehanne de France laisse la latitude [à] la sensibilité de substituer un ou plusieurs mots, un mouvement de mots, ce qui forme la forme, la vie du poème, le simultanisme
>
> (Francastel, 1957: 112)

> [*Prose du Transsibérien* leaves the sensibility the freedom to substitute one or more words, a movement of words, which forms form, the life of the poem, simultanism].

In the final comment of this passage, Delaunay refers to the 'contraste de mots simultanés' [contrast of simultaneous words] as the source of a new aesthetic fit for the age; and that new aesthetic, for him, as for Apollinaire perhaps, involves the discovery of a universalizing language, where linguistic abstraction is the route to the universal. We cannot doubt that he saw Apollinaire's work as paralleling his own: 'Je pense que les *Fenêtres* marquent ce qu'Apollinaire appelait la *peinture pure*, comme il a cherché une poésie pure' (Francastel, 1957: 171) [I think that the *Windows* mark what Apollinaire called *pure painting*, just as he pursued pure poetry].

The relationship between acoustic simultaneity and the temporal sequence of reading or hearing remains something of a textual mystery. But the phenomenon of rhyme seems to confirm that the inner ear can, by suspending and 'spreading' sound—presumably at the expense of other sounds—hear as 'single' an acoustic event which the reading eye/ear can only register as the consecutiveness of two sounds. Literary reading requires us to read suspensively, activating as much short-term memory as possible, so that we can also listen synthetically, combinatorially and inclusively.[10] What we must learn to listen to are the very materials of language, and this involves a prismatic dismantling of language into its primary elements, phonemes, morphemes and lexemes. The continuity of the voice-stream directs us towards the retrieval of meaning, as it surfaces; but we must also gather in what lies below this surface, the unconscious of language, or the raw percepts of language, or the repressed expressivity of language's intimate constituents. Consider, for a moment, the relationship between vowels and consonants.

Relations between vowels and other vowels, and between consonants and other consonants, are essentially paradigmatic ones: each vowel or consonant conceals behind itself those vowels and consonants which might replace it. Relations between vowels and consonants, on the other hand, will be syntagmatic, with vowels as potential syllabic nuclei exerting a power of attraction over consonants. The basic relations just described have different temporal and mental implications, as Saussure reminds us:

> Le rapport syntagmatique est *in praesentia*; il repose sur deux ou plusieurs termes également présents dans une série effective. Au contraire le rapport associatif [i.e. paradigmatic relation] unit des termes *in absentia* dans une série mnémonique virtuelle
>
> (1972: 171)

> [The syntagmatic relation is *in praesentia*. It is based on two or more terms that occur in an effective series. Against this, the associative relation [i.e. paradigmatic relation] unites terms *in absentia* in a potential mnemonic series (1974: 123)].

Within these 'primitive' phonemic relationships, therefore, there is at once a here and now of text-on-the-page, ever in the process of relating with itself; and there is a virtual or hypothetical text, a text of memory and projection, analeptic and proleptic.

Pierre Garnier (1968: 42) refers to 'les voyelles-lumière' [the vowels-light] and 'les consonnes-architecture' [the consonants-architecture], while Roland Barthes (1973: 89) speaks of 'la patine des consonnes' [the patina of consonants] and 'la volupté des voyelles' [the voluptuousness of vowels]. The articulation of vowels involves the opening of the mouth, while that of consonants involves different kinds of closure (Straka, quoted in Jakobson and Waugh, 1979: 85). Consonants are more informative, more responsible for the differentiation of meaning, than vowels. Consonants are characterized by their noise, vowels by their sonority. Any table of phonetic distinctions, identifying more complex permutations, whatever its particular terminology, will begin to make the phonemic structure of the language look like the acoustic equivalent of one of Delaunay's colour discs:

	grave diffuse	acute diffuse	compact
abrupt	p	t	k
	b	d	g
continuant	f	s	ʃ
	v	z	ʒ

Here we might also associate the contrast between voiceless consonants and their voiced partners with Delaunay's contrasting of transparent and opaque versions of the same colour. And the elements of such a table will all have certain psycho-physiological connotations for the speaker: some sounds will seem more assertive, more insinuating, more restful, and so on. Indeed, as Benjamin Whorf suggests, we have at our disposal automatic chains of association just waiting to be released by particular sounds:

> In the psychological experiments human subjects seem to associate the experiences of bright, cold, sharp, hard, high, light (in weight), quick, high-pitched, narrow, and so on in a long series, with each other; and conversely the experiences of dark, warm, yielding, soft, blunt, low, heavy, slow, low-pitched, wide, etc., in another long series (Carroll, 1956: 267).

Not only that—such experiments may suggest, too, certain equivalences between vowels and consonants: high-pitch/low-pitch in vowels is equivalent to stridency/mellowness in consonants, or to the unvoiced/voiced distinction.

About sound symbolism in general I do not want to say more than that the evidence is too substantial to be ignored (see, for example, Grammont (1911), Bolinger (1950), Marouzeau (1965), Delbouille (1961; 1984), Genette (1976), Magnus (2001)). As a single example we might cite what Mallarmé has to say about the word-initial cluster *fl-* in the English language: '[F] forme avec *l* la plupart des vocables représentant l'acte de voler ou battre l'espace, même transposé par la rhétorique dans la région des phénomènes lumineux, ainsi que l'acte de couler, comme dans les langues classiques' (2003: 984) [[F] forms with *l* the majority of words representing the act of flying or beating the air, even transposed by rhetoric into the field of luminous phenomena, as well as the act of flowing, as in the classical languages]. Let us describe *fl-* otherwise, as a gliding, glancing motion followed by a swift eruption, a flowing movement which climaxes in an explosive burst of energy: flip, flash, flare, fly, flit, flap, fling, flick, flush. Clearly monosyllabicity is a prerequisite for the words' explosiveness. Dissyllables tell us about the dispersal of that stored energy: flitter, flutter, flicker, flurry, fluster, flatter. Since Delaunay is our target, we need, as here, to draw these accounts of sound away from symbolism, away from interpretation, away from emotion, towards the psycho- and neuro-physiological, towards buccal sensation, towards experience in the mouth.

In trying to think our way systematically through the different functions and colorations of phonemes, in trying to identify the linguistic sensations that might be associated with them, we need to develop a new mode of reading, of apprehending the text, not one which separates sounds from words and from prosody, listening to them for their own sakes, listening for pure acoustic symbolisms, but one which sees the reading consciousness as a dispersive and multiplying agent, which throws language(s), sound, typography into an expanding turbulence. What we mean by a performance of, or in, a text is the setting in motion of this dispersive and volatile mix of constituents. Reading/translation asks questions about language, not about its meanings in particular configurations, but about its energies and propensities, about its proliferative impulses, its awakenings of, leanings towards, and filterings into, other languages. This is to take the road back from articulation to pronunciation, from pheno-text to geno-text (Kristeva, 1974: 83–6; 1984: 86–9), and to suggest that the signifier is an animal still not properly domesticated, still not sure of its place, its affiliations, its appropriateness, still not sure where it came from. If a colour, varying in saturation but not hue, and lying in the wavelength range of 585 to 575 nanometres (*Collins English Dictionary*, 2000: 1767) is 'yellow', then one must ask how it relates acoustically to /jɛləʊ/ or indeed to /ʒon/ or indeed to /gɛlp/, where all these relationships, while being opaque and without the need to demonstrate any acoustic kinship, create a nexus of interwoven auditory sensations and questions: why are /ɛ/ and /l/ shared tones in the English and German perception of yellow; why does the German without its /l/ come into the French territory of the aggressively yellow—/gɛp/ ('guêpe'), a beast that might produce an unnatural segmentation and pronunciation of the English (yell! ow! /jɛlaʊ/) or remind us of the proximity of 'gelb' to 'yelp' (/jɛlp/), where there is also a yellow insinuation; has 'jaune' (/ʒon/) a certain circumscribability thanks to 'zone' (/zon/, or /zəʊn/) or 'Zone' (/tso:nə/); why are the French and English versions voiced from beginning to end, while the German modulates into the unvoiced /p/; why does the German give us a consonantal modulation, while the dissyllabic English word provides a modulation of vowels; and in what conditions might we hear a schwa at the end of the single-minded French /ʒon(ə)/?

This is the space in which, to use Deleuze's term, language 'stutters'. But this is also the space to which any language and all language refers: it is the free world of linguistic and acoustic ecology, a real world of multiple resource, the world of the linguistic blind field, a kind of logical consequence of the dispersive thing that the text itself is. The mechanism entailed here is very different from that usually posited for, say, the Mallarméan sonnet, where the text's inner dynamism is reckoned to be directly proportional to the firmness of its frame, its formal closedness. Delaunay's *Fenêtres simultanées* not only explore a wide variety of formats (square, oval, horizontal, three-part), but they open on to a blind field, in two senses: the dynamism of colours is in excess of the frame, reverberates across the frame, as in *Les Fenêtres simultanées sur la Ville [1ère partie, 2e motif, 1ère réplique]* (1912), and radiates to infinity (the fourth-dimensionality of colour); at the same time, the window of colour-vision is set within, opens out on to, an interior space, the apartment/studio, the real environment of the optical transformation (see *Fenêtre aux rideaux orange* (1912)). In this way, the frame captures or engenders a depth as much as an extent, and the tension between the two kinds of blind field holds in equilibrium the at once abstract and indexical, virtual and referential, nature of Delaunay's work.

Both Delaunay's paintings and Apollinaire's text provide a static set of triggers which the eye, or the eye and the ear, set in motion, reap the sensations of, make sense of. Criticism makes a twofold mistake in relation to this material: (i) it does not imagine what the activity generated by those triggers consists of, largely because it cannot: we know, for example, that in reading we do not enunciate successions of separated phonemes, ticked off, as it were, as they are encountered; we enunciate a soundstream in which several phonemic elements are fused together.[11] And just as we cannot predict the eye-motions of the reader of a tabular text, so we cannot predict the ocular trajectories of a viewer of a Delaunayan window, nor the psycho-physiological 'visual babble' which will ensue. (ii) we return to the pre-experiential fact (i.e. the canvas, the text) to account for the experience, assuming that the experience lies in the canvas or text, in its static structures and dispositions. Accordingly, the reading aloud of poetry is imagined as a presentation of the text, not of what is going on in the mind and body of the reader, as if the text by itself were expressive. We silently accept that this experience of the reading or looking mind and body is inaccessible to criticism. But we would argue that it is accessible, if not completely so, to translation, and can, through the act of translation, be written back into the source. Consequently we must adapt our approach to the source and acknowledge that its experience does not inhere in it, that it is not to be recovered from the text/canvas as a set of answers or solutions or keys (interpretation), but rather that it can only be prepared for by our identifying potentialities, provocations (motive forces). As we therefore make remarks about, say, alliteration or assonance, we are not reading off achieved moments of literariness, consolidations of a given structure, which exert certain prejudicial obligations on the reader; we are, rather, trying to capture text-genetic impulses, sources of possible acoustic intensities and densities, the possible materials of acoustic memory and simultaneity. But what uses the reader will put these observations to, what patterns in the carpet the reader will respond to, we cannot say.

Let us, for a moment, consider the two 'refrain' lines in 'Les Fenêtres' connected with the opening of the window:

Et maintenant voilà que s'ouvre la fenêtre	4 > 4 > 4
La fenêtre s'ouvre comme une orange	3 > 2 > 5

This /u/ ('s'ouvre') is the /u/ of the word 'couleur', absent from the text but ever-present as a phantom assonance, particularly in the word 'coule'. Eyes do not 'run' or 'weep', but flow, spread into colour. Why is it that 'Vancouver' must be twice present, if not because /vãkuvɛR/ takes us from 'couleur' and 'rouge' towards 'vert'? Elsewhere /u/ appears in 'tout', 'se mouchait', 'soulèveras', 'Oursin', 'couchant', 'Tours', 'mourir', 'où'. If in these words we may hear 'couleur', we shall also hear 'rouge', sometimes in the 'reversed' form /uR/, sometimes with its voiced /ʒ/ unvoiced to /ʃ/, always with this sense that we are passing through different shades and hues.

One might also pick out 'jaune' (/ʒon/) because /ʒ/ is in 'rouge', 'géant', 'message', 'jolie', 'jeune', 'neige', 'orange', because /ʒ/ , as we have just noticed, plays so often against its voiceless partner /ʃ/, because /o/ in its other appearances is often in the vicinity of /R/, as it is in the opening /RuʒovɛR/: 'traumatisme', 'pauvre', 'rideau', ['beauté'], 'repos', 'chaussures', ['Ô'], ['beau']. Or again, we might fix on the doubling of vowels in 'aras', 'natales', 'abatis', 'pihis', 'téléphonique', 'cravate', 'vagabondes', 'oua-oua', 'pelleteries' (supposing a 'full' pronunciation: /pɛlətəRi/), 'fuit l'hiver'.

As we look at these phonemic recurrences, we must beware of treating them as a set of identical acoustic markers disposed across an immobilized textual surface. Simultaneity presupposes a reading that has never done with a text. Consequently, these apparently identical sounds are not unchanging, but constitute a mobile network of relationships which are permutating, and in which the 'colours' of the phonemes are constantly being given new 'hues' by contextual sounds and by acoustic slippages (homophones, allophones, modulations across languages). The rhythmic envelope is another influence on acoustic 'hue': at its first appearance (l. 11), 's'ouvre' is the final element in the medial tetrasyllabic measure of an *alexandrin trimètre*; at the second (l. 36), it is a disyllabic measure that closes the first hemistich of a 'Romantic' decasyllable (i.e. divided 5//5 rather than 4//6). Similarly, 'la fenêtre' is first the final measure (4) of the alexandrine, and then the initial measure (3) of the decasyllable.

But if we are able to enjoy these acoustic associations and permutations principally as a set of self-motivating particles constantly to be re-absorbed into the process of reading, a set of particles demanding their own language within language, generating an activity of language beyond meaning, we might point to two particular factors which help produce an acousmatic or 'schizophonic' (Smith, 2003: 127) auditory effect—that is, language detached from a source, utterance detached from a speaker. The first is, quite simply, collaged language, the language of the *poème-conversation*, language issuing from multiple, no longer identifiable sources. 'Les Fenêtres' does not mean as a cohesive discourse, with a cumulative semantic momentum, but rather as a set of discontinuous, undeveloped impulses, within which one can always start again. We have already explored these linguistic conditions in Chapter Three, apropos of our translation of 'Lundi rue Christine', and, as there, we might speak of the poem's power as deriving from the dynamic *between* lines rather than from the meaning made progressively *within them*. Accordingly, as before, we might draw upon a cinematic model for their unfolding, and, once again, on Dziga Vertov's theory of intervals.

The second factor lies in Apollinaire's attraction towards the monolexical or monophrasal line. On the proof of the catalogue version (Vriesen and Imdahl, 1967: 48) Apollinaire not only gives instructions that 'Tours les tours ce sont les rues' should make two lines ('Tours/Les Tours ce sont les rues) and that 'Vancouver' (first appearance) should be given a line of its own, but also seems to intend that the 'Puits' lines should run:

> Puits
> Puits
> Ce sont les places
> Puits

In the event, the second 'Puits' becomes the headword of the line 'Puits ce sont les places' to create the echo with 'Les Tours ce sont les rues'. About these purely substantival lines, two things should be said:

(i) these words lose their clear enunciatory origin and become words that might be read off from a shop-front, a book, a newspaper, an advertising hoarding. And even if we do imagine them as having an enunciatory origin, we cannot tell who speaks them, nor with what intention, nor with what expressivity.

(ii) these lines change the consecutive, the sequential, the linear, the authorially chronometric, into the enumerative, the potentially appositional, the tabular, the readerly durational. They create a linguistic situation in which there are no syntagmatic restraints on the multiplication of the paradigmatic. To take but one small example. Originally 'Étincelant diamant Vancouver' constituted one line, with the implication that 'Étincelant diamant' was a pre-appositional description of Vancouver. As separate lines, we can treat them more easily as discrete items, in an enumeration that does not constitute a progression. But, equally, we can continue to read them as appositionally related, not only to each other, but also to the presiding noun, 'Les Fenêtres', with which all lines in the poem have, or may have, an appositional relationship. That a window might be described as an 'Étincelant diamant' is no surprise. That Vancouver should be an apposition to 'Les Fenêtres' is less obvious, but no more surprising: Delaunay's windows draw into their coloured ambit not only the immediate cityscape of Paris, but the whole world; and Vancouver contains within its phonetic composition, as we have already seen, the opening window ('s'ouvre'), two of the colours of the first line—'rouge' and 'vert'—and the /ɑ̃/ that we find in 'maintenant' and 'orange', and in many other lexical participants.

In order, then, to capture something of this transformation of the lyrically grounded utterance into the acousmatic and schizophonic, and also to convey something of the permutative interactions of acoustic particles, I let my first version run thus:

<table>
<tr><td><table>
<tr><td>Red</td><td>Tout</td><td>O</td><td>red</td><td></td></tr>
<tr><td>Ou</td><td>VERT</td><td>Green</td><td></td><td></td></tr>
<tr><td>Rouge</td><td>reD</td><td></td><td>rot</td><td>Ne</td></tr>
<tr><td>Jau</td><td>Green
Eau</td><td>Gelb</td><td></td><td>green</td></tr>
</table></td><td>Yell</td><td>Ell</td><td>Lo</td><td>w</td></tr>
<tr><td>Caw</td><td>Ow</td><td>Low</td><td>Mc</td><td>Arara</td></tr>
<tr><td>Gib</td><td>Ma</td><td>CAW</td><td>Trees</td><td>Pi</td></tr>
<tr><td>caw</td><td>Lets</td><td>street</td><td></td><td>Hi</td></tr>
</table>

The Chromatic and the Acoustic

There's a poem to be written about the 1-winged **the windows**
bird

We'll send it as a textmessage

ICU
monoplane
UR plumed with
mischief
2 not in wing but in
poste de pilotage
canoodling biplane

SEI8SMIC TRAUMATISM/~~IQUE~~

It makes your eyes water
An eye-catching girl among the Turinaises looklookLOOK
The poor young man used his white tie as a handkerchief
Is that still Tender Buttons?
You will lift the curtain

And now SEEsee the *window opens*
SPIDERS WHEN HANDS WOVE THE LIGHT
BEAUTY PALLOR ~~OF~~ UNFATHOMABLE VIOLETS
We'll try *fruit*lessly to get some rest

It'll begin at midnight
Lee told me he'd suddenly come to a vivid understanding
Of non-comprehension
When you've got the *Mail* you've got the *Express*
Winkles
Monkfish
multiple Suns
and the Sea-urchin
of sunset
An old pair of yellow shoes by the window

T e
O r
W s

The **towers** are the **streets**

For the Simultaneous Delaunay, to whom I dedicate this poem

You are the brush he dips in light

Wells

Wells are the **squares**

S

L

L

E

W

Hollow trees which shelter nomadic mulatresses

The Chabins sing songs to die of

To runaway Chabines

And the oua-oua goose trumpets northwards

Where the raccoon hunters

Scrape clean their pelts

Sparkling diamond [Vancouver

Where the train white with snow and ~~gold-lit with~~ night-lights outruns winter

O Paris

From red to green all the yellow fades
Paris Vancouver Lyon (?) Hyères Maintenon New York and the Antilles

Refreshers Philip Browne Carman's Bakery

Gong tom-tom Zanzibar jungle beast X-rays express scalpel symphony
The *window opens like an* ooorange

The windows of my poetry are wide open to the boulevards and in its shop windows

The plump *fruit* of **LIGHT**

If, in the opening three lines of my translation, I have laid out my linguistic 'primary elements' in a grid, it is designed to suggest not only

Delaunay's colour-grids but the system of differentiation which holds a language in a stable state. But, clearly, my system is both out of shape and extremely precarious: it suggests that the elements listed define themselves anarchically and occur in very heterogeneous relationships with each other. There is, here, after all, a mixture of languages, a mutually enriching Babel of languages, just as there is a mixture of lexemes, morphemes and phonemes. What such a grid as this seeks to establish is not so much that a set of lexemes, morphemes and phonemes has achieved the stability of a system, nor that they are meaningful by virtue of the binary differentiations that the system creates, but that such a systematization of elements generates endless permutations, permutations not only of relationship but also of metamorphosis: /u/ *becomes* /o/, etc. What I want to suggest is that language itself invades and subverts the language system; that the language system is not watertight, but is extendable, can be added to, and that with each addition, the system is pushed further out of shape. Language becomes a disorderly sprawl. The carefully framed system conceals a linguistic energy which is always bound to run into the blind field, the blind field of other languages, the blind field of onomatopoeia, the blind field of acoustic variation and variability. And the translator is complicit in this subversion. He/she responds to the urgings of language and lends his/her sensibility to language's (self)-outworking. With each new performance of language that a translation is, new linguistic competences are necessitated.

Elsewhere, the poem draws, if only passingly, on sounds directly heard and transcribed, on onomatopoeia: the oua-oua of the goose. But the opening grid invites us to an extendable possibility. What if all words, when broken down into morphemes and phonemes, were seen as combinations of onomatopoeias? So that words suddenly found in themselves a multi-dimensional synaesthesia? What if whole words were onomatopoeias that we had always overlooked in our hurry to get to meaning? But this language is janus-faced, for not only does it invite us to identify direct sensory notations, text-external phenomena, whether they be of touch, or smell, or sound, or taste, or sight, it invites us, too, to explore language as the repository of its own abstract constituents, sounds, shapes, elements without pre-assigned meanings, looking to define themselves in their own activity. My opening 'table' tries to create a symphony of colours that give off sounds, and sounds that may suggest colours, and other sensory experiences, through the agency of their metamorphic dynamism. Changes of font and language take red, green and yellow through varied shimmerings, yellow releases its loud yell, but its 'low', too, which is also 'lo(ok!) W', its 'ell' which is l, which is also /lə/. The macaws let us hear their 'caw', which, because of its distribution across the grid, sounds like another colour. The fabulous bird, the one-winged pihi, sounds like a combination of single phonemes: p (/pi:/, or is it really /pə/) and h (but in a new phonetic guise, not /eltʃ/ but /hi:/). A 'street', we realize, is 'trees' with its /z/ unvoiced to /s/ and shifted from one end of the phonemic string to the other, with its former place taken by t. And so on. And my translation of Apollinaire's 'message téléphonique' (more like 'telegram' than 'telephone message'—see Steegmuller, 1973: footnote, 203–4) as 'textmessage', the text message itself being a poem about the one-winged pihi, is not just an attempt to find a modern equivalent, but a desire to indicate that contemporary communicative language continues to explore and exploit this re-orientating abstraction of language.

But I do not wish to turn the entirety of Apollinaire's poem into a grid of phonemes, morphemes and lexemes, because this grid represents a mode of linguistic perception rather than a new language. I want this opening grid to be the necessary window through which we, as it were, optically process, read, the remainder of the text. The reading of the text thus becomes the opening of the window that the poem describes. But we will not perceive the cityscape that lies beyond the window with new eyes, unless we keep the lens of the window imaginatively in front of our faces. We thus enable ourselves to see, with the help of typographic enhancement it is true, that whole words, too, have potentialities as natural sounds, as styles of architecture, as olfactory sensations, as new acoustic experience which we, blinded by an overriding concern for meaning, have not before perceived.

This is a language that has little or no *origin* in the speaking voice, but invites the voice to re-imagine itself, to re-inhabit language without the reassuring envelope of its own informing discursivity. It is as if we were trying to create words which have a free consciousness, a consciousness not bound into a given temporal sequence, into linearity, into the syntagmatic and the metonymic—all these latter are governed by a voice establishing itself as proprietorial, as linguistically colonizing, as able to assert its rights of occupation by making meaning, by taking possession of the means of expression, by generating the need to be listened to. Now the voice participates, as it were, in the free play of oral consciousness, where it is the vehicle of an indeterminate orality rather than of an individuating identity, and this process closely relates to the destruction, or radical diminution, of syntax.

'J'ai fait mon possible pour simplifier la syntaxe poétique et j'ai réussi en certains cas, notamment un poème: « Les Fenêtres » [...]' (2005: 71) [I have done my utmost to simplify poetic syntax, and I have succeeded in certain cases, notably a poem called 'Les Fenêtres'], Apollinaire wrote to Madeleine Pagès on 1 July 1915. However mixed were Apollinaire's feelings towards Futurism, we might suppose that in this syntactic respect he would have endorsed Marinetti's view that syntax mediates (or, rather, interferes with) our contact with the world, by operating as a force for anthropomorphization, as a certain human point of view, as a set of evaluative criteria:

> Only the asyntactical poet with words set free will be able to penetrate the essence of matter and destroy the mute hostility that separates [matter] from us. [...] [Syntax] has been a sort of interpreter, a monotonous tour-guide. We must suppress this intermediary so that literature can directly enter into the universe and become one body with it ('Technical Manifesto of Futurist Literature (May 1912)'; Rainey, 2005: 18–19).

The unsyntactical poet is the poet whose communicative faculty is intuition, the faculty of communication both with the world (organic and inorganic) and, through language, with the reader. Marinetti triumphantly asserts: 'We are entering the boundless domains of free intuition' ('Technical Manifesto'; Rainey, 2005: 19). Syntax enacts the laws of perspective, ensures a point of view, orientates itself on its vanishing-point, the full stop. With Marinetti and Delaunay and Apollinaire, we move into a planar world, a world of distances, and depths and reliefs, with multiple and free-ranging points of view.

Apollinaire's moves to desyntacticalize his poem are to be found in (i) the suppression of punctuation (because punctuation presupposes voice as an animating presence, breathing life, rhythm, articulatedness, into word-strings); (ii) the naturally paratactic nature of collage-writing; (iii) the purely presentative nature of the discourse—'Voilà', 'Voilà que', 'Il y a', and so on; (iv) the device of purely substantival lines, e.g. 'Abatis de pihis'; 'Traumatisme géant'; 'Beauté pâleur insondables violets' (in the catalogue version 'Beauté Pâleur d'insondables violets'). And, as a result of these devices, an indefinite power of selection is released: as we have already observed, there are no syntagmatic restraints on the multiplication of the paradigmatic. Furthermore, because these objects/words have no enunciatory envelope, have not been possessed by anyone, they are open-ended, or what one might call 'abstract'. We are, as it were, outside discourse; the basic elements of language are no longer mediated to us by a representation, or representational function.

My own translation attempts to dramatize Apollinaire's thinking about syntax and lineation by making visible the revisionary process and by taking some of the revisions a few stages further: thus I maintain the 'Vancouver' revision as a mooted intention, but further devocalize and make more abstract the 'Towers' and the 'Wells', by changes of font, counter-cultural directions of reading and phonemic dispersal; as the tabular is substituted for the linear, so these words become even more radically isolated from discourse. But, equally and oppositely, I have also tried to respond to the pulls in the direction of the indexical, tried to imagine ways in which the poem might constantly re-ground itself in the environmental hubbub of ongoing history, as part of its destiny as a *poème-conversation*, a text grounded in multiple voices, a direct transcription of words and sounds heard or read in particular settings at particular times. Accordingly, I have added, as part of the process of re-installing Apollinaire's text in another point in time, and of making the writing of the poem happen in my own consciousness, two transcriptions of comments from a seminar on early twentieth-century art trends:

> *Is that still* Tender Buttons

and

> *Lee told me he'd suddenly come to a vivid understanding*
> *Of the non-comprehensible*

and a sequence of shop-signs seen as I passed one day (Friday, 14 October 2005) down Guildhall Hill in Norwich:

> *Refreshers Philip Browne Carman's Bakery.*

[All these items are in italics to indicate that they are insertions into Apollinaire's text].

I have also included citational transcription in my translation, a quotation of lines from Blaise Cendrars's 'Tour' [(Eiffel) Tower] (1st pub. November 1913):

> *For the Simultaneous Delaunay, to whom I dedicate this poem,*
> *You are the brush he dips in light*

and

> *Gong tom-tom Zanzibar jungle beast X-rays express scalpel symphony*

and from his 'Contrastes' [Contrasts] (1st pub. January 1914):

> *The windows of my poetry are wide open to the boulevards and in its shop windows*

These two poems, collected in *Dix-neuf poèmes élastiques* (1919), are products of Cendrars's long association with the Delaunays, to whom he was introduced by Apollinaire in October 1912. Quotations might appear to be textual fragments at one remove, acting in two places at once, inhibited by a particular kind of textual self-consciousness. But, conversely, in a montaged poem, this material can also participate in the self-improvising immediacy of the text, can recover its first-handness as an *objet trouvé*, as if it had never really existed before, as if, only now, it had discovered its spontaneous desire to be, in a particular environment.

It seems to me crucial, therefore, that we allow both that the pull towards the indexical, towards the sense of the direct transcription of life embodied in the *poème-conversation* and in collage, is a vital part of the poem's effect and that the two elements we have considered, the abstract, or non-objective, and the environmental, are, despite appearances, intimately connected. There are two reasons for making this claim, the first of which lies with Delaunay himself. The year of Delaunay's window series, 1912, is the date carried by Kandinsky's *Über das Geistige in der Kunst* (actually published in December 1911), the first confrontation with abstraction, the investigation of painting's underlying language—line and colour, but in this text, more colour than line—shorn of any obligations to imitation or representation. But while Kandinsky's delight in the abstract is motivated by the renewal of spiritual values, by the activation of 'inner resonances', Delaunay's work explores the optical experience, the effects on the spectator's eye, of the interactive dynamics of colour-shapes. While Kandinsky's abstraction tends towards[12] the symbolic (what does this colour mean?), Delaunay's non-objective painting is, by persuasion if not in fact, indexical: it derives from the direct observation of light and seeks to provoke a rich neuro-physiological response in the spectator. In a letter to August Macke of 1913, Delaunay writes:

> Une chose indispensable pour moi, c'est l'observation directe, dans la nature, de son essence lumineuse. Je ne dis pas précisément avec une palette à la main (quoique je ne suis pas contraire aux notes prises d'après la nature immédiate, je travaille beaucoup d'après nature; comme on appelle cela vulgairement: devant le sujet). Mais où j'attache une grande importance, c'est à l'observation du mouvement des couleurs. C'est seulement ainsi que j'ai trouvé les lois des contrastes complémentaires et simultanés des couleurs qui nourrissent le rythme même de ma vision
>
> (Francastel, 1957: 186)

> [Indispensable for me is the direct observation, in nature, of its luminous essence. I don't exactly mean with a palette in hand (although I am not against notations taken directly from nature, that's the way I often work; as it is commonly called: in front of the subject). But what I attach a great importance to, is the observation of the movement of colours. It is only in this way that I've discovered the laws of the complementary and simultaneous contrasts of colours which fuel the very rhythm of my vision].

The question to ask of a Delaunay window is not 'What does it mean?' but 'How does it act on me?' We are left, then, with something of a paradox: a kind of painting which is abstract and, at the same time, vividly embedded in living reality.

The final act of this chapter consists of two further translations of 'Les Fenêtres' in the form of photo-poems, both of which contain photographed text. The first of these is based on a second translation of 'Les Fenêtres', building on my previous version. In this second translation I moved to increase the degree of indexicality of the text by incorporating more onomatopoeic features and by more lexical dislocations. I also introduced painted colour 'notes', in a limited and unsophisticated fashion, about which the following should be noted:

1. I used watercolours, for their transparency, desirable both in relation to Delaunay's practice and for the continuing legibility of what is overpainted.
2. In the opening grid I (a) gave colour-words their appropriate colour, except where 'green' and 'red' were invaded by their complementary colour; (b) gave the repeated 'caw' different colours, to suggest different notes or timbres, and varied relationships with the other elements in the grid; (c) painted remaining areas, but not all, in colours dictated by my own perceptual impulses. If I left some areas unpainted, it is

because this text is a *movement towards* colour, not a *representation of* colour.

3. Thereafter, I simply divided the keyword 'window(s)' into three elements 'w-in-(d)ow(s)' and applied to those elements the three colours of the first line 'red-green-yellow'. However, as far as possible, I varied the shades of each colour in order to capture the fact that orthography and phonetics do not always correspond: e.g. w (/w/) v. wh (/h/) = whom; /In/ v. /Iŋ/; in (/n/) v. in (/ɛ̃/) v. in (/in/) = curtain, Chabins, Chabines; /əʊ/ v. /aʊ/ = ow, low, dow, but tow(ers), *Browne*. I also introduced blue, the third primary and a key to green; if red, green and yellow are the window, then blue is the light which is reflected on to the window and shines through the window. 'Vancouver' is blue because its phonetic structure is, as we have seen, a synthesis of many of the poem's vital acoustic components. Other place names also attract colours.

I then problematized the greater degree of indexicality by photographing this new text haphazardly, cutting up the results and collaging them as a radiation from the opening grid (Fig. 25). In Chapter One, in our rendering of 'Chevaux de frise', I also used photographs of text, but in that particular context the photographs were of books and of text-in-books, so that their sense related to the ambience of reading, as a potential critique of what reading too easily elides. In this instance we are operating with close-ups of text itself (although there are variations of scale).

The camera is a mediating consciousness, which by this mediation creates not a reading consciousness but a consciousness of reading. These photographic fragments are a *record* of a (translated) text; they change the status of the text and our relationship with it: it is no longer a text situated in a present-for-reading; it is, rather, a text consigned to a past-of-having-been-read, a text become document, a text become historical artefact, a text become disposable (as the cutting proves), at the expense of its readability. The text is an event in the universe that has taken place and that we can no longer get back into. This is not entirely true, because it still advertises itself with glimpses of words, phrases, typefaces, and these glimpsed elements may act as affects or memories; but they have a knowledge that we can, it seems, no longer fully retrieve. This, one might argue, is an intensification of the very spirit of the photographic: that making patent which is a withholding, those casual, unselfconscious images which are the subject of anxious and frustrated interrogation. These photographic fragments deprive

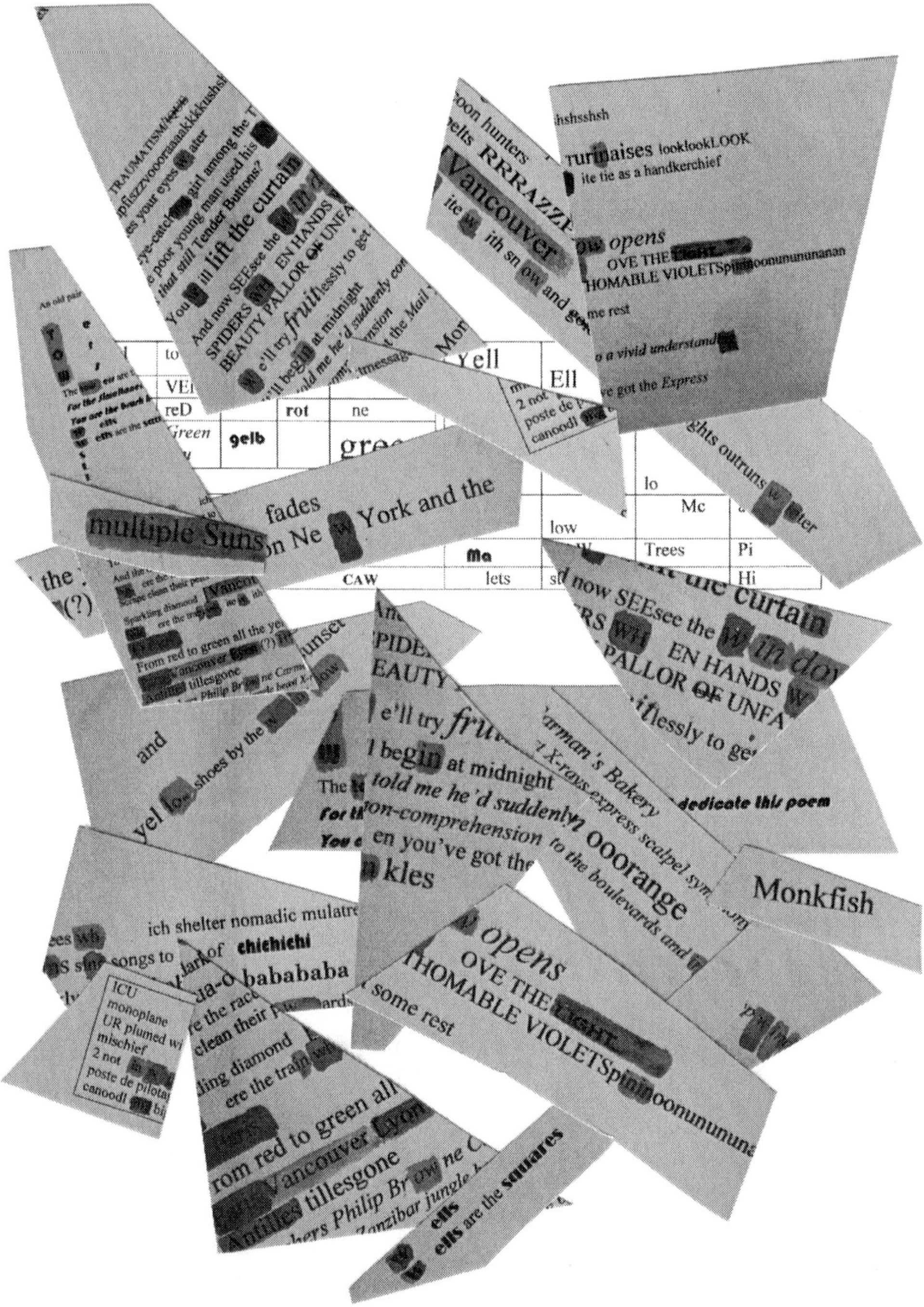

Figure 25: Translation, with photographed textual fragments, of ‘Les Fenêtres’

us of text not only in their fragmentation but in their preservational capacity: they are offered to us as simulacral aides-mémoire, but at the cost of direct sensory contact.

By virtue of its metalinguistic status, then, this translation becomes a translation of a translation, a translation of the text after textual experience. If in Chapter Two we investigated, through the notions and practice of the variant and variation, what translation might be in the way of a pre-textual activity, an activity plunging into the proliferative nature of language as a text-genetic infinity, then we might also wonder about translation's potentiality as a post-textual activity. Translation might be, as here, a memorial to text (ST and TT), something which, by indication and recognition rather than by inhabitation, evokes an event of translation now past.

But there is something text-genetic here, too, something proleptic co-habiting with the analeptic, but again more to do with the consciousness of reading than with reading consciousness. Collage itself has this proleptic drive, and in two senses. First, the various fragments may suggest to us the relativism and perspectivism of future readings, or the complex multifariousness of the text's becoming, its many lives as intertext, as an agent in literary consciousness. Such a translation as this incorporates the envisageable fortunes of the ST/TT, not as actualities but as virtualities. Second, the very act of cutting makes possible further acts of cutting, but cutting into different shapes, into different distributions, into different kinds of dynamic. The text is still to be made, still to be infinitely re-imagined. And since cutting is the incision of time, and of consciousness, into the text, so each new time demands a new cutting as much as it demands a new consciousness. These fragments call out for their blind field, but the blind field is now both the framed whole of the text seen in its totality and the unframed and unframable totality of the future of the ST in manifold varieties of itself and of possible TTs. Collage will always have this proleptic, revolutionary or avant-garde attraction, because it offers us not a writing but the organization of writing, not just images but the formal reconstruction and organization of images. It is the cutting of collage which turns the event of the photograph into an advent—that is, an event which does not just happen but which makes possible, which does not close time down but opens it up, and transforms the mere passage of time into an elastic consciousness of time.

My second photo-poem also looks at the text 'from the outside' and, from the outside too, at Delaunay's paintings and at the world (Fig. 26). This outside derives not only from the fact that 'live' elements

Figure 26: Contact-sheet photopoem translation of 'Les Fenêtres'

are reduced to photographs—it is also clear in some half-dozen of the Delaunay images that these images are derived from books—but also from the diminutive size of the photographs themselves. This is a contact sheet, which casts the image as reference, as mnemonic shorthand, as mock-up, and the sheet itself as storage unit. These are images that one may, indeed, inspect, but not so much *as images* but rather *for their viability as images.* Consequently the emphasis here is once again on the proleptic: even if the contact sheet is a record of a shoot, or of several shoots, it asks questions about the future of the photographs, about what the accidents of encounter and vision will resolve themselves into, what kind of historicity they will participate in, what consequences they might have. Usually, like translation, the contact sheet (variants) resolves itself into choice(s) and the obliteration of other images from spectatorial consciousness; but we have located the business of translation firmly within the field of metamorphosis, of variational infinity, of looking among. So the contact sheet indefinitely suspends its imminence and holds the world open.

In fact, the contact sheet is, precisely, homologous with the Delaunayan window, but it is a Delaunayan window where looking-among involves jolts of optical re-adjustment as we pass between different orders of perception. The real world, for example, is no longer chromatically absorbed into the interactions and modulations of colour-shapes, into the dialogue between opacity and transparency, as are the Eiffel Tower and the Great Wheel in Delaunay's work; the real world is *resistantly* present as a distinct order of being and apprehension. But the format of its images declares its unanimity, its co-existential parity, with the orders of painting and text, and thus emphasizes compossibility. Thus, while the street-photographic images oppose the images of painting and text—these latter confront you, ask questions about readability, demand an exclusive attention—by proposing an escape into an ambient world which is haphazard and self-diversifying, and constantly scatters or redirects attention, they also propose themselves as something which might act coextensively in consciousness with painting and text, not only as the blind field of those activities, but as necessary to them, as an environment, everywhere in the world, which must be incorporated into the work as a reflection or trace or echo, in a new 'chromatemology' or 'acoustemology'.[13] This is indeed to suggest that the direction of Apollinaire's creative thinking, particularly as it assimilates the phonograph and cinema, is that all art must adopt the creative posture of the *poème-conversation.* These street photographs remind us that any time whatsoever and any space whatsoever are full of perceptual rewards, and that these perceptual rewards do not require the application of an interpretative mechanism, that they are psycho-physiological and to do with the orchestrations of sensation.

There are moments, then, when translation needs to be post-textual, meta-textual, conceptual, in order to take stock of itself, in order to re-affirm its psycho-physiological and phenomenological drives. At these moments, translating a text is translating the perception of a perception of text. We do not ask how to read the photographed text; we ask how to read its unreadability. We do not ask how translation might take us into a reading of the ST, but how it might take us out of reading the ST into an image of that text's modes of cultural operation. What these images depict no longer inhabits my reality; I cannot go towards them, as I could if I were holding the camera that took them (even though I did take them). They are now subjects of disembodied looking. In these two photopoetic translations, the photograph as mediating consciousness has placed the text at a distance from its readability, where we are confronted with its after-life in a cultural community. We are confronted with a reading, not of the text, but of its 'situation' or 'significance' or 'potentiality'. These photopoems help us to imagine a translation which is a retreat from the travails of pure linguisticity, a positioning of translation outside the boundaries of the linguistic medium, the possibility of putting translation in the space of event, and of projecting translation beyond the act of translation.[14]

6

New Sounds, New Languages

This final chapter takes, as its point of departure, what is perhaps Apollinaire's ultimate linguistic provocation and the penultimate poem of *Calligrammes*, 'La Victoire', first published in *Nord-Sud* on 15 March 1917. I present a translation without further ado (see Appendix I (xi) for French text):

1. A cock crows I dream and the osiers shake
2. Their leaves which look like poor sailors

3. Winged and downward-spiralling like Icarus the false
4. Blind men gesticulating like ants
5. Gazed at their reflections in the mirrors of the rainy pavement

6. Their laughter clumped together in grape-bunches

7. Don't walk out on me diamond that spoke/speaking diamond
8. Sleep peacefully you are at home everything is yours
9. My bed my lamp and my punctured helmet

10. Precious looks sapphires cut near Saint Claude
11.   Your cheeks the weeks were a pure emerald

12. I remember you city of meteors
13. They blossomed in the air in the nights when nothing sleeps
14. Gardens of light where I picked bouquets

15. You must have had your fill of putting fear into this sky
16. Let it swallow its hiccup

17. It is difficult to imagine
18. Just how stupid and unthinking people are after success

19. At the institute of the young unsighted they were asked
20. *Isn't one of your number winged*

21. O Mouths mankind is in search of a new language
22. One that will leave grammarians of every language speechless

23. And these aged languages are so close to dying
24. That, truly, it's only from habit or lack of nerve
25. That they're still put to work in poetry

26. But they are like the sick and spineless
27. My God people will soon get used to silence
28. Mime is plenty good enough for film

29. But let's stick with speaking
30. Let's keep our tongues wagging
31. Let's launch some spluttering
32. We want new sounds
new sounds
new sounds
33. We want consonants without vowels
34. Consonants farting sotto voce
35. Imitate the sound of the spinning top
36. Let bubble up an unbroken nasal sound
37. Make your tongue click
38. Use the muffled noise of the sloppy eater
39. The indrawn hawking of spittle would also make a pleasant
consonant

40. The varied labial buttputtbbpps would lend resonance to your
utterances too
41. Get used to burping at will
42. And what letter incises like a bell-ring

Into our memories
We love too little the joy
Of seeing beautiful brand-new things
O my friend make haste
Fear the day a train leaves you
Unmoved
Look at it faster for you
These railway networks
Will soon play no more part
They'll be handsome and ridiculous
Two lamps burn before me
Like two women laughing
I sadly bow my head
Before their ardent mockery
Their laughter spreads
Everywhere
Speak with your hands snap your fingers
Tap on your cheek as on a drum
O words
Into the myrtle grove they follow
Eros and Anteros in tears
I am the city's sky

Listen to the sea

The sea moaning in the distance and crying out all alone
My voice faithful as the shadow
Wishes at last to be the shadow of life
Wishes to be o living sea as faithless as you
The sea that has betrayed countless sailors
Swallows up my great cries like drowned gods
And the sea in the sun bears up only the shadow
Cast by the outspread wings of the birds

Speech is sudden and it's a God who trembles
Come forward and sustain me I miss the hands
Of those who held them out and together adored me

77. What oasis of arms will welcome me tomorrow
78. Do you know the joy of seeing brand-new things

79. O voices I speak the language of the sea
80. And in the port at night the last taverns
81. I who am more pigheaded than no the Lernan hydra

82. The street where my two hands swim
83. With their subtle fingers feeling out the city
84. Goes off
                    but who knows if tomorrow
85. The street growing motionless
86. Who knows which way my way would lie
87. Think that the railways
88. Will be out of fashion and quickly abandoned
89. Look

90. Above all Victory will be
91. A clear long-sightedness
92. An inclusive
93. Near-sightedness
94. And that everything
                    be newly named

[Notes on the translation: l. 11. I revert to the manuscript and *Nord-Sud* versions: 'Tes joues étaient', maintaining the acoustic relationship between 'jours' and 'joues', by translating 'jours' by 'weeks'; l. 21. I have retained the capital letter ('Bouches') from *Nord-Sud*; l. 32. I have retained the stepped layout of the manuscript and *Nord-Sud*; l. 84. The manuscript and *Nord-Sud* have this as two lines: 'S'en va/Mais qui [...]'; I step the line, as with l. 32; l. 94. The same applies here as in l. 84; manuscript and *Nord-Sud* have 'Et que tout/Ait [...]'].

In attempting to bring this poem to sense[1] I start from the two dimensions of language identified visually in the final lines, the view long-sighted both in space (the cosmic, sea and sky) and time (the mythic), and the near-sighted view, the view that emanates from the perceiving body. Apollinaire's attention to the close-up view (ll. 29–43), is often seen as a tongue-in-cheek, if not mocking, endorsement of so-called 'bruitist' trends, whether in Futurist writing or the poems of

Pierre Albert-Birot. But there are plenty of good reasons to suppose that Apollinaire means what he says in these lines (see Boschetti, 2001: 218–20), however much he may warn against confusing acoustic raw materials with finished utterance (1991: 947) or falling into Futurist onomatopoeic descriptivism (1991: 971). In fact, these lines align themselves with the similar sentiments expressed in Valery Larbaud's 'Prologue' (1996: 23–4) to the first part of *Les Poésies de A.O. Barnabooth* (1908): the poet's song of himself will include the 'borborygmes' [intestinal rumblings], the 'chuchotements irrépressibles des organes' [the irrepressible whisperings of the organs], the 'inévitable chanson de l'œsophage' [the unavoidable song of the œsophagus]. There can be no doubt, however, as this poem amply demonstrates (ll. 74–7), that Apollinaire confronted with deep apprehension that sacrifice of his lyric identity which a poetry of free-wheeling environmental and bodily consciousness seemed to entail. The 'editorial' of the issue of *Nord-Sud* in which 'La Victoire' first appeared, an editorial written by Apollinaire but signed N.S., might lead one to believe that the poet was envisaging for himself an almost *post-productive* glory as the totemic figurehead of new trends in poetic expression: 'Naguère, les jeunes poètes allèrent trouver Verlaine pour le tirer de l'obscurité. Quoi d'étonnant que nous ayons jugé le moment venu de nous grouper autour de Guillaume Apollinaire. Plus que quiconque aujourd'hui, il a tracé des routes neuves, ouvert de nouveaux horizons. Il a droit à toute notre ferveur, à toute notre admiration' (quoted by Boschetti, 2001: 217) [Previously, young poets went looking for Verlaine, to drag him out of obscurity. Where is the surprise, then, that we have judged it the right moment to muster round the figure of Guillaume Apollinaire. More than anyone else today, he has mapped out new routes, opened up new horizons. He has a right to all our enthusiasm, all our admiration].

At all events 'La Victoire' is perhaps not so much a call to explore all the scatological possibilities of the vocal tract, so much as (a) to understand language not as an average middle ground, which evacuates all extremities from readerly consciousness, but a dialectical weaving together[2] of the infra-linguistic[3] and the ultra-linguistic, of the near-sighted and the long-sighted, bifocalizing the ear, creating productive tensions at the heart of the average, at the heart of what we too comfortably possess; (b) to feel, consequently, that these two dimensions, in no way beholden to the average, but enjoying their own particular anarchies, might be extended, added to, fourth-dimensionally so to speak, and thus correspondingly expand our sensory range (particularly listening) and our powers of linguistic intuition.

In Apollinaire's treatment of the long-sighted, the cosmic and the mythic, a relatively straightforward drama is played out. The poet, son of Apollo, the sun which etches out shadows remarkable for their faithfulness, their lack of ambiguity, their charge of eternity ('Ma voix fidèle comme l'ombre', l. 67), looks for a voice which is charged with the faithlessness of the sea:

Veut être enfin l'ombre de la vie
Veut être ô mer vivante infidèle comme toi (ll. 68–9)

The sea consumes those submerged in it (the sailors), or those who, on false wings, attempt to dissociate themselves from it (Icarus). The sea, with its constant and unpredictable metamorphoses, its transience, makes blind people of us all.[4] The sea is no *langue* in which we might feel (too much) at home, but a *langage* whose modes of operation we can only guess at. In order to become a living shadow, we must find the true wings of the sea-bird and fly poised between sea and sun, across the sea's surface:

A l'institut des jeunes aveugles on a demandé
N'avez-vous point de jeune aveugle ailé (ll. 19–20)

Et la mer au soleil ne supporte que l'ombre
Que jettent des oiseaux les ailes déployées (ll. 72–3)

Here the shadow is the undulant and fragmented, the fleeting, the passage of the new and its vocal capture.

But the winged bird does not eradicate the blind, does not act as a permanent alternative to immersion/submersion in a world always likely to make a mockery of us (ll. 6, 53–8). When we do not see, we feel our way with our hands, with gestures which themselves might seem like mockeries ('agitent', 'gesticulant'), a prey to comic self-delusions:

Se miraient sous la pluie aux reflets du trottoir (l. 5)[5]

But as the poem proceeds, there are redemptions to be found, even in the blind condition. Hands, too, become the source of a new language:

Parlez avec les mains faites claquer vos doigts
Tapez-vous sur la joue comme sur un tambour (ll. 59–60)

and have previously been the signs of acclamation of the poet's own achieved poethood:

> Avance et soutiens-moi je regrette les mains
> De ceux qui les tendaient et m'adoraient ensemble (ll. 75–6)

And as the poet returns to the streets of the city, which in their fluidity and transience have become water channels, his hands are the fish feeling out the city's secrets.[6]

The sea, as we have observed, is *langage*, inclusive, multiform, polymorphous, the instrument of infinite variation. We must underline the collision in lines 21 and 22 of *langage* and *langue*, a collision which underpins our own translational ethos: translation must always open up national languages to the whole medium, must open up *langue(s)* to *langage*. Renewal of language lies in what *langage*, and the rhizomatic proliferation of *langage*, can do for *langue*; to work in the volatile and protean spaces of *langage* is to leave the grammarian of any *langue* without points of either reference or orientation (ll. 21–2). *Langue* is almost by definition dead, the agent of habit and imaginative immobilization (ll. 84–6), something that even now might become the paralyzing outcome of *langage*.[7] Perhaps the poem's central line is:

> O voix je parle le langage de la mer (l. 79)

About this line we might observe three things. First, the poet becomes the channel of other voices. Not only does 'Ma voix' (l. 67) become 'O voix', but we might assume, as I have, that by analogy with 'O bouches' (l. 21)—the physical place, the near-sighted version, of 'voix'—that 'voix' is plural. We might suppose, too, that the moans and cries we hear in the sea are the accumulated cries of all those submerged there:

> La mer [...]
> Engloutit mes grands cris comme des dieux noyés (ll. 70–1)

Second, while the sighted see new things, speech and hearing are peculiarly the resources of the blind, and, as the last lines remind us, new modes of seeing create the need for new names; the visionaries need the blind. Third, 'parler' bifurcates into two conceptions of language: *langage*, on the one hand, and 'parole', on the other. If *langage* is the undifferentiated and mercurial medium (the body, the cosmos), 'paroles' are isolated and lapidary utterances belonging to the mythic world:

> O paroles
> Elles suivent dans la myrtaie
> L'Éros et l'Antéros en larmes (ll. 61–3)

And if authority is something characteristically embodied in 'paroles', that authority proportionately increases as the 'paroles' become more peremptory:

> La parole est soudaine et c'est un Dieu qui tremble (l. 74)

Décaudin (2002: 96) relates this line to language's inexhaustibility and unpredictability. We might add that language, in the end, has an authority greater than those who speak it: language speaks language, generating its own unsuspected powers and directions; this is the gamble of the new; this is what makes a god tremble; this is the authority that the poet must surrender, without knowing what his future might be (ll. 74–7).

If translation is to be the agent of a new language, always reaching beyond the frontiers of the known, nomadic, then it must substitute a centrifugal approach to text for a centripetal one. A centripetal approach insists on a continual return to the source text (ST) as its unchanging point of orientation, on the grounds that the ST fully possesses itself, in its linguisticity, in its literariness and in its meaning, however polysemic that may be. The centrifugal practice of text, on the other hand, believes that the text is constantly in search of itself; that it does not comprehend itself; that it has yet to fulfil itself, in paralinguistic realizations, in synaesthetizations, in extensions of its own language; that, consequently, it owns neither its linguisticity nor its literariness, but that these features are unstable, continually re-inventable, always at the text's widening periphery.

This translational project, this use of translation to mobilize language at its limits, entails the abandonment of that putative literary ideal of organicity, the organic wholeness, the integratedness, of form and content which safeguards ultimate untranslatability. Organicity assumes that, in poetry, the arbitrariness of the relationship between signifier and signified, this inbuilt inadequacy of language, is overcome or overridden, largely by the self-reflexivity that form is able to generate and which allows poetry to define the linguistic rules of its own game, to create its own self-sufficient and autonomous language-universe. There are three correctives to apply to this vision: (i) form is dynamic and serves the process of reading as much as it does that of writing, but in a different way. It is fallacious to think that the reader gets out of a poem what the writer puts in, and it is misguided to think that a perfect coincidence of writerly input and readerly output is the optimal relationship between writer and reader. Quite simply, there is no process of interlocution, no present addressee to act either as a genetic force, or as a communicative stabilizer for the text; the written text always has the freedom to work at, and beyond, the limits of *immediate* intelligibility. Correspondingly, misunderstanding and misappropriation have a certain legitimacy. (ii) As a result of reading, it is not the thereness/objectness of the poem which is established, but its ability to accommodate multiplicity and to trigger multiplicity, a multiplicity of the idiosyncratic. The power of the poem lies in what it can suggest and what it can tolerate. (iii) We should avoid the assumption that we are always engaged with a source language's (SL's) strengths (and not its weaknesses) in relation to other languages, simply because it is the language of the original utterance. Translation does not move in just one direction, from ST to target text (TT). We need, too, to imagine translation as a reversible procedure. How adequate would the ST be as a back translation of the TT? The notions of strengths and weaknesses belong to an unreconstructed translational criticism which is driven by a pious but unjustified defence of the irrefrangibility of the ST.

Acoustic perception is one source of the discrepancy between writerly input and readerly output. We know that the attribution of meanings to sounds remains speculative and crude, and has two underlying channels of enquiry: (i) the pure sound made (phonetic rather than phonological) which is given semantic values, particularly by differential experimentation: which is darker/warmer/softer: /u/ or /i/? (ii) the articulatory mechanism, and the itineraries of sounds in the mouth. But the attribution of values, whether of an expressive or psychoanalytic colouring, remains tentative, highly uncontrolled and idiosyncratic, and governed by the awareness that different linguistic contexts can produce different values in the same sound. It is also clear that our sound-sense is rudimentary, that sounds need to be much better understood in relation to the soundscapes in which they appear, and that we do need to find some way of extending our perceptual capacity from the consideration of isolated phonemes towards something that better approximates to the perceptual experience of speech-flow and of other sounds in time. But it is not just our sense of the linguo-acoustic context that we need to refine, it is also the acoustic environment beyond language. And here it is not just traditional onomatopoeic or ideophonic effects of which we should speak, it is, as already intimated in the previous chapter, of (a) the onomatopoeization of all language and of (b) our capacity to increase, or make more vivid, the psycho-physiological dimensions of language. By the onomatopoeization of all language I mean an ability to listen to language as if all its sounds were telling you something about origins in the environment, origins which might be of a multi-sensory or synaesthetic nature. All language, that is, would be full of perceptual, rather than semantic, information [e.g. 'parfum' (/paRfœ̃/) = the sound a smell makes as it hangs on the air (/paR/), before diffusing itself (/fœ̃/); or the way in which smell works on memory (/paR/), before opening a door of recognition (/fœ̃/)]. The capacity to heighten the psycho-physiological dimensions of language may involve not only the orthographic manipulation of words in their accepted forms, but also the creation of new diacritical marks to achieve maximal sensory immediacy. If I translated, 'I slowly turned over the leaves one by one' (Wilkie Collins, *Basil* (1852), Part I, ch. 8) by:

> I S$_{low}$Ly tu<uu>r<n>ed over the le[gliphgliph]aves one by one

what would one conclude about the posture, the gestures and the mood of the narrator? Words are not about a correct orthography, but about how you choose to spell and write or print them in order to get the most out of them. The synaesthetic experience that words are full of will perhaps emerge only if coaxed out by typographic versatility (see Marinetti's 'free expressive orthography'). This is all to refer ourselves back to Steven Feld's notion of 'acoustemology' (2003). We do not ask ourselves what sounds mean so much as what framework of relating (to the environment, to ourselves) they project, and what particular kind of listening sensibility they activate: 'Soundscapes are invested with significance by those whose bodies and lives resonate with them in social time and space' (2003: 226).

But acoustemology has further linguistic applications in the way we listen to other languages, an experience explored by homophonic translation, a form of translation whose general significance has been seriously underrated. There seem to be two ways of responding to homophonic translation: (i) homophonic translation is an onomatopoeic account in one's own language of a text in a foreign tongue. Homophonic translation activates and explores inaccurate listening, stereotyped listening, approximate listening, selective listening, conventional (lexemic) listening. (ii) Homophonic language is a way of listening the sound-sense relations of one language into the sound-sense relations of another. A certain arrangement of sounds re-arranges sense as one crosses a linguistic border. The homophonic translation of Catullus by Celia and Louis Zukofsky (1969) brings this latter point home more immediately perhaps: I present for reference three lines of their translation of poem VIII, with Catullus inserted interlinearly:

> Billowed in tumultuous joys and affianced,
> IBI ILLA MULTA TUM IOCOSA FIEBANT,
> why you would but will it and your girl would have it.
> QUAE TU VOLEBAS NEC PUELLA NOLEBAT.
> Full, sure, very candid the sun's rays glowed solace.
> FULSERE VERE CANDIDI TIBI SOLES. (ll. 6–8)

The Zukofskys show us how the translator can begin to work towards the signifier of the source text, rather than towards its signified, and in so doing to make the target language (TL) (English) bi-focal: the Latin source multiplies the Englishes present in the translation, in terms both of history and register, and draws out of those Englishes a fund of unsuspected expressive energies; conversely, the sounds of the TL become the acoustic access-points to Roman sensory experience, an experience outside their normal range.

Translation, then, is centrally about language acquisition. But we would wish to set the process of learning against the process of knowing. The clear assumption, mistaken it seems to me, behind the process of knowing is that there is something to be known. But if language is for ever caught in a state of disequilibrium, of constant variation, if language is not a stable system, then there is nothing to be known except change. Learning a language is learning language, for ever feeling one's way forward into a field whose contours are changing, in a process which is never at an end. While coming to know a language implies a circumscribed space, a framed space, whose constituents are progressively ticked off, learning language is an advance into a space which is constantly being unframed, into a material which proliferates and will not hold still. The acquisition of linguistic knowledge is connected with the fulfilment of a method, a particular itinerary. Learning can start at any point and is bound to be fragmentary. What we aspire to is a linguistic nomadism, not a nomadism that is tribal, that is still governed by knowledge of territories and cycles of departure and return, but a deterritorialized free-roaming nomadism.

In devoting translation to the creation of new language, we must understand what kind of new language we mean. We do not mean the creation of a total language system, which it becomes translation's task to exercise and impose. The TT is too small a space to institute anything systematic; indeed, the TT's small-scale experimental status is the perfect pretext for generating novelty unsystematically, ad hoc, unpredictably, in order to achieve a variety of ends:

(i) to remind us that innovation *within* language systems is itself unsystematic, a necessary feature of the continual historicization of language;

(ii) to accept that language (conceived of as the mutilingual, as both oral and visual languages, as the languages of typography, etc.) is a constant invitation to innovation—that is, that innovation does not *change* language, since it is an inbuilt virtuality of language;

(iii) to project from linguistic innovation within the frame of the TT a powerful blind field which would include:

   (a) possible new language systems;

   (b) the totality of all languages;

   (c) any linguistic extension/option the reader cares to imagine.

This in turn implies that the training/preparatory work of translators should encompass not only the study of foreign languages but also familiarity with artificial, imaginary and science-fictional languages (through the work of, e.g., Genette (1976), Eco (1995), Yaguello (2006), Conley and Cain (2006)), but also the experimental adventures of bruitism, *zaum*, Lettrism, concrete poetry, *poésie sonore* (see, e.g., Rasula and McCaffery, 1998). The readiness to invent language is not an attempt to outwit any putative untranslatability of the ST, or to capture its 'poetry', nor systematically to pursue any programme of foreignization. Translation is designed not so much expressively to renew and flexibilize the TL as to explore and exhibit the linguistic resources available for the capturing of readerly experience, so that all options are in the melting pot, so that language recovers its multiform undecidedness and its capacity for metamorphic slippage. The dissatisfactions that the translator works with are dissatisfactions not with the constraints of the TL but with the constraints of language's underlying givens: the alphabet and orthography as transcriptive mechanisms, and as measures and modes of audibility; lexis as the vehicle of perceptual, affective and conceptual consciousness; syntax as the regulator of categorial hierarchy and of the delivery and flow of information.

These constraints can, in my view, be outwitted by extending resources for the physical presentation of language, and, in particular, as already argued (2012a; 2012b; see also Chapter Three and Appendix II), by the re-activation of handwriting and the associated activities of the hand, and by the translation of the linear into the tabular. Handwriting is the graphic performance of the voice, of paralanguage; handwriting performs the kinesics of the hand; handwriting performs the psyche, breaks free from the codedness of the alphabet, becomes the instrument of desire, in illegibility, crossing out, doodling, and other forms of graphism. The tabular, for its part, enacts a paradigm shift in the reception of the word, a shift in which a format (the linear) which encourages the *acceptance* of language, as if it were all already there, as if pleasure in language *depended upon* perceiving it as fluent and untroubled, is required to give way to a format (the tabular) which refuses to let language pass, which subjects it to many kinds of scrutiny, but allows words to enjoy all their mutabilities, words whose every position re-defines them, reconfigures their relationships and their expressive relief; with the tabular, paginal space initiates new kinds of ocular activity, new kinds of audibility.

I would like to draw together, in a short sequence of translations of Apollinaire's 'Le Voyageur' (*Alcools*, 1913), the several threads that this chapter has followed in pursuit of a new language appropriate to translation, and to move a step further, beyond presentational modes into novel linguistic structures. These novel linguistic structures will not be a brand new language, beyond any recognition, nor will they be *a* language; they will, rather, be language. While a poetic text may seem to propose a language, or indeed languages, as its blind field, the text itself, as we have already argued, is committed to metamorphic principles, and to the performative, and will resist any dealings with codedness or non-improvisatory system-making. You can learn these new manifestations of language only piecemeal; they will trigger certain recognitions and familiarities, but you will never come to know them in any meaningful sense. And they will seem to be fashioned on other languages, like a dialect. But the reader must not translate them to a source, must not seek to solve them, by decipherment.

Are these manifestations of language condemned then, by their very evanescence, to extinction? This is the wrong question to ask, because it imagines a desire for stability, stabilization. New translational language will embody the very spirit of mobile polymorphousness, the principle of change and extension and adaptability, and while remaining within the orbit of known languages, sternly refuse to comply with, or reduce itself to, any one of them. In this sense, new translational language will be fugitive language, thriving on linguistic *bricolage*, always seeking to exist just beyond reach, to maintain an unpredictability. But, to facilitate my further thinking about this use of language, I would like to turn to a constituted language, that language called Riddleyspeak, the language of Russell Hoban's *Riddley Walker* (1980).

What problems face the creator of an alternative language derived from a national language, such as Riddleyspeak? Two misapprehensions are encouraged by Russell Hoban himself, when he writes:

> Riddleyspeak is only a breaking down and twisting of standard English, so the reader who sounds out the words and uses a little imagination ought to be able to understand it. Technically it works well with the story because it slows the reader down to Riddley's rate of comprehension (2002: 225).

There is a great temptation to treat alternative Englishes as if they should be translated *back* into Standard English in order to be understood (our old quarrel with the translation of linguistic performance into linguistic competence). Of course our knowledge of SE helps us to measure and relish the perceptual differences that we find in Riddleyspeak. But in fact, we should be translating the other way, from SE into the new language, so that we can ourselves *linguistically undertake* the shift in perception, so that we can better inhabit, give ourselves up to, new language as part of our readerly/writerly becoming.

Secondly, we tend to treat deviation from standard language as having historical or social causes. Riddley uses the language he does because he is slow-witted; Riddley uses the language he does because he is operating in a post-holocaust Kent where the holocaust has had a regressive effect. Even though R.D. Mullen's exhaustive linguistic examination of Riddleyspeak (2000) demonstrates that it is structurally principled and consistent with itself, it is referred to by Christine Wilkie as 'a broken-down and vernacular language' (1989: 15), by I.F. Clarke as 'adding to the impression of social degradation and vernacular corruption' (1993: 210), and by Steven Connor as 'an impenetrably degenerated language' (1996: 219). Even though Mullen reminds us that regional dialects are not corruptions of standard language (2000: 394), we condescend to this language, believing it to be 'uneducated' or anachronistic or quaint. But Riddley knows less than the reader only in certain respects; in others, he knows more, or at least differently. Riddley's language does not square with the standard because the standard does not square with the perceptual experience available to Riddley.

Thus, we imagine our own variation on Riddleyspeak as flexible, structurally unprincipled, ad hoc, orthographically free; we are looking to create a new kind of translationese, a third language which comes into existence after initial acts of conventional translation. This new kind of translationese grows out of a proleptic view of translation, which posits that any work, in its will to survive, to exist for posterity, must inevitably will itself to be other than it is, must foster a desire to become strange to itself; and it is translation which consummates this desire. Already, as the ST arrives at the translator, it is deep in the process of othering itself; the translator develops and expands this process, projecting the ST out across its future in an ever-widening arc. It cannot be sufficiently emphasized that although much of the richness of the third language may derive from its relationship with the second language, and perhaps even with the first, its real value lies in its reordering of linguistic processes, in the way it relates mind to language, in the way it uses language as a sensory liberator, as a proliferator of possible universes.

What are the principles of this third language?

1. It is made of puns, hybridizations, orthographic and phonetic invention, an integral part of the language's metamorphic drive to multiply perceptual relating and sensory association. Imagine 'fruit' as not only frewt, frute, froot, but also froat, frait, fraut. One has both a sense of fruit itself in a whole variety of conditions (picked v. unpicked, summer v. autumn, ripe v. unripe, where in our language adjectival supplementation would be necessary) but also in different relations with the world, as a swallowable commodity, as load in a basket or on a trailer, as something upon which a drama is focused or which is attended by peril. The third language is a language in which perception always multiplies, in which perception is always likely to slide over into hallucination.
2. It is designed to activate both visual and vocal paralanguage. By visual paralanguage we mean any 'message' to the eye, any visual evidence, which may inflect our attitudes towards, or generate the multi-sensory in, the performative realization of the written text. In this sense, photographic fragments

may act both as an added 'foreign' language and as a visual paralanguage.

3. It has a fluid relationship with etymology. By 'fluid' I mean etymology slides between learned, folk and fictional etymologies, and between historical periods. Let us suppose that 'pigeon' is reckoned to derive not from Latin pipio [young bird] < pipire [to chirp] but from a combination of pigge [C13th, of obscure origin] and aiōn [Gk, C17th, an infinitely long time]. What new zoological affiliations are suggested for this plump, grey bird, what role in the unfolding of the cosmos?

But there is another, slightly different, but equally important way in which we may think of this third language as the language of translation itself. This proposition requires us to refer ourselves to the short story by the Oulipian Harry Mathews entitled 'The Dialect of the Tribe' (1980), in which Pagolak, 'the speech of a small hill tribe in New Guinea' (Mathews, 2002: 8), is explored. Pagolak, 'while it produced translations that foreign listeners could understand and accept, [...] also concealed from them the original meaning of every statement made' (2002: 8), because it '*was* the very process of transforming language that I expected it to be *about*. It was not an account of the process, it was the process itself' (2002: 10). This is difficult to grasp. Pagolak is a language caught between; to speak it is already to leave, or have left, an origin and to reach for a destination, but a destination never fully arrived at, as a consequence of which individual words are in the process of being re-shaped, finding new roles and expressive dimensions for themselves. For that reason, as the narrator points out: '(The dictionaries turned out to be useless. They had been compiled for traders and had only an arbitrary, mercantile utility. The problem, in any case, was not one of particular words)' (2002: 9). Pagolak's comprehensibility is deceptive; the source of its linguistic motion is no longer retrievable, its semantic objectives not (yet) divinable. It can be made *practical* use of, apparently, only if one ascribes to it powers not of transformation but of exchange, utilitarian functions. This kind of third language, if caught on a page, in print, would be a chimaera, its stability a mirage, completely arbitrary: it can only be imagined as both manifest and elusive, protean, withdrawing what it offers.

Can my translations of Apollinaire's 'Le Voyageur' (see Appendix I (xii) for French text) engineer a gravitation towards a linguistic equivalent of Pagolak? First, I present a conventional translation; the text shifts between the left- and right-hand margins to capture the changing direction of the current in the Euripos, the strait between Euboea and the Greek mainland, flowing alternately north and south:

THE TRAVELLER

To Fernand Fleuret

This door, I'm knocking, in tears: please – open it

Life is changeable no less so than the Euripos

You watched
a bank of clouds, coming down

With the orphaned steamer towards future fevers
And all those regrets, those moments of remorse
Do you remember them
Waves curving fish flowers on the water
One night, the sea
And the rivers spreading into it

I remember, I still remember

One evening I went down to a sorry-looking inn
Near Luxembourg
At the back of the saloon a Christ took wing
Someone had a ferret
Someone else a hedgehog
There were games of cards
And you, you had forgotten me

Do you remember the long orphanage of the stations
We crossed cities that turned all day like roundabouts
And at night spewed up the daytimes' sun
O sailors, o dark-mooded women and you my fellow-travellers
Remember it all

Two sailors who had never been apart
Two sailors who had never spoken to each other

The younger, dying, fell upon his side

O you, cherished fellow-travellers,
Electric bells in the stations, song of the women at harvest,
A butcher's sled regiment of countless streets
Cavalry of bridges nights ashen with alcohol
The cities I saw lived like madwomen.

Do you remember the suburbs and the lowing herd of landscapes

The cypresses cast their shadows in the moonlight
That night at summer's close I listened
To a bird, languid and tirelessly testy,
And to the never-ending sound
of a wide, dark-watered river.

And while all the looks, all the looks of all the eyes,
Tumbled, dying, towards the estuary
The banks were deserted, grassy, silent
And the mountain on the farther shore
was brightly lit

Then in silence, with not a living thing in sight
Against the cliff-side passed perennial shadows,
In profile or suddenly turning their dimly-featured faces,
With the shadows of their lances
thrust forward

The shadows against the steeply rising cliff-face
Grew tall or sometimes slid down sharply
And these bearded shadows shed human tears
As, step by step, they slipped
over the bright-lit mountain

Who then do you recognize in these old photos
Do you remember the day when a bee fell into the fire
It was – do you remember – in late summer
Two sailors who had never been apart

The elder wore an iron chain around his neck

The younger his blond hair braided

Please – open this door; I'm knocking and in tears

Life is changeable no less so than the Euripos

Then I move to a new-language account of the first ten lines. Here I should just note that I have diversified typeface to suggest different paralinguistic inflections, both vocal and visual, or different manifestations of selfhood, and adopted a layout somewhat akin to Roland McHugh's *Annotations to 'Finnegans Wake'* (3rd edn, 2006), so that we can see the associative echoes of the words, not exhaustively, but as the beginnings of signifying chains or aural fantasies:

ThizdoH r Im nokking in tiers: pliz opn nit

nuklnokking tiernokking trickletiers pleads opnful

sydfisnokking (showt)nokking strimytiers opnjar

Live iz chanjumble nolesso thumb thə yourhippos

chain-jungle Urhippos

Luv erz

Uw otchit

əbangc əvclows kumin do OO wuun

if-clows dowtords

myte-clows dowinter

wivthə orfannt stimə tords fewtchə freeverz

vapeur **vapid vappa F**ieber

unawl dozer egrets, dozem omenz əvrəm horse

beeawl

dozawl

duwUw ri-membrem

wave scur vinkfish flour zonthə wort her

w Av_e

warippvele

won nytethə C

undthə riff her spredddddinin toowit

flie ru-membr, eyestill rum-embr

So each throw of the linguistic dice begins to generate its own metamorphic series, by a process which is a combination of acoustic distortion (vocal idiosyncrasy) projected into the alphabet, and of alphabetic invention (free orthography) projected as performativity (verbal and visual paralanguages). The intention is threefold:

1. That the segmentation of a normally analytic language should become uncertain, tentative, so that language drifts in the direction of the agglutinative, and of synthesized or compound sensations.
2. That the mode of transcription should open up a direct path, by infinite modulation, into other languages and other forms of language, thus encouraging us to redefine our perceptions of morphemic, lexemic and etymological sources and destinations.
3. That the listening mechanism itself should not settle on what it perceives as correct or appropriate, but should be ready to float, listening towards sounds and sound-combinations, and listening away from them. Passive listening commodifies the object, transforms the text into work, institutionalizes reading. We must listen the intentional towards the intentionless, towards what is available to privacy, to piracy, towards what does not signify, but has sense in its very variability.

The language we invent might be oral in origin (the oral transcribed), but nobody really knows how to pronounce it, what its paralinguistic range is; its speaking is thus also to be invented. Nor is it meant to be learned to be known, inasmuch as it has no *necessary* further applications, outside the text; there is, for example, no further literature to be read in this language; it is to be learned only in its ability to effect linguistic transition, to expand linguistic capacities, to engage with the multi-sensory. This is language which will never be complete and therefore can never be truly understood.

For my next version, I zoom in on just the first two lines, and add: a desultory handwritten account of lines 11–15, as a ghost of the whole text acting simultaneously in the reader's mind; a 'decoration' in enamel paint and watercolour; and five clusters of cropped and overlapping contact prints (Fig. 27). The doodles in enamel paint and watercolour are not only the abstract, chromatic vagaries of associative consciousness, but are also a painterly equivalent of that linguistic doodling which produces new language forms, and of the visual doodling that produces photographic clusters; they are thus a founding tracery which binds all activities together synaesthetically. The clusters of contact prints, for their part, are designed to capture, within the dynamic of the painted doodles and the wayward self-improvising handwriting, a visual imagination which moves towards moments of complex associative focus but cannot solve its own perceptual riddles, cannot find its way in the dialogue of the conscious and the unconscious, the motivated and the haphazard, the attentive and the absent-minded. Standard interpretative moves (see, e.g., Lockerbie, 1969) find in the poem a record of Apollinairean themes and biographical episodes, as if something were being stood for, represented, something prior to language; but our translator/reader approaches this language as something which has a future only as a multi-evocative medium, which has reached a point, a textual manifestation, only to begin again, in other directions, towards proliferating performance.

There are two principal ways in which these clusters of contact prints can be seen as performances of text. First, in the sense suggested by Margaret Iversen (2007: 91–108), the photographs participate in 'the recording of an ongoing, open-ended event open to unanticipated consequences' (102); the camera is an instrument of discovery, forward-looking, no longer interested in achieving autonomy for its images, not concerned to illustrate or to *justify* the text, but to respond to the text's own challenge to find paths out of text. Second, these photographs are a visual paralanguage; they are an element added to the text in order to realize it in performative activity—that is, in the realm not of the text itself, but of the text read. The small scale of the photographs, their not being 'full' images, means that they are, as it were, inflections of the visual imagination, which in turn inflect the voice in its exploration of the text's expressivity. Their influence is equivalent to that of different typefaces, or punctuation, or handwriting.

At another level these image-clusters shadow the formation of the new language. The new language is a phonetic and graphic and morphological undoing and deformation of conventional, 'unified'

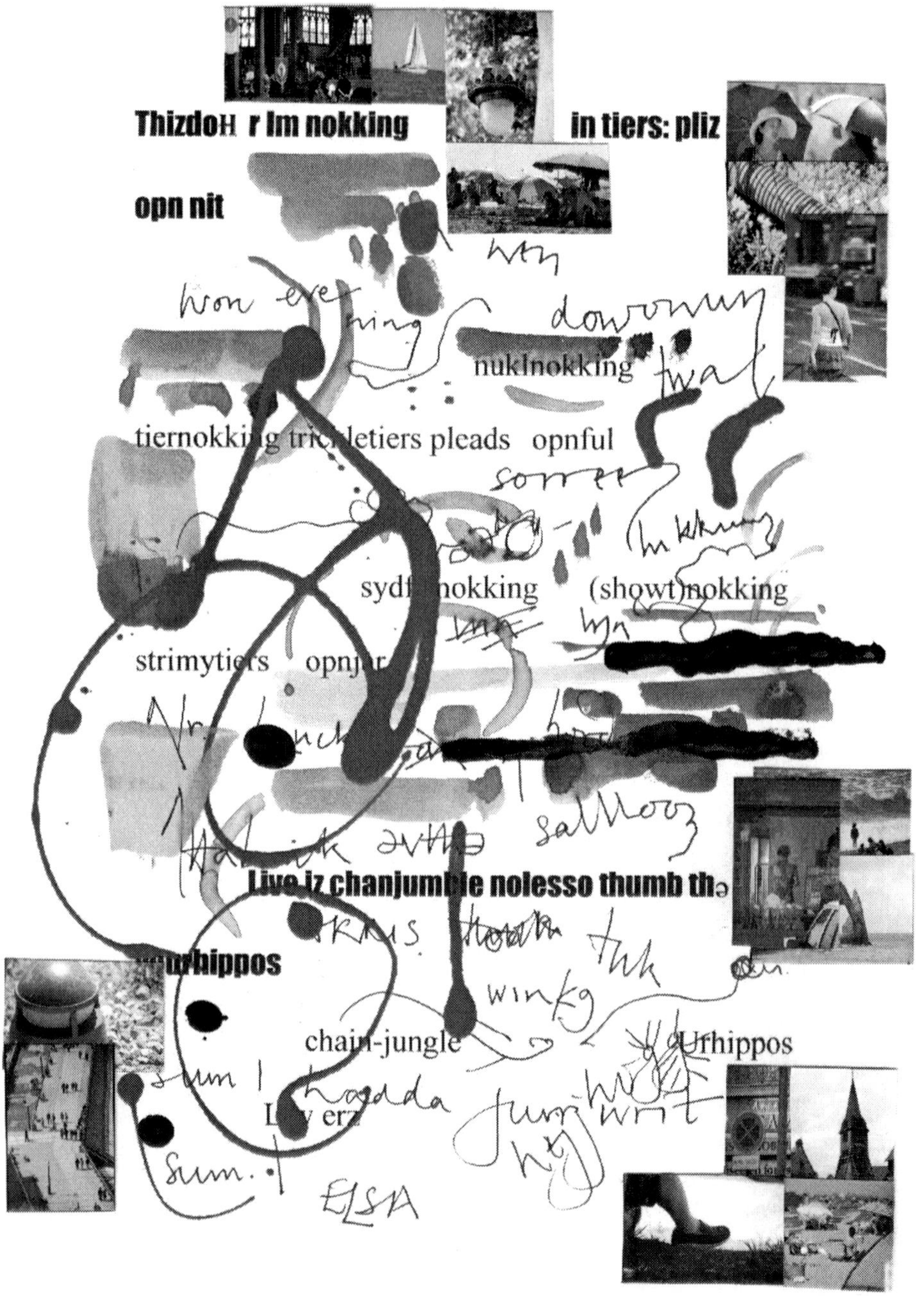

Figure 27: Translation of fragments of 'Le Voyageur', with photo-collage, handwriting, and doodles in enamel paint and watercolour

lexemes in such a way that new itineraries of acoustic, orthographic and morphemic connection are broached. Correspondingly, the photographic images become a bundle of self-disseminating visual impulses, whose elements are sometimes closely related, sometimes more distantly so. These images are tantamount to being new morphologies of the image, new morphemic compounds, looking to re-morphologize themselves with other image-clusters.

For my final translational foray into linguistic renewal I want to pick up the thread of linguo-painterly connections broached in our treatment of 'Les Fenêtres' by turning to Apollinaire's poem dedicated to the work of Marc Chagall, 'A travers l'Europe' (*Calligrammes*, 1918) (see Appendix I (xiii) for French text). In an article of 2 June 1914 for *Paris-Journal*, announcing the exhibition of Chagall's work at the Der Sturm gallery in Berlin, Apollinaire observes: 'Je préfère ses dernières œuvres et surtout son *Paris vu par la fenêtre*' (1991: 746) [I prefer his most recent works and, above all, his *Paris seen through the Window*]. Chagall took his place, alongside Delaunay and others, in Apollinaire's programme for Orphism and the Orphic artist (see Hicken, 2002). There are indeed unmistakable connections between Delaunay's 1912 'Windows' and Chagall's *Paris seen through the Window* (1913), but while Delaunay's vision is of a Paris dissolved by light and resurrected in colour, the subject of a new, forward-looking, 'non-objective' pure painting, Chagall's picture is dominated by the Janus-faced artist/poet (Apollinaire), caught between past and future, between Vitebsk, or Monaco, or Nice, and Paris; the light of vision emanates not from the sun but from the poet's head; and, far from being 'non-objective', Chagall's canvas is littered with emblematic and allegorical items (Hicken, 2002: 95–8, 130, 134). At the same time, however, *Paris seen through the Window* is segmented by Cubistic planes and colour contrasts and 'fades' made grid-like by the window-panes. The colours we see in the window-frames— red, yellow, blue, green—are colours to be found in the daylight of 'A travers l'Europe':

> Un jour fait de morceaux mauves jaunes bleus verts et rouges

and indeed in many of Chagall's images, including *The Cattle-Dealer* (1912), an image of even greater importance, perhaps, for Apollinaire's poem.

This latter claim may seem rather odd, particularly in the light of Hicken's suggestion that Apollinaire's declared preference for *Paris seen through the Window* related to his general favouring of Chagall's depictions of Paris, the *Ville Lumière* (2002: 60), as against his reworkings, in Paris, of Russian motifs, however attractive their Slavic flavour may have been (2002: 59). Chagall had come to Paris in August 1910. Once installed in a studio in La Ruche, passage de Dantzig 2, hard by the Vaugirard slaughterhouses, in the winter of 1911/12,[8] he came to know both Apollinaire and Cendrars, the latter more closely (see, particularly, the fourth ('I. Portrait, II. Atelier') of Cendrars's *Dix-neuf poèmes élastiques* (1919)).

My first version of Apollinaire's poem is as follows:

To M. Ch.

Rotsoge
Your scarlet face your biplane convertible into hydroplane
Your round house where a smoked herring swims
I need the key to eyelids
Luckily we saw M. Panado
And our mind is at rest on that score
What do you see my dear old M D
90 or 324 a man in the air a calf looking out of the belly of its mother

I've searched long and long along the roads
So many eyes are closed at the roadsides
The wind brings tears to the clumps of willows
Open open open open open
Look but please do look
The old man washes his feet in the basin
Una volta ho inteso dire Chè vuoi
I started to cry as I remembered your childhoods
And you show me a terrible violet

The small picture depicting a cart reminded me of the day
A day made of mauve yellow blue green and red patches
When I went to the country with a charming chimney with its bitch on a leash
There's no more you no longer have your little reed-flute
The chimney smokes Russian cigarettes far off from me

The bitch barks at the lilacs
The night-light has sputtered out
Petals have fallen on the dress
Two gold rings beside the sandals
Have been set ablaze by the sunlight
Your hair is the trolley-bus
Across Europe decked out in little multicoloured lights

We cannot be sure when this poem was first written. Bohm-Duchen tells us:

> The painting [*Homage to Apollinaire* of 1911–12] seems to have been given its present title in 1913, when Apollinaire [...] visited Chagall's studio for the first time and pronounced favourably on his work. (1998: 71)

This seems erroneous on two counts: first, about the dating of *Hommage à Apollinaire*—although others also offer the date 1911–12 (e.g. Baal-Teshuva, 2008: 47), Wullschlager gives 1913–14 (2008: 175–6), as does Hicken, with a comprehensive justification (2002: 129–32). Second, Apollinaire's visit to Chagall's studio in La Ruche, during which he uttered the word 'surnaturel' as a judgement of Chagall's paintings, and the day after which he sent Chagall a first draft of the poem (written on a napkin?),[9] is likely to have occurred fairly shortly after Chagall's installation, during 1912, rather than in 1913. At that point, the poem was entitled 'Rodztag' (red day), in probable acknowledgement of Chagall's cultivation of the colour (see, for example, *Dedicated to my Fiancée*, 1911, *The Violinist*, 1911, *I and the Village*, 1911). Thereafter, the poem was published in *Les Soirées de Paris* (15 April 1914) and in *Der Sturm* (May 1914), where it acted as a curtain-raiser to Chagall's June–July exhibition; in both instances it appeared with the title 'Rotsoge' (red trails, red vortices). Adéma and Décaudin (Apollinaire, 1965: 1085) offer this further information:

> Une maquette conservée au Fonds Doucet est composée de papiers découpés et collés; les deux premiers vers sont manuscrits; successivement ont été rayés les titres *Rotsoge* et *Prophétie et Vision*
>
> [A mock-up held at the Doucet Archive is composed of cut and pasted papers; the first two lines are handwritten; the titles *Rotsoge*

and *Prophecy and Vision* have been crossed out, one after the other]

The convertibility of the biplane into the hydroplane takes us back to arguments explored in Chapter Two and suggests that Chagall's world is a soft world of ongoing metamorphosis—that is to say that his 'surrealism' does not, though it may seem to, deal in metaphor, an achieved figure, a stable equation or identification, to be 'worked out', but is, rather, a mobile world of fluid conjunctions, passing relationships, without semantic objective. In Chagall's world metamorphosis is a kind of susceptibility that objects/figures have, a chameleonic capacity of adaptation to various existential environments. At the same time the conversion of air to water—that is, the cross-fertilization of elements—means that habitats can re-locate and dialogues between different orders of existence can be established. Once again, it is the liberating, involuntary, uncoercive availability of metamorphosis that generates the poetic, not the compulsion of metaphor, nor its pointedness, nor its ingenuity. So the smoked herring can leave its container and swim again in the seas of Chagall's studio. And this state of affairs reflects, and is reflected in, the nature of Yiddish, itself a mobile language; spoken as a vernacular by European Jews and emigrant Jews in other parts of the world, it is a dialect of High German leavened with a mixture of words from Hebrew, and words of Romance and Slavonic origin. Its written form usually employs the Hebrew alphabet.

I start by restoring my text to prose, so that, in the further processes of translation and back-translation that I envisage for it, the processes of textual transformation will be less prejudiced by lineation. I then undertake a translation into and out of Hebrew:

> Rotsoge your face Scarlet 2-the wings of the aircraft into the Round House conversion hydroplane that swimming herring smoked me the key to eyelids fortunately we m. Panado mind is at rest that indicates what you'll see my 90 d of m or a round in the air looking for out of 324 belly of his mother already was looking for a long long time so many roads closed eyes on the way to the spirit brings tears vlill to chgianom willows open open open open open appearance But please the old man cleans his feet on uNA Voltabasin Ho inteso vuoi Chè apartment I started to cry and then I remembered childhoods you can show me a terrible breath that describes a small picture day reminded me of mauve yellow blue green and Red patches I went to Palestine a chimney with its lovely bitch שהפסטיבל you no longer must be no more than a small

reed-flute שהארובה smokes cigarettes is Russian bitch at me, barks LILACS that night light has sputtered out petals fell in two gold rings Next to the sandals are set ablaze by the sunlight on your hair is a trolley-bus in Europe including the multi-coloured little lights

Next I produce a translation into and out of 'traditional' Chinese, which I re-lineate to create a text of thirty-one lines, rather than the original's twenty-nine. This translation employs three typefaces—Times New Roman, MS Mincho and Arial Unicode MS—to enact adjustments of consciousness which may also correspond to a typical Apollinairean polyvocality (modulation of personal pronoun):

Rotsoge
Stops where you can convert
your wings airship smoked herrings
swimming round house you
Scarlet face I need the key to eyelids
fortunately we see M.Panado Our thoughts are
still at this point do you see
my dear old M D 90 Or 324 In the air of a man
I searched for a long time and so many eyes
are closed roads along
the road and its mother's abdomen
looking calf wind's eye
Tear old man washing his feet in open open
open open open look of willow but please
do not look at the plex in basin u na Woertehe
inteso Terrible Chè vuoi I started to cry I remember
your childhood and your small pictures
depicting a shopping cart display
purple reminded me of my terrible day
mauve After yellow blue green and
Red patches to the countryside
Days of no more smoke you no longer
have your little reed flute
Smoking chimney Russia from as far

away as I sputtered out in the night light
below the petals of LILACS bitch bark
Sandals next to two gold rings with fire
Clothes dog under the
Sun with its bitch charming chimneys and your
hair is an electric trolley bus throughout
Europe bright color small Lamp

These may look like rather unsubtle and automatic procedures, just one trick from the box of tricks that the computer is. But their conceptual value far outweighs their technical facility. These kinds of back-translation make the TT into a new ST, make of the old ST a text of passage, a generator of multiple kinds of foreignness: that is, it is not the ST that foreignizes the TT—after all, we already know the nature of the SL—but other languages which we thought had no part in this particular linguistic transaction. These procedures also introduce the element of chance ('incomprehension' or mistranslation in the filter-language), as one might use chance to gain access to the unconscious beneath the conscious, the invisible that the visible so well conceals. They take the TT momentarily out of the translator's control and re-arrange the energies in language according to other perceptual and linguistic imperatives. As in our experiment with 'Le Voyageur', back-translations deform language as given, without creating a lasting, systematic alternative; which is to say that they present us with change which is as virtual as it is actual, as much aspiration beyond the frame as achievement within it. At the same time they thicken the flesh of text. By that I mean that they shift the ground of the text from a certain coded organization (*langue*), a certain anticipated comprehensibility (decodability), to something more opaque, more visceral, whose enunciatory sources lie not in a fluency produced by syntax but in an obstructedness created by the body, by a pathology, by a psycho-physiology, by affective strain.

So these kinds of translation/back-translation offer us two stories. The first allows a text/language (TT/TL) to be manhandled by other languages, whose gauntlet it has run. In a translation which is something like a syntactic equivalent of a homophonic translation, one language (TL) desires that we hear through it the actualized and *physical* demands and configurations of another language. Chinese, for example, might leave on the 'original' English some of the marks of an isolating language (despite the persistent pronouns, articles, possessives, tenses, etc.). What we aspire to are processes of pidginization in which the linguistic results are much more complex and flexible, much more resourceful and expressive, than those of 'standard' pidgins, with contexts correspondingly much more varied than those of trade or tourism. But such an analogy would need to be treated with the utmost circumspection: the superstrate language (here English) makes little room for the substrate languages; but, on the other hand, like pidgins, these languages are not indigenized (as creoles are), and more importantly, they exist only in situations of contact, they grow only from contact in makeshift ways; they do not, like standard translation, involve transfer from one language to another.

The second story asks us to confront and combat what syntax deprives us of in the actuality of our perceptual experience, what syntax seeks to persuade us to, against our deeper wishes and needs. Syntax is an *image* of resolved thought, in a flowing and unproblematic temporality. In these translations, in this story, the identity of the filtering language—whether Chinese, Hebrew or Hungarian—hardly matters: each new language is just another order of consciousness, another possible way of configuring the magma of association, memory and sensation that language triggers and attracts. Indeed, one might argue that these translations seek to transform words and their arrangement from tools of meaning into receptors of sense, simply by re-activating processes of linguistic negotiation and engagement. It is important, too, in these translations, that the texts, in line with the Apollinairean source, are not punctuated. The absence of punctuation better enables the voice to tumble headlong, hardly in possession of itself, anticipating, catching up, in a turmoil of word-making which grows from the multidimensionality and the polyphony of perceptual/conceptual activity. Syntax insists on the one-at-a-time, on the even, consecutive delivery of its discourse; these back-translations seem to strive for the near-simultaneity of manifold enunciations through unimpeded speed alone, impatiently sweeping aside syntactical *triage*.

To the last of my versions (Fig. 28), which is a compound back-translation of several linguistic filters, I have added a photographic back-translation of Chagall's work into and out of the work of Francis Bacon. This is partly because Bacon's work is itself concerned with processes of deformation and pictorial re-direction induced by a factor of chance or accident,[10] and partly because Bacon himself uses photographic sources as the trigger and challenge for assimilative transformations, and to exercise painting's ability to turn what, in the photograph, is mediated into the unmediated.[11] It is also partly

Figure 28: Translation, with photo-collage (Chagall and Bacon), of ‘A travers l’Europe’

because Bacon brings so disruptive a language into Chagall's universe. In Chagall there is no eruption of forces from within the flesh, no dynamic apart from the effortless and pliable expression of lyrical and oneiric momentums. Chagall's pictorial world is one of social rituals and conditions, codes and symbols, in which questions of scale, or relations of horizontal to vertical, or planar recession, can be treated as cavalierly as caprice demands. Bacon's world, on the other hand, is concerned with the physiological-existential, an Artaudian theatre of cruelty in which a language of significations has no purchase, in which beings are uttered by the unquietness of their flesh, trapped in theatrical-clinical settings to act out their ungovernable drives. Denied, by the parasitism of the Baconian fragments, the characterful autonomies they usually enjoy, Chagall's figures are subjected to the transformational morphing which is the currency of Bacon's work. But, from another point of view, Bacon's figures seem to crave admission to Chagall's world, to discover a new ease, a new integratedness, a recovery of social function.

This reciprocal interpenetration of Chagall and Bacon parallels the interpenetration of the Apollinairean and Chagallian worlds in the text, which is constructed of: shifting pronouns themselves used as shifters; the expressive values of colours; snippets of *poème-conversation*; dialogue between motifs from Chagall's painting and motifs from Apollinaire's poetry (e.g. lines from 'La Clef', insistence on looking at the new, the meaning of desire, childhood memories). It is as if, in Chagall's studio in La Ruche, Apollinaire had surrendered himself to stream of consciousness, to Chagall's 'surnaturel'. The multi-filtered text of Fig. 28 remixes this dialogue as an hysterical divagation, as a mind overwhelmed by its own contents, a ragbag of existential clues and self-scattering perceptual seed, which no syntax can sow, but from which the reading mind might grow its own crop. In this context, the Chagall/Bacon collage encourages the eye likewise both to explore the Chagall/Bacon exchange and to go beyond it, to imagine that both painters are engaged in processes of re-arranging materials in order to discover what point the painterly medium has reached, what it has become expressively capable of, what paths of plastic enquiry it might pursue. This photo-collage then becomes an image of translation's most precious functions: to find out where we are now in relation to the past, or to another place and culture; to practise our own stylistic transformations so that the source can re-immerse its *langue* in *langage*, which is the medium, and thus renew its capacity for dissemination, its migration across its own metamorphoses; to multiply contacts so that translation is not a one-to-one transfer but the activation of a mutually enriching circulation of languages.

It is photography which allows paintings to become part of a collage—that is to say, to participate directly in confrontations, encounters, reciprocal self-insinuations, to re-assess their relationship with history, to find ever-new areas of activity, to cast aside the invulnerability of their aura. In their printed forms, photographs are a kind of paper, a kind of surface (matt/gloss), a kind of size (6" x 4", contact sheet) and shape. For the translator these material features are of paramount importance, and for two reasons. First, it is by the choices made among these material variables, and their manipulation, that the translator expressively assimilates a photographic input into the constitution of the poetic page, *where the page as a whole, rather than the mere text, is the totality that the poem aspires to, is what constitutes the poem.* The page itself creates a space of textual activity, involving different typefaces and dispositions, and/or the addition of other graphic and pictorial modes (handwriting, painting, photography), and thus already initiates, within itself, within its own textuality, the text's blind field. But the page itself is also a frame, so that the blind field *within* it generates a blind field *outside* it, so that performance in the page-text generates performance of the page-text, so that the associative ambience released in the page, as part of the translational process, opens on to the physical ambience of its being read, the reading environment. Second, the materiality of the photograph allows it to be cut. This cutting of the image and the resultant fragments in turn have two effects. First, they imitate that paradoxical process by which the eye is caught, that mixture of accident and focus, which creates the possibility of *hasard objectif*, the chance encounter with suppressed trauma, or desire, or preoccupation; or, if unmotivated, the possibility of opening up fruitful fissures in habit or *studium*. The rectangularity of the whole image is a model of abatement, of the in-place, of considered framing, of cool intentionality, which must at all costs be ruptured. Second, the multiplicity of fragments, with their variable size and shape, maintain the restlessness and uncertainty of perceptual consciousness and thus strengthen that metamorphic principle which we would place at the centre of translational enterprise. When we speak of translation as a centrifugal practice, we think of the centrifuge not as a force of dissipation or entropy but as the multiplier and distributor of energies along proliferating series and sequences.

Conclusion

Repetition, Difference, Representation

What I wish to develop in these closing pages is an argument derived from Deleuze's *Différence et répétition* (1st pub. 1968), but which draws very selectively upon it, not as a total system but as a repository of certain ideas and suggestive propositions, justified by their appropriateness to ways of envisaging translation.

Our first supposition is that a text repeats itself as it constantly affirms its singularity across space and time. A text repeats itself in new editions, in quotations, in allusions, in adaptations, in imitations and in translations. In Deleuzian terms, repetition belongs neither to the order of resemblances nor to that of equivalences, and thus is susceptible neither to exchange nor to substitution. In other words, it is wrong to think of textual repetition (or indeed translation) in terms of a side-by-side, a juxtaposition, which might be imagined as a superimposition; repetition is a body's movement *through* its own self-renewing singularity. To this last statement two observations need to be added: (i) the forward momentum that is realized in repetition is *generated* by self-differentiation. This difference that a work generates out of itself is not that 'margin of error' or 'margin of tolerance' that one might find in resemblance or equivalence, but is the 'margin of differentiation' which affirms movement itself, the will to repeat and the inimitability of the work's previous manifestation. For Deleuze, the effectiveness of this forward movement, its regenerative capacity, is related to its natural antagonism to memory and habit. We might agree about habit, but in translation memory remains a crucial element in the self-differentiating process; what we remember as translators is always different, and the repetition that is translation favours the Bergsonian view whereby the past is not behind the translator, but a cumulative part of his/her present. (ii) Because movement is a constant re-affirmation of a work in its self-renewing singularity, it must not be immobilized in representation or concept; we must find ways to capture the lived experience of movement, or as Deleuze puts it:

> Il ne leur suffit donc pas de proposer une nouvelle représentation du mouvement; la représentation est déjà médiation. Il s'agit au contraire de produire dans l'œuvre un mouvement capable d'émouvoir l'esprit hors de toute représentation; il s'agit de faire du mouvement lui-même une œuvre, sans interposition; de substituer des signes directs à des représentations médiates; d'inventer des vibrations, des rotations, des tournoiements, des gravitations, des danses ou des sauts qui atteignent directement l'esprit
>
> (2011: 16)

> [It is not enough, therefore, for them to propose a new representation of movement; representation is already mediation. Rather, it is a question of producing within the work a movement capable of affecting the mind outside of all representation; it is a question of making movement itself a work, without interposition; of substituting direct signs for mediate representations; of inventing vibrations, rotations, whirlings, gravitations, dances or leaps which directly touch the mind (2004a: 9)].

What the capturing of movement entails, if it is to outwit representation and concept, is performance, and, as we constantly remind ourselves, this as much might mean performance in the text as performance of the text:

> Dans le théâtre de la répétition, on éprouve des forces pures, des tracés dynamiques dans l'espace qui agissent sur l'esprit sans intermédiaire, et qui l'unissent directement à la nature et à l'histoire, un langage qui parle avant les mots, des gestes qui s'élaborent avant les corps organisés, des masques avant les visages, des spectres et des fantômes avant les personnages—tout l'appareil de la répétition comme 'puissance terrible'
>
> (2011: 19)

> [In the theatre of repetition, we experience pure forms, dynamic lines in space which act without intermediary upon the spirit, and link it directly with nature and history, with a language which speaks before words, with gestures which develop before

organised bodies, with masks before faces, with spectres and phantoms before characters—the whole apparatus of repetition as a 'terrible power' (2004a: 12)].

There are two things we should note in this paean to performance: repetition, this thrust of singularity in its interiority, is pre-predicative and pre-conceptual, 'a language which speaks before words'. Words themselves are bound to concept, to finite comprehension, to systematization (the dictionary), to a different, 'external' kind of repetition: 'Le mot possède une compréhension nécessairement finie, puisqu'il est par nature objet d'une définition seulement nominale' (2011: 22) [Words possess a comprehension which is necessarily finite, since they are by nature the objects of a merely nominal definition (2004a: 14–15)]. This second kind of repetition is distinguished from the first by Deleuze in the following terms:

> L'essentiel pour nous [...] est alors de démembrer la causalité pour y distinguer deux types de répétition, l'un concernant seulement l'effet total abstrait, l'autre, la cause agissante. L'une est une répétition statique, l'autre, dynamique. L'une résulte de l'œuvre, mais l'autre est comme 'l'évolution' du geste. L'une renvoie à un même concept, qui ne laisse subsister qu'une différence extérieure entre les exemplaires ordinaires d'une figure; l'autre est répétition d'une différence interne qu'elle comprend dans chacun de ses moments, et qu'elle transporte d'un point remarquable à un autre (2011: 32)
>
> [[...] it is essential to break down the notion of causality in order to distinguish two types of repetition: one which concerns only the overall, abstract effect, and the other which concerns the acting cause. One is a static repetition, the other is dynamic. One results from the work but the other is like the 'evolution' of a bodily movement. One refers back to a single concept, which leaves only an external difference between the ordinary instances of a figure; the other is the repetition of an internal difference which it incorporates in each of its moments, and carries from one distinctive point to another (2004a: 22–3).

Rather confusingly, what we are calling the 'first' kind of repetition (singular and internal) appears in Deleuze's differentiations as the second ('the other'). What is important for us is that singular and internal repetition, pre-predicative repetition, repetition by self-differentiation, is the core and cause of external repetition (identity of concept, representation): 'Les deux répétitions ne sont pas indépendantes. L'une est le sujet singulier, le cœur et l'intériorité de l'autre, la profondeur de l'autre. L'autre est seulement l'enveloppe extérieure, l'effet abstrait' (2011: 37) [The two repetitions are not independent. One is the singular subject, the interiority and the heart of the other, the depths of the other. The other is only the external envelope, the abstract effect (2004a: 27)].

If we then return to our argument about the word, we might say that performance (speaking, writing) is the repetition that lies at the heart of a product (words) which is another form of repetition, but which, in the case of literary language, does not impede or block singular repetition in its forward career. Indeed, we might suppose that literary language is able to maintain in itself something of the pre-predicative and pre-conceptual, something which resists the signified, something which resists nominal definition, not only in the way it transforms/deforms/stutters language, but also through the incorporation of the non-verbal arts (graphism, photography, painting); to think of our inserted photographic fragments as illustrations or decorations of the text, as any kind of post-textual commentary, is to miss the point. In our introductory remarks we argued that photographs have a natural temporal and perceptual priority over text; our photographic fragments are part of the undifferentiated experiential flux which precedes, and urges itself into, text. These raw materials help literary language to gravitate 'inwards', towards 'primary' repetition, towards 'singularity without concept', as Deleuze puts it:

> On répète une œuvre d'art comme singularité sans concept, et ce n'est pas par hasard qu'un poème doit être appris par cœur. La tête est l'organe des échanges, mais le cœur, l'organe amoureux de la repetition
>
> (2011: 8)

> [The repetition of a work of art is like a singularity without a concept, and it is not by chance that a poem must be learned by heart. The head is the organ of exchange, but the heart is the amorous organ of repetition (2004a: 2)].

This remark might lead us towards another supposition, to wit: that a translation built on interpretation, on any meta-process, will translate primary repetition into secondary repetition, will translate sensory encounter into achieved concept, textual body into textual representation, while the phenomenological mode of translation that we are canvassing will keep the primary repetition of the source text (ST) intact. In saying this, I am aware that *all* translational processes will end in words, and that words will always threaten to divert or conceptualize the singular and evolving. As we have intimated, it is up to translation to find ways of expressing movement, the process of becoming, the dynamics of self-differentiation, and for this reason translation must work in the mode of the experimental. Deleuze himself singles out kinds of linguistic activity which express in themselves the principles of primary repetition: homonymy [and homophony?], rhyme ('elle est bien répétition verbale, mais répétition qui comprend la différence entre deux mots et qui l'inscrit au sein d'une Idée poétique, dans un espace qu'elle détermine' (2011: 33) [it is indeed verbal repetition, but repetition which includes the difference between two words and inscribes that difference at the heart of a poetic Idea, in a space which it determines (2004a: 24)], and rhythm (in distinction to the secondary repetition of metre, or 'mesure' (trans. 'cadence')):

> La mesure n'est que l'enveloppe d'un rythme, et d'un rapport de rythmes. La reprise de points d'inégalité, de points de flexion, d'événements rythmiques, est plus profonde que la reproduction d'éléments ordinaires homogènes; si bien que, partout, nous devons distinguer la répétition-mesure et la répétition-rythme, la première étant seulement l'apparence ou effet abstrait de la seconde
>
> (2011: 33)

> [Cadence is only the envelope of a rhythm, and of a relation between rhythms. The reprise of points of inequality, of inflections or of rhythmic events, is more profound than the reproduction of ordinary homogeneous elements. As a result, we should distinguish cadence-repetition and rhythm-repetition in every case, the first being only the outward appearance or the abstract effect of the second (2004a: 23–4)].

From one point of view, therefore, we might say that the target text (TT) is a homonym of the ST, or a rhyme, or a development of its rhythm. The TT performs the ST which is already a performance. But, even as we say this, we need to ask ourselves where exactly difference might take place. It may, quite clearly, take place in the work, in the text; but it may also take place in the field of perception of the work. In most cases it takes place in both work and perceptual field, but, on occasion, it may occur only in the latter (e.g. Pierre M[é]nard's 'translation' of *Don Quixote* in Borges (2000: 33–43)).

But, as I have made clear elsewhere (2012b: 166), I would not, in relation to my own terminological sympathies, want to hook the self-differentiation of textual evolution too much to difference, particularly if difference itself were to be equated with differentiation of identity and were to lead to self-affirmation by confrontation, resistance, intractability, conflict. I want self-differentiation to derive from, and to promote, diversity—that is, the simple multiplication of cohabiting othernesses. This introduces a lateral movement of spatial extension into the linear movement of becoming; it is as if movement forwards necessarily generates out of itself lateral radiations. But these radiations do not create sedentary structures of representation, as if distilled from the forward impetus of repetition; in true Bergsonian fashion, they are gathered up into that impetus and become the makers of its inevitable expansion. In other words, diversity does not set up territories of settlement for its proliferating manifestations; these manifestations have a 'nomadic' distribution:

> Tout autre est une distribution qu'il faut appeler nomadique, un *nomos* nomade, sans propriété, enclose ni mesure. Là, il n'y a plus partage d'un distribué, mais plutôt répartition de ceux qui *se* distribuent dans un espace ouvert illimité, du moins sans limites précises
>
> (2011: 54)

> [Then there is a completely other distribution which must be called nomadic, a nomad *nomos*, without property, enclosure or measure. Here, there is no longer a division of that which is distributed but rather a division among those who distribute *themselves* in an open space—a space which is unlimited, or at least without precise limits (2004a: 45–6)].[1]

What, finally, we need to make clear about this self-diversifying nomadism is that the process of individuation is a perpetual process, designed to renew the singularity of the text without allowing it to become an identity. The principle of identity is a presupposition of representation (2011: 70; 2004a: 60). A translation cannot be true to a ST because the ST has no pre-existent identity (it cannot even be true to itself); but a translation can participate in and contribute to the ST's capacity to move forward through time and space by tireless self-individuation and, conversely, to individuate itself by being drawn through time and space. Self-individuation thus understood is a process of self-accumulation which never comes to an end in identity and is ever reaching for otherness. Diversity simply multiplies in otherness, and singularity remains singular by othering itself. Diversity does not operate in degrees of differential relationship, cannot, as in difference, lead to the extreme of opposition. I call opposition that degree of difference which grounds the notion of untranslatability.

In order to be consistent with my own thinking, which shares much with the writing of Victor Segalen and Édouard Glissant, I am here opposing diversity as an affirmative expression of the free-multiple to difference as a negative principle which immobilizes what it differentiates by limitation and opposition (contradiction). But my thinking is only an adjustment of Deleuze's terminology. Deleuze distinguishes between difference and diversity thuswise: 'La différence n'est pas le divers. Le divers est donné. Mais la différence, c'est ce par quoi le donné est donné. C'est ce par quoi le donné est donné comme divers. La différence n'est pas le phénomène, mais le plus proche noumène du phénomène' (2011: 286) [Difference is not diversity. Diversity is given, but difference is that by which the given is given, that by which the given is given as diverse. Difference is not phenomenon but the noumenon closest to the phenomenon (2004a: 280)]. Difference, in this particular sense, is the motor-principle of diversity, not the differentiated (difference between) but the agent of differentiation (difference of). Difference [diversification] is that by which things come into existence as diverse. In another context, my 'diversity' has real affinities with Deleuze's 'free differences', as opposed to that simplifying difference based on conflicting/comparable identities. The former is the presupposition, or originating state, of the latter:

> Chaque fois que nous nous trouvons devant ou dans une limitation, devant ou dans une opposition, nous devons demander ce qu'une telle situation suppose. Elle suppose un fourmillement de différences, un pluralisme de différences libres, sauvages ou non domptées, un espace et un temps proprement différentiels, originels, qui persistent à travers les simplifications de la limite ou de l'opposition. [...] Les oppositions sont grossièrement taillées dans un milieu fin de perspectives chevauchantes, de distances, de divergences et de disparités communicantes, de potentiels et d'intensités hétérogènes; et il ne s'agit pas d'abord de résoudre des tensions dans l'identique, mais de distribuer des disparates dans une multiplicité
>
> (2011: 71)

> [[…] every time we find ourselves confronted or bound by a limitation or an opposition, we should ask what such a situation presupposes. It presupposes a swarm of differences, a pluralism of free, wild or untamed differences; a properly differential and original space and time; all of which persist alongside the simplifications of limitation and opposition. […] Oppositions are roughly cut from a delicate milieu of overlapping perspectives, of communicating distances, divergences and disparities, of heterogeneous potentials and intensities. Nor is it primarily a question of dissolving tensions in the identical, but rather of distributing the disparities in a multiplicity (2004a: 61)].

And if we have spoken of diversity as lateral radiations accumulating around the momentums of repetition, we might quote what Deleuze further has to say about 'free differences': 'Partout les couples, les polarités supposent des faisceaux et des réseaux; les oppositions organisées, des rayonnements en toutes directions' (2011: 72) [Everywhere, couples and polarities presuppose bundles and networks, organised oppositions presuppose radiations in all directions (2004a: 62)]; 'Ce n'est pas la différence qui suppose l'opposition, mais l'opposition qui suppose la différence' (2011: 73) [It is not difference which presupposes opposition but opposition which presupposes difference (2004a: 62)]. Further on, Deleuze will directly relate movement to the teeming proliferation of diversity ('free differences') (2011: 78; 2004a: 67); difference, in this sense, can thrive only in 'un monde compliqué, *sans identité*, proprement chaotique' (2011: 80) [a complicated, properly chaotic world *without identity* (2004a: 69)].

What this consideration of mechanisms of self-differentiation reveals is an unrelenting hand-to-hand struggle against the fossilizing tendencies of the representational. There are two immediate senses in which the ST is already a representation. First, the printed text itself is a conventionalized and 'muted' transcription of what we might imagine as a creative event in the mind/body of the writer: its mutedness lies principally in its erasure of prosodic and paralinguistic indications (it is phonetically 'abstract', without specific timbre, resonance, pitch, etc.); the text is a featureless transcription of an originating performance in the writer, and it is translation's business to re-awaken those performative origins, however little these may correspond to the actual originating performance itself. But any text also drifts towards the representational inasmuch as it is a machinery to produce certain effects, inasmuch as it treats language mediationally, inasmuch as it embraces certain aesthetic codes (generic, rhetorical, etc.) and inasmuch as it seeks a certain unanimity of interpretative response. With the representational, we submit to the rules of the game in order to earn the rewards that the text offers us on that condition. Comments such as 'A fine performance' or 'A searching interpretation' tell us that parameters of justified expectation have not been transgressed, that a perceptible tradition has been added to. How does translation break down these representational forces at work in the text it translates? By the processes of constant self-differentiation we have just explored, such that the text always eludes itself, almost runs away from itself, is always orientated towards non-teleological futures. There are, as we have seen, many operations by which this might be achieved: one treats the text as a field of energies, constantly able to redispose itself, to release in itself new morphologies, new dispositions of intensity, new projective capacities; one re-geneticizes the ST—that is to say, the translator does not represent the ST in the TT, but inhabits the ST such that its founding materials, real and speculative, become available again to inaugurative possibility in the TT; by recourse to the tabular, one puts the language of translation into an interrogative space, a space in which we have to reinvent the processes of reading and writing, and which will thus positively *necessitate* further translations. These further translations will be the further expression of that process of continuous variation which takes place in the making of each.

Each individual translation achieves a form, of course, even if only provisionally, but the form achieved does not derive from the active exclusion of alternatives, does not depend on choice, on decisions about the more or less felicitous, the more or less faithful, the more or less correct, and still less on the objective of the fairest of fair copies. When the translator translates for the polyglot reader, as we propose, all such considerations are without relevance, since the polyglot reader already fully possesses the ST. The translation achieves form by the simple arrestation or interruption of its ongoingness; that is to say, the space of 'choice' is occupied by a word which is *a transition between* others, that exists by virtue of having others alongside, absent but implied. The moment of arrestation, of textual pausing, that translation is, is perhaps best compared with the frame of a film waiting to be re-activated in the resumed momentum of 24-frames-per-second. And, like the film, the translation generates a blind field which it might always move into. But, unlike the film, it also generates, as we have seen, blind fields which do not lie in the path of the ongoing sequence and which have the same purview as the blind field of a still photograph—that is to say, an infinite lateral and temporal extension, a play of virtualities renewed with each translation. Each translation, then, both takes part in its own series of variations and is traversed by other series of variations.

We also rescue translation from the representational mode by insisting on a translational procedure which is less 'translation of' and more 'translation out of and translation into'. With this distinction we return to our distinction between jump-thinking (from one language directly to another, between two independent language systems) and morph-thinking (sliding from one language into another and into others, a deformative, transformative, reformative journey between languages). The most obvious model of this latter procedure is to be found, as we have indicated, in homophonic translation. But it need not, of course, be confined to morphing between sonorities, but will encompass morphing between rhythmic configurations (see 2012a: Chapter 6), between verbal languages, between the languages of the page (punctuation, typefaces, paginal disposition) and between media. What is crucial to this procedure is that the translator should treat all relationships as indeterminate; that is to say, the distance between languages, between different elements of language, between media, is indeterminate, and each reader/translator measures and spans this distance differently, takes different journeys between their two points. Translation tends to assume that the distance between, say, 'rouge' and 'red', is the same for every reader, the jump almost automatic, that there is only one journey to take, via a mental or actual dictionary, where, in fact, the ways of getting from one to the other are innumerable.

In relation to our own particular photographic concerns, we might single out the frame as an insidious instrument of the representational. Anything framed, whether by art or science, whether in the gallery or in the laboratory, as an object of contemplation or investigation, is a gift to the representational, both by its exemplarity and by its entry into a self-sustaining circuit of values. Inasmuch as boundedness acts as an index of self-sufficiency and completion, the framed work proposes itself as something which can be superimposed on what it depicts, as an adequate account, as a substitute, as something which deserves to be treated as already there. But our own endeavours to resist representation have, ironically, been abetted by the presence of photography. For even where the photographic image is whole and framed (contact print), it is subject to the peculiar paradox of its dual nature: as an icon, the photograph must strive to affirm its frame, as a release from any obligations to its blind field; but as an index, it must treat its frame as a masking device which conjures up the blind field and urges it into existence. The photographic fragment, for its part, discards its frame by cutting and enters into its blind field as a free agent, indeed recasts its blind field, not as a potentially particular space but as any space whatever.

In speaking of repetition and difference in relation to translation, we speak much of self-differentiating singularity. But we must not think of singularity as a singleness, as an unfolding straight line, but rather as something which begets a rhizomatic becoming, something which generates its own expanding multiplicity. And what is important about multiplicity is that it is trying not to find its way to a synthesising universal but to establish 'les conditions sous lesquelles se produit quelque chose de nouveau (*creativeness*)' (Deleuze, 2003: 284) [the conditions under which something new is created (*creativeness*) (Deleuze, 2007: 309)]. Translation Studies suffers from an anxiety of self-justification; it worries about its rigour as a discipline; it seeks refuge in methodologies and analytical systems of classification. But there is always a danger that methodologies themselves become solutions, universals, and translations their almost accidental spin-off. Methodologies threaten to become the great signifiers. They define what we can perceive, what we can know. That may be better than perceiving and knowing nothing. But it is no consolation if it constitutes *all* that we can perceive and know. If a text is a singularity which, through translation among other things, begets a multiplicity, a historicity without history, a becoming without an object, then as translators we must be careful not to close down experimental channels, the ways towards the new, the 'tangente de déterritorialisation' (Deleuze, 2003: 15) [tangent of deterritorialization (Deleuze, 2007: 15)]. The translator, like Deleuze, might best eschew systems whose coordinates are the Identical, the Similar and the Analogous, and instead seek out the system which is not only in perpetual heterogeneity but is itself a *heterogenesis* (2003: 338; 2007: 365). The argument for translation as a multilinguality, or *langage*, which subsumes the languages of the other media, as well as the national languages and the typographic languages, and indeed pre-textual and post-textual languages, is an argument for heterogenesis.

Appendix I

Texts

(i) Chevaux de frise (1965: 302–3)

Pendant le blanc et nocturne novembre
Alors que les arbres déchiquetés par l'artillerie
Vieillissaient encore sous la neige
Et semblaient à peine des chevaux de frise
Entourés de vagues de fils de fer
Mon cœur renaissait comme un arbre au printemps
Un arbre fruitier sur lequel s'épanouissent
                        Les fleurs de l'amour

Pendant le blanc et nocturne novembre
Tandis que chantaient épouvantablement les obus
Et que les fleurs mortes de la terre exhalaient
                        Leurs mortelles odeurs
Moi je décrivais tous les jours mon amour à Madeleine
La neige met de pâles fleurs sur les arbres
  Et toisonne d'hermine les chevaux de frise
    Que l'on voit partout
      Abandonnés et sinistres
        Chevaux muets
  Non chevaux barbes mais barbelés
    Et je les anime tout soudain

En troupeau de jolis chevaux pies
Qui vont vers toi comme de blanches vagues
Sur la Méditerranée
Et t'apportent mon amour
Roselys ô panthère ô colombes étoile bleue
O Madeleine
Je t'aime avec délices
Si je songe à tes yeux je songe aux sources fraîches
Si je pense à ta bouche les roses m'apparaissent
Si je songe à tes seins le Paraclet descend
O double colombe de ta poitrine
Et vient délier ma langue de poète
Pour te redire
Je t'aime
Ton visage est un bouquet de fleurs
Aujourd'hui je te vois non Panthère
Mais Toutefleur
Et je te respire ô ma Toutefleur
Tous les lys montent en toi comme des cantiques d'amour et d'allégresse
Et ces chants qui s'envolent vers toi
M'emportent à ton côté
Dans ton bel Orient où les lys
Se changent en palmiers qui de leurs belles mains
Me font signe de venir
La fusée s'épanouit fleur nocturne
Quand il fait noir
Et elle retombe comme une pluie de larmes amoureuses
De larmes heureuses que la joie fait couler
Et je t'aime comme tu m'aimes
Madeleine

(ii) Marizibill (1965: 77)

Dans la Haute-Rue à Cologne
Elle allait et venait le soir
Offerte à tous en tout mignonne
Puis buvait lasse des trottoirs
Très tard dans les brasseries borgnes

Elle se mettait sur la paille
Pour un maquereau roux et rose
C'était un juif il sentait l'ail
Et l'avait venant de Formose
Tirée d'un bordel de Changhaï

Je connais gens de toutes sortes
Ils n'égalent pas leurs destins
Indécis comme feuilles mortes
Leurs yeux sont des feux mal éteints
Leurs cœurs bougent comme leurs portes

(iii) Annie (1965: 65)

Sur la côte du Texas
Entre Mobile et Galveston il y a
Un grand jardin tout plein de roses
Il contient aussi une villa
Qui est une grande rose

Une femme se promène souvent
Dans le jardin toute seule
Et quand je passe sur la route bordée de tilleuls
Nous nous regardons

Comme cette femme est mennonite
Ses rosiers et ses vêtements n'ont pas de boutons
Il en manque deux à mon veston
La dame et moi suivons presque le même rite

(iv) *La Nuit d'avril 1915 (1965: 243–4)*

A L. de C.-C.

Le ciel est étoilé par les obus des Boches
La forêt merveilleuse où je vis donne un bal
La mitrailleuse joue un air à triples-croches
Mais avez-vous le mot
Eh ! oui le mot fatal
Aux créneaux Aux créneaux Laissez là les pioches

Comme un astre éperdu qui cherche ses saisons
Cœur obus éclaté tu sifflais ta romance
Et tes mille soleils ont vidé les caissons
Que les dieux de mes yeux remplissent en silence

Nous vous aimons ô vie et nous vous agaçons

Les obus miaulaient un amour à mourir
Un amour qui se meurt est plus doux que les autres
Ton souffle nage au fleuve où le sang va tarir
Les obus miaulaient
Entends chanter les nôtres
Pourpre amour salué par ceux qui vont périr

Le printemps tout mouillé la veilleuse l'attaque
Il pleut mon âme il pleut mais il pleut des yeux morts

Ulysse que de jours pour rentrer dans Ithaque
Couche-toi sur la paille et songe un beau remords
Qui pur effet de l'art soit aphrodisiaque

Mais
orgues
aux fétus de la paille où tu dors
L'hymne de l'avenir est paradisiaque

(v) La Porte (1965: 87)

La porte de l'hôtel sourit terriblement
Qu'est-ce que cela peut me faire ô ma maman
D'être cet employé pour qui seul rien n'existe
Pi-mus couples allant dans la profonde eau triste
Anges frais débarqués à Marseille hier matin
J'entends mourir et remourir un chant lointain
Humble comme je suis qui ne suis rien qui vaille

Enfant je t'ai donné ce que j'avais travaille

(vi) Lundi rue Christine (1965: 180–2)

La mère de la concierge et la concierge laisseront tout passer
Si tu es un homme tu m'accompagneras ce soir
Il suffirait qu'un type maintînt la porte cochère
Pendant que l'autre monterait

Trois becs de gaz allumés
La patronne est poitrinaire
Quand tu auras fini nous jouerons une partie de jacquet
Un chef d'orchestre qui a mal à la gorge
Quand tu viendras à Tunis je te ferai fumer du kief

Ça a l'air de rimer

Des piles de soucoupes des fleurs un calendrier
Pim pam pim
Je dois fiche près de 300 francs à ma probloque
Je préférerais me couper le parfaitement que de les lui donner

Je partirai à 20 h. 27
Six glaces s'y dévisagent toujours
Je crois que nous allons nous embrouiller encore davantage
Cher monsieur
Vous êtes un mec à la mie de pain
Cette dame a le nez comme un ver solitaire

Louise a oublié sa fourrure
Moi je n'ai pas de fourrure et je n'ai pas froid
Le Danois fume sa cigarette en consultant l'horaire
Le chat noir traverse la brasserie

Ces crêpes étaient exquises
La fontaine coule
Robe noire comme ses ongles
C'est complètement impossible
Voici monsieur
La bague en malachite
Le sol est semé de sciure
Alors c'est vrai
La serveuse rousse a été enlevée par un libraire

Un journaliste que je connais d'ailleurs très vaguement

Écoute Jacques c'est très sérieux ce que je vais te dire

Compagnie de navigation mixte

Il me dit monsieur voulez-vous voir ce que je peux faire d'eaux-fortes et de tableaux
Je n'ai qu'une petite bonne

Après déjeuner café du Luxembourg
Une fois là il me présente un gros bonhomme
Qui me dit
Écoutez c'est charmant
A Smyrne à Naples en Tunisie
Mais nom de Dieu où est-ce
La dernière fois que j'ai été en Chine
C'est il y a huit ou neuf ans
L'Honneur tient souvent à l'heure que marque la pendule
La quinte major

(vii) *Zone (1965: 39–44)*

Yes
In the end
You're tired of
This antiquated world

Shepherdess O Eiffel Tower
The flock of bridges bleat
This morning

You've done with living
In antiquity
Greek *and* Roman

Here even the motor-cars
Look out of date
Only religion is the latest thing
Religion
As simple as the hangars
At Port-Aviation

Christianity you alone
In Europe
Are not old-fashioned
And you Pope Pius X
Are the modernest
Of Europeans
And you you
Observed by windows
Held back by the restraining arm
Of shame
Cannot bring yourself to enter
A church to make confession
You read the brochures the catalogues and posters
Which sing out loud
So much for poetry

This morning
And for prose there are
The newspapers
Instalments at 25 centimes a-piece full
Of detective stories portraits of great men
And a thousand varied titles

This morning
I saw a street
Whose name escapes me
Easy on the eye
Spanking new and hygiene-clean the clarion of the sun
The managers the workers the elegant
Shorthand typists pass by
Four times a day
From Monday morning to Saturday evening
And three times every morning
The siren wails
While at about midday
A bell beside itself
Clangs clangs clangs clangs
The signs the graffiti
Nameplates and notices
Screech like parrots
I love the supple ease of this industrial street
In Paris somewhere between
The rue Aumont-Thiéville and the avenue des Ternes.

So that's the fresh-faced street and you're still only a child
And it's only blue and white
That your mother lets you wear
Devout and like your oldest friend René
Dalize you think there's nothing
To beat the ceremonies
Of the Church it's nine o'clock
The gas is lowered to a glowing blue

You slip out of the dormitory unobserved
And spend the whole night at your prayers
In the school chapel
While the lustrous glory of Christ
For ever wheels
Adorable depths of amethyst without end
It's the beautiful lily we all grow
It's the red-haired torch impervious to the wind
It's the pale vermilion-tinted son of the *mater dolorosa*
It's the ever thick-leaved tree of all the prayers
It's the double-gibbet of eternity and honour
It's the six-armed star
It's God who died on Friday and rose again the Sunday after
It's Christ who climbs the skies more nimbly than aviators
Holder of the world altitude record

Pupil Christ of the eye
Twentieth pupil of the centuries it has the art
And turned to a bird this century soars
Like Jesus
The devils in the dark abysses lift their heads
To see it fly they say it's aping
Simon Magus in Judaea
If it can fly let's call it fly in flapping and filching
They cry meanwhile the angels
Flutter round the graceful flutterer
Icarus Enoch Elias Apollonius of Tyana
Swoop around the first aeroplane
They sometimes make a passage for those
Transported by the Holy Eucharist
These priests eternally ascending
Elevating the host
The aeroplane touches down at last
Without folding its wings the sky fills
With countless swallows

In a flurry of flying come the crows the falcons the owls
The ibis the flamingos the marabout
Head in from Africa
The Roc celebrated by poets and
The tellers of tales
Glides overhead the skull of Adam the first head
In its talons
And uttering a loud cry the eagle
Swoops from the far horizon
From America
Hums in the humming-bird
And from China
Come the pihis supple sleek
The birds with one wing who fly
In couples
Then there's the dove the Spotless Spirit
Accompanied by the lyre-bird and the Argus-eyed peacock
And the phoenix the funeral pyre of
Self-re-engenderment
Veils all with its burning ashes
For just one moment
And leaving behind their perilous straits
The sirens arrive
Singing beautifully
All three
And all
Eagle phoenix and Chinese pihis
Consort with the flying machine

Now you're walking in Paris
Alone in the milling crowds
Herds of lowing omnibus drive by
Close to you
Love's pains contract around your throat
As if you were bound
Never to be loved again

If these were days gone by you'd
Join the brotherhood of monks
Shame takes a grip when
You catch yourself in prayer
You're the derisory butt
Of your own derision
And your laughter crackles
Like hellfire
Its sparks glowing in the depths
Of your existence
It's like a picture hanging
In a shadowy museum
And you from time to time
Squint at it close up

Today you're out walking
In Paris
The women bloodied,
It was
If only I'd forget
Beauty's dismantlement.

Herself encircled by 'a fervency of flames'
The eyes of Notre-Dame
Rested on me in Chartres
And in Montmartre
The blood of your Sacré-Cœur
Left me submerged
I am sick of giving ear
To the glad tidings
The love I suffer from's
An illness I'd rather not admit to
The image you're possessed by
Keeps you going
Through the sleepless nights
Through the obstinate distress

This passing image
Never leaves your side

Now you're by the Mediterranean
Under the lemon trees
In flower all the year
You're on a boat-trip with your friends
One from Nice one from Menton
And two from La Turbie
Our hearts in our mouths we
Watch the squid down in the murky depths
While among the seaweed swim
The Christian emblems
Fish

You're in the garden of an inn
On the outskirts
Of Prague
In good spirits a rose on the table
And instead of penning your narrative in prose
You watch the beetle sleeping
In the rose's heart

Terror-stricken
You see yourself engraved
In the agates of Saint Vitus
You were dispirited enough to die
The day you recognised yourself
You're like Lazarus driven spare
By the daylight
The hands of the clock in the Jewish quarter
Go backwards
As you go backwards slowly through your life
Climbing to the Hradchin
And in the evening
Listening to the singing of Czech songs

Translating Apollinaire

In the taverns

Here you are in Marseille among the watermelons

And here in Coblenz at the Hôtel du Géant

And here in Rome sitting under a Japanese medlar

And here in Amsterdam with an ugly girl you find attractive
She's set to marry a student
From Leyden
They let rooms in Latin *Cubicula locanda*
I remember yes
I spent three days there
And as many at Gouda

You're in Paris
Hauled before the examining magistrate
You're under arrest
No better than a common criminal

You journeyed
Both with spirits raised
And spirits trampled down
Before encountering lies
And the burden of the years
At twenty and at thirty years of age
Love made you suffer
I've lived demented and I've squandered time
You cannot bring yourself
To contemplate your hands
And unrelentingly
I feel the urge to tearfulness
For you for the one I love
For everything that's struck your heart
With fear

You watch

Eyes pricked with tears
These pitiable emigrants
They believe in God they pray
The women suckle their children
The station concourse
At Saint-Lazare
Is suffused with their smell
They like the Magi
Have faith in their star
They're looking to earn some silver
In Argentina
And then come home again
Having struck it rich
A family transports a red
Eiderdown as you transport
Your heart
This eiderdown our dreams
Are equally unreal
Some stay here
At shabby addresses in
The rue des Rosiers or the rue des Écouffes
I've often seen them in the street
Taking the air
At evening
Like chess-pieces
They rarely move
They're mostly Jews their wives wear wigs
And sit anaemically
In the backs of shops

You standing at the counter
Of a seedy bar
Drinking a cheap coffee
Among the down-and-outs

It's night

You're sitting
In a fancy restaurant

These women mean no ill and yet
They've plenty on their minds
They've all even the ugliest
Given lovers a hard time

She's a Jersey policeman's daughter

Her hands I hadn't seen them
Chapped and calloused

I feel great pity for the
Stitched wounds
On her belly

My mouth does servile service
For a poor *pute* whose laughter
Makes me shudder

No one else about morning soon
Milkmen clank their cans along the streets

Night melts away as if her blood were mixed
Ferdine the False or Léa the Solicitous

And alcohol runs down your throat
As scorching as your life
Which you knock back like eau-de-vie

You make towards Auteuil
Heading home on foot to sleep
Among the fetishes collected
From Oceania
From Guinea
They are the Jesus Christs of other rites
And other beliefs the lesser Christs

Of hopes less well defined

Goodbye goodbye

Sun the neck
Of a decapitated head.

(viii) Zone, lines 121–34 (1965: 43)

Tu regardes les yeux pleins de larmes ces pauvres émigrants
Ils croient en Dieu ils prient les femmes allaitent des enfants
Ils emplissent de leur odeur le hall de la gare Saint-Lazare
Ils ont foi dans leur étoile comme les rois-mages
Ils espèrent gagner de l'argent dans l'Argentine
Et revenir dans leur pays après avoir fait fortune
Une famille transporte un édredon rouge comme vous transportez votre cœur
Cet édredon et nos rêves sont aussi irréels
Quelques-uns de ces émigrants restent ici et se logent
Rue des Rosiers ou rue des Écouffes dans des bouges
Je les ai vus souvent le soir ils prennent l'air dans la rue
Et se déplacent rarement comme les pièces aux échecs
Il y a surtout des Juifs leurs femmes portent perruque
Elles restent assises exsangues au fond des boutiques

Weeping you watch the wretched emigrants
They believe in God they pray the women suckle their infants
They fill with their smell the station of Saint-Lazare
Like the wise men from the east they have faith in their star
They hope to prosper in the Argentine
And to come home having made their fortune
A family transports a red eiderdown as you your heart
An eiderdown as unreal as our dreams
Some go no further doss in the stews
Of the Rue des Rosiers or the Rue des Ecouffes
Often in the streets I have seen them in the gloaming

Taking the air and like chessmen seldom moving
They are mostly Jews the wives wear wigs and in
The depths of shadowy dens bloodless sit on and on

(trans. Samuel Beckett (1986: 148))

(ix) *1909 (1965: 138–9)*

La dame avait une robe
En ottoman violine
Et sa tunique brodée d'or
Était composée de deux panneaux
S'attachant sur l'épaule

Les yeux dansants comme des anges
Elle riait elle riait
Elle avait un visage aux couleurs de France
Les yeux bleus les dents blanches et les lèvres très rouges
Elle avait un visage aux couleurs de France

Elle était décolletée en rond
Et coiffée à la Récamier
Avec de beaux bras nus

N'entendra-t-on jamais sonner minuit

La dame en robe d'ottoman violine
Et en tunique brodée d'or
Décolletée en rond
Promenait ses boucles
Son bandeau d'or
Et traînait ses petits souliers à boucles

Elle était si belle
Que tu n'aurais pas osé l'aimer

J'aimais les femmes atroces dans les quartiers énormes
Où naissaient chaque jour quelques êtres nouveaux
Le fer était leur sang la flamme leur cerveau

J'aimais j'aimais le peuple habile des machines
Le luxe et la beauté ne sont que son écume
Cette femme était si belle
Qu'elle me faisait peur

(x) *Les Fenêtres (1965: 168–9)*

Du rouge au vert tout le jaune se meurt
Quand chantent les aras dans les forêts natales
Abatis de pihis
Il y a un poème à faire sur l'oiseau qui n'a qu'une aile
Nous l'enverrons en message téléphonique
Traumatisme géant
Il fait couler les yeux
Voilà une jolie jeune fille parmi les jeunes Turinaises
Le pauvre jeune homme se mouchait dans sa cravate blanche
Tu soulèveras le rideau
Et maintenant voilà que s'ouvre la fenêtre
Araignées quand les mains tissaient la lumière
Beauté pâleur insondables violets
Nous tenterons en vain de prendre du repos
On commencera à minuit
Quand on a le temps on a la liberté
Bigorneaux Lotte multiples Soleils et l'Oursin du couchant
Une vieille paire de chaussures jaunes devant la fenêtre
Tours
Les Tours ce sont les rues
Puits
Puits ce sont les places
Puits
Arbres creux qui abritent les Câpresses vagabondes
Les Chabins chantent des airs à mourir
Aux Chabines marronnes
Et l'oie oua-oua trompette au nord
Où les chasseurs de ratons
Raclent les pelleteries

Étincelant diamant
Vancouver
Où le train blanc de neige et de feux nocturnes fuit l'hiver
O Paris
Du rouge au vert tout le jaune se meurt
Paris Vancouver Hyères Maintenon New-York et les Antilles
La fenêtre s'ouvre comme une orange
Le beau fruit de la lumière

(xi) La Victoire (1965: 309–12)

Un coq chante je rêve et les feuillards agitent
Leurs feuilles qui ressemblent à de pauvres marins

Ailés et tournoyants comme Icare le faux
Des aveugles gesticulant comme des fourmis
Se miraient sous la pluie aux reflets du trottoir

Leurs rires amassés en grappes de raisin

Ne sors plus de chez moi diamant qui parlais
Dors doucement tu es chez toi tout t'appartient
Mon lit ma lampe et mon casque troué

Regards précieux saphirs taillés aux environs de Saint-Claude
Les jours étaient une pure émeraude

Je me souviens de toi ville des météores
Ils fleurissaient en l'air pendant ces nuits où rien ne dort
Jardins de la lumière où j'ai cueilli des bouquets

Tu dois en avoir assez de faire peur à ce ciel
Qu'il garde son hoquet

On imagine difficilement
A quel point le succès rend les gens stupides et tranquilles

A l'institut des jeunes aveugles on a demandé
N'avez-vous point de jeune aveugle ailé

O bouches l'homme est à la recherche d'un nouveau langage
Auquel le grammairien d'aucune langue n'aura rien à dire

Et ces vieilles langues sont tellement près de mourir
Que c'est vraiment par habitude et manque d'audace
Qu'on les fait encore servir à la poésie

Mais elles sont comme des malades sans volonté
Ma foi les gens s'habitueraient vite au mutisme
La mimique suffit bien au cinéma

        Mais entêtons-nous à parler
        Remuons la langue
        Lançons des postillons
On veut de nouveaux sons de nouveaux sons de nouveaux sons
On veut des consonnes sans voyelles
Des consonnes qui pètent sourdement
        Imitez le son de la toupie
Laissez pétiller un son nasal et continu
Faites claquer votre langue
Servez-vous du bruit sourd de celui qui mange sans civilité
Le raclement aspiré du crachement ferait aussi une belle consonne

Les divers pets labiaux rendraient aussi vos discours claironnants
Habituez-vous à roter à volonté
Et quelle lettre grave comme un son de cloche
        A travers nos mémoires
Nous n'aimons pas assez la joie
De voir les belles choses neuves
O mon amie hâte-toi
Crains qu'un jour un train ne t'émeuve
                Plus
Regarde-le plus vite pour toi
Ces chemins de fer qui circulent
Sortiront bientôt de la vie
Ils seront beaux et ridicules
Deux lampes brûlent devant moi

Comme deux femmes qui rient
Je courbe tristement la tête
Devant l'ardente moquerie
Ce rire se répand
Partout
Parlez avec les mains faites claquer vos doigts
Tapez-vous sur la joue comme sur un tambour
O paroles
Elles suivent dans la myrtaie
L'Éros et l'Antéros en larmes
Je suis le ciel de la cité

Écoutez la mer

La mer gémir au loin et crier toute seule
Ma voix fidèle comme l'ombre
Veut être enfin l'ombre de la vie
Veut être ô mer vivante infidèle comme toi

La mer qui a trahi des matelots sans nombre
Engloutit mes grands cris comme des dieux noyés
Et la mer au soleil ne supporte que l'ombre
Que jettent des oiseaux les ailes éployées

La parole est soudaine et c'est un Dieu qui tremble
Avance et soutiens-moi je regrette les mains
De ceux qui les tendaient et m'adoraient ensemble
Quelle oasis de bras m'accueillera demain
Connais-tu cette joie de voir des choses neuves

O voix je parle le langage de la mer
Et dans le port la nuit les dernières tavernes
Moi qui suis plus têtu que non l'hydre de Lerne

La rue où nagent mes deux mains
Aux doigts subtils fouillant la ville
S'en va mais qui sait si demain

La rue devenait immobile
Qui sait où serait mon chemin
Songe que les chemins de fer
Seront démodés et abandonnés dans peu de temps
Regarde

La Victoire avant tout sera
De bien voir au loin
De tout voir
De près
Et que tout ait un nom nouveau

(xii) Le Voyageur (1965: 78–80):

A Fernand Fleuret

Ouvrez-moi cette porte où je frappe en pleurant

La vie est variable aussi bien que l'Euripe

Tu regardais un banc de nuages descendre
Avec le paquebot orphelin vers les fièvres futures
Et de tous ces regrets de tous ces repentirs
Te souviens-tu

Vagues poissons arqués fleurs surmarines
Une nuit c'était la mer
Et les fleuves s'y répandaient

Je m'en souviens je m'en souviens encore

Un soir je descendis dans une auberge triste
Auprès de Luxembourg
Dans le fond de la salle il s'envolait un Christ
Quelqu'un avait un furet
Un autre un hérisson
L'on jouait aux cartes
Et toi tu m'avais oublié

Te souviens-tu du long orphelinat des gares
Nous traversâmes des villes qui tout le jour tournaient
Et vomissaient la nuit le soleil des journées
O matelots ô femmes sombres et vous mes compagnons
Souvenez-vous-en

Deux matelots qui ne s'étaient jamais quittés
Deux matelots qui ne s'étaient jamais parlé
Le plus jeune en mourant tomba sur le côté

O vous chers compagnons
Sonneries électriques des gares chant des moissonneuses
Traîneau d'un boucher régiment des rues sans nombre
Cavalerie des ponts nuits livides de l'alcool
Les villes que j'ai vues vivaient comme des folles

Te souviens-tu des banlieues et du troupeau plaintif des paysages

Les cyprès projetaient sous la lune leurs ombres
J'écoutais cette nuit au déclin de l'été
Un oiseau langoureux et toujours irrité
Et le bruit éternel d'un fleuve large et sombre

Mais tandis que mourants roulaient vers l'estuaire
Tous les regards tous les regards de tous les yeux
Les bords étaient déserts herbus silencieux
Et la montagne à l'autre rive était très claire

Alors sans bruit sans qu'on pût voir rien de vivant
Contre le mont passèrent des ombres vivaces
De profil ou soudain tournant leurs vagues faces
Et tenant l'ombre de leurs lances en avant

Les ombres contre le mont perpendiculaire
Grandissaient ou parfois s'abaissaient brusquement
Et ces ombres barbues pleuraient humainement
En glissant pas à pas sur la montagne claire

Qui donc reconnais-tu sur ces vieilles photographies
Te souviens-tu du jour où une abeille tomba dans le feu
C'était tu t'en souviens à la fin de l'été

Deux matelots qui ne s'étaient jamais quittés
L'aîné portait au cou une chaîne de fer
Le plus jeune mettait ses cheveux blonds en tresse

Ouvrez-moi cette porte où je frappe en pleurant

La vie est variable aussi bien que l'Euripe

(xiii) *A travers l'Europe (1965: 201–2)*

A M. Ch.

Rotsoge
Ton visage écarlate ton biplan transformable en hydroplan
Ta maison ronde où il nage un hareng saur
Il me faut la clef des paupières
Heureusement que nous avons vu M. Panado
Et nous sommes tranquilles de ce côté-là
Qu'est-ce que tu vois mon vieux M. D…
90 ou 324 un homme en l'air un veau qui regarde à travers le ventre de sa mère

J'ai cherché longtemps sur les routes
Tant d'yeux sont clos au bord des routes
Le vent fait pleurer les saussaies
Ouvre ouvre ouvre ouvre ouvre
Regarde mais regarde donc
Le vieux se lave les pieds dans la cuvette
Una volta ho inteso dire Chè vuoi
Je me mis à pleurer en me souvenant de vos enfances

Et toi tu me montres un violet épouvantable

Ce petit tableau où il y a une voiture m'a rappelé le jour

Un jour fait de morceaux mauves jaunes bleus verts et rouges
Où je m'en allais à la campagne avec une charmante cheminée tenant sa chienne en laisse
Il n'y en a plus tu n'as plus ton petit mirliton
La cheminée fume loin de moi des cigarettes russes
La chienne aboie contre les lilas
La veilleuse est consumée
Sur la robe ont chu des pétales
Deux anneaux d'or près des sandales
Au soleil se sont allumés
Mais tes cheveux sont le trolley
A travers l'Europe vêtue de petits feux multicolores

Appendix II

The Case for the Tabular

The Politics of Tabularity

1. Tabularity turns linear text into experimental writing and in doing so implicitly offers a critique of linear thinking. Glissant associates linearity with normativity, History and the legitimization of atavistic cultures (1997: 113). Thus, conversely, tabularity becomes the agent of what Deleuze and Guattari would call a minor literature, or the foreign language within the native language (1975; 1986).
2. Tabularity is politically utopian. The tabular page re-disposes the single-minded, paternal authority of the linear—a principle to which writing concedes—in such a way that a federation emerges. The tabular page admits all immigrants; but it views the relations of its constituents as modulations—that is, as both autonomous and inseparable. This is equally its attitude to languages. What it resists is the sense of the universal, of integration in the name of some transcendent principle, some linguistic hegemony.
3. Linearity and tabularity are two conflicting attitudes to the *management of the page.* An empty page is the field of scriptural action for the person who sits before it:

    > In front of his blank page, every child is already put in the position of the industrialist, the urban planner [...] (de Certeau, 1984: 134).

    But here, according to his own terms, de Certeau turns the writer into a strategist rather than a tactician (as he himself admits, 135): the page is a space into which a model of structure can be introduced; that model is then followed, complied with, by the reader. In that the linear model embodied in a text has a prior existence, the text is not so much produced as reproduced. The linear text thus not only predicts the relationship between reader and writer, by making the 'submissive' or 'compliant' response of the reader predictable, but it predicts the relationship between the source text (ST) and the target text (TT). The tactician, or tabular writer, coming across the linear text, subverts it, trespasses upon its territory, scattering the pieces of its game, re-writing its rules. The intruder has no real text of his own; he has insubordinately performed someone else's text, according to his own whims, which themselves demand a new order of decipherment, a new approach to reading unguided by a code.

4. The tabular text entails the destruction of the mediating subject in favour of a dispersal of subjectivities. In tabularity, subjecthood is 'dis-assigned', transformed into an availability of subject positions. There is subjecthood neither of the author nor of the translator, but, rather, an inhabitable space of subjective consciousness (non-perspectival).

Tabularity and Language

5. The tabular text turns text into event, into a becoming, into process; tabular layout is not so much a pattern as a field of energies released, where those energies are multilingual. In other words, the tabular text is not so much interested in meaning as a product as in sense-making as an activity, not so much interested in *signification* as in *signifiance*. Tabularity is less utterance than an enquiry into language. Correspondingly, the formal morphology of the tabular text is always on the point of adopting new configurations.
6. The very act of choosing a support for the text in tabular writing figures the intervening consciousness of the translator. And every typographic deviation or variation within that screen becomes, as it were, a point of renewed (self-)consciousness. Translation more frequently concerns itself with the translation of texts without a perceived support or screen, for which any support will do, since linearity constantly accommodates itself to the support or annexes the support to itself. In tabular translation, one translates towards the indispensability of the support, as that which ensures the obstructive materiality of language, its opacity, its resistance to conceptual appropriation, its affirmation of perceptual density.
7. The tabular text lets the reading consciousness into the heart of the text and squares with modern theatrical and musical attempts to destroy the idea of a performing space, a stage, *specially* set aside and at a distance from the audience. The performative transformation of the work from object into event, experienced in its ongoingness from within, as an immersion, relativizes hearing and means that different ears have different mixes of the same sounds. If the reading eye constantly adopts new

positions within the text, the text becomes a multi-dimensional acoustic experience made up of shifting proximities and distances.

8. We tend to think of the translational condition as post-Babelian: Babel is what condemns translation to everlasting dissatisfaction with itself; Babel is what translation sets out to redeem. Tabular textuality gives the process of redemption a new chance, because, in some sense, the Babelian curse is not so much the multiplication and separation of languages as the fact that languages can only repeat themselves—that is, repeat their isolation from each other—by constantly reproducing a given linguistic order. The tabular text undermines that linguistic order and provides the opportunity to develop a 'maximal language', one that is inclusive, infinitely extendable, able to encompass all languages and all shades of language, which has at its disposal the entire range of visual and verbal paralanguages and all scales of language, from the macro to the micro (discursive, phrasal, lexical, morphemic, phonemic, graphemic).

9. The tabular text re-introduces the alphabet—which in linear writing is predominantly pared down to phonogrammatic being—to the presence within itself of potential ideograms and pictograms, and indeed to a different way of being phonogrammatic. What do we mean by 'a different way of being phonogrammatic'? Two things really:

   (a) A situation in which acousticity exceeds the task of producing a particular signifier and confirming its meaning (by the Saussurean process of phonetic differentiation) and achieves an expressive autonomy which, like line and colour in abstract painting, either seems to gravitate towards anarchy (the whims of the individual unconscious, the purely associative) or towards community (prelinguistic, the collective unconscious, the organic).

   (b) An invasion of the text by paralanguage (tone, intonation, differential accentuation, change of tempo, expressive pausing, variations of voice timbre).

   We might say that the tabular text de-alphabetizes the alphabet, introduces it to another order of being and acting. In the early ideographic systems of Mesopotamia, Egypt, China, the ideogram is 'un signe que l'on interroge, un signe susceptible d'assumer des fonctions verbales très différentes selon le contexte où il apparaît' (Christin, 1995: blurb) [a sign to be interrogated, a sign susceptible of assuming a range of very different functions according to the context in which it appears]. Tabularity de-stabilizes the alphabetic character by multiplying its functions and applications.

10. A tabular text cannot be quoted—it can only perform itself or be performed, as it is *on the page*—or shifted to a support with a different format. AND YET the tabular text is the text which invites infinite reconstruction, making room for re-dispositions and additions, alerting the reader to the play of potentialities. The tabular text is thus perpetually

unique and perpetually a draft-text. Tabularity is the interrogative form of translation: it is the disposition by which translation, the TT, seeks to become part of the ontogenesis of the ST; in this process of perpetual questioning, it cannot expect an answer; indeed, an answer would indicate that the ST, and the world, had stopped being/becoming. The translator attempts to capture answers but only *in their formation*, as a process of emergence rather than a teleology.

11. The tabular text is informed by textual futurity in a way that the linear text is not. We are always in a position to endow a text with a future: we adapt, translate, re-interpret and so on. But translation is not merely a process which bestows, by gracious gift as it were, a future on a text (for as long as the translation lasts); it also creates a text which demands futures, presupposes futures, has futures in its own instability and reconstructibility.
12. The tabular text is at best a language we know, translated into an enunciatory activity we are unfamiliar with, at worst an enunciatory schema deriving from a language we do not know. Either way, we do not know how to read this text; we have to read it as a language coming into existence, a language whose rules we do not know and whose signifiers provide no guarantees of known signifieds. The linear become tabular is a process whereby the excess of the signifier is steeply increased and the ability to close on signification is removed. Tabularity, then, produces a version of language endowed with a new viscerality and reading remains experimental, innocent or endlessly inventive, improvised. How does one write tabular? This question is significant in two respects. First, one says that writing tabular cannot be taught—it is not a system like linear writing, even if it draws on the same alphabet. The translator is not drawing on a linguistic knowledge so much as learning an appropriate knowledge, a knowledge appropriate to the ST, by a process of trial and error. Second, it reminds one that while languages evolve naturally, writing and its associated scripts do not. The discrepant, diglossic relationship between writing and speech makes writing a relative failure in relation to speech, but is potentially an advantage in tracking the psychic and cognitive processes of the reader and registering his/her inner duration. Once writing engages with an alternative phonatory range and takes us out of the familiar articulatory routines, so it can shape a different kind of language for different uses, not to communicate with other beings so much as to explore our own relationship with language, with a text, with our perceptual processes and processing. So tabular writing is at once more visceral and more psychic.

Tabularity and the Voice

13. Tabularity reminds us that *mise-en-page* is *mise-en-scène*, the text both as performance and for performance. And here we need to remind ourselves

of the difference between these two possible manifestations of text, a difference pointed out by Henri Meschonnic (1982: 308): performance *in* the text entails, precisely, the inscription of the 'action' and gestural body within the textual space, while performance *of* the text involves the inscription of the text in an action and a gestural body.

14. Tabularity multiplies margins and in so doing destroys the single enunciatory position. Translation shifts the ST towards the heteroglossic and multivocal.
15. But it is not just the number of potential voices that is multiplied, it is also the number of potential modes of voicing—that is, vocalization pure and simple gives way to a sliding scale from vocalization through devocalization to various kinds of oralization (noises), so that speech mode listening becomes non-speech mode listening (Tsur, 1992).
16. The difference between the linear and the tabular is also covered by Johanna Drucker's distinction between the unmarked text (literary, the text speaks for itself) and the marked text (commercial, evidence of intervention) (1996: 94–7). Of the unmarked text, Drucker writes: 'All interference, resistance, must be minimized in order to allow the reader a smooth reading of the unfolding linear sequence' (95). In the marked text, on the other hand, 'different parts of it appear to "speak" differently, to address a reader whose presence [is] inscribed at the outset by an author in complicity with the graphic tools of a printer who recognized and utilized the capacity of typographic representation to manipulate the semantic value of the text through visual means' (95). The marked text, we might say, transforms the reader as third person into the reader as second person. But the addresser has not the integrated identity of a single first-person voice, but is, instead, a strange mixture of a disembodied, performative voice playing different roles, and a non-voice of verbal presentation.

Tabularity and Rhythm

17. The shift from linear to tabular text produces a cinematization of discourse. Verse sacrifices the articulation of discursive syntax to the splicing together of cuts, to 'editing' by 'shot'. The tabular introduces the ethos of montage: anything can enter, can be montaged into its self-adapting structure (expanding text). This rhythm of adjustment, this preparedness to re-orientate structural and emotional drives, is the essence of this kind of reading. Rhythm lies not in syntagmatic continuities, but in the enchained discontinuities of shot, in what is put together with what.
18. Linear text has traditionally encouraged an analysis of rhythmic properties based on syllabic values and accentuation, and has assumed that these characteristics motivate performance, whatever other paralinguistic

features might be activated by performance. Much modern French poetry deactivates syllabic numeracy (counting is no longer reliable) and makes accent *discursively* insignificant (word-fragmentation, monolexical lines). Tabular texts are a continuation and exacerbation of these trends. Additionally, as promoters of performance, tabular texts make the suprasegmental effects—tone, intonation, loudness, tempo, sense-stressing, voice-timbre—perceptually more conspicuous, and more significant as rhythm-giving features.

Tabularity and Time

19. In the tabular text, time is located in the page rather than in the text. Another way of putting this: a linear text is like a train passing through an empty landscape. The train is set in motion by the reading eye; the text's lines are the lines. This is regulated travel, with destinations and timetables and the injunction to move on. In tabular text, the text itself is the country through which the train passes—but it does not pass, because this is the landscape of a marshalling yard, of sidings and shuntings and endless formations and deformations of trains.
20. The tabular text is the text without beginning or end. No correct reading shape is achieved, no reading pathway is predicted or privileged. This increases both the responsibilities and the vulnerabilities of the reader. That is to say, a time which is teleological, directional, homogeneous, made up of isochronous intervals, is replaced by a time whose very continuity is made up of its heterogeneity, elasticity, digressiveness. The tabular text does not play out an average, unpossessed, homogeneous time as the linear text does; and therefore, correspondingly, it does not make the assumption, which criticism implicitly makes about linear texts, that all readers read at the same pace with the same degree of attention. The tabular text allows readers to individuate themselves by *living out* their heterogeneous Bergsonian durations in a highly variable, readerly experience, so that the objective least sought by the text is interpretative unanimity and that most sought is text-experiential diversity. The linear page is the page we pass through; the tabular page is the page we spend time in.
21. Tabular text takes specificity, unpredictability, formal contingency, its boundedness in the time of its making, to the extreme. At the same time, and necessarily, it maximizes the arbitrary. But this is not a gratuitous (unjustified) arbitrary, nor the arbitrary which is sustained by convention alone, but the arbitrary of the inimitable, of non-rule-governed will, of a discretionary right driven by intuition, caprice, impulse. This seems to run directly against the principles of translation, because it is in translation's nature to be guided by the discipline of rational decision, the kind

of decision that can be submitted to peers for judgement. Let us then express it this way: STs are, of course, historical products and embedded in history. But this remark requires two qualifications. First, if the ST is to be re-contextualized, in new cultural histories, then it must be worked loose from its own genetic history, re-geneticized. Secondly, the ST needs to become part of the translator's history, of his/her history as a writer. There is an important sense in which the space of the tabular text is the space of the translator's writing, a very exact point in the translator's history; we are always, alas, inclined to believe that the translator serves the ST, rather than the other way round, that the ST helps the translator to a particular kind of writerly consciousness.

Tabularity and Space

22. The tabular text fully activates blank space as an expressive constituent of the page. Meschonnic is no doubt right to differentiate between the qualities of blank space that different poets cultivate (Mallarmé, Claudel, Apollinaire, Reverdy) (1982: 310–16). But readerly subjectivity also finds countless options open to it. We might speak of space as a new polysyntax, as a source of sense. Words generate spaces, traversals, durations, rhythms of scale, the meanings of space (desert, precipice, galaxy, room, city, solitude). Once space, as in linear texts, becomes standardized—between words, for example—consciousness departs from it and it assumes a uniform visibility/intelligibility in the text. It acts as a border, a point of disjunction rather than of articulation. Tabular space, on the other hand, is infinitely a metaphor of spaces that consciousness can create.
23. Tabular space, more completely than the linear, achieves the dissolution of reader into writer, partly because space compels the *scriptible* (see Barthes, 1970: 9–12; 1974: 3–6). But space must be inhabited to the same degree by the reader as by the writer, expressing not the text, or not only the text, but the nature of reading itself, its impulses, intensities, anxieties, delights, imaginings.
24. The tabular text replaces perspectival space with planar space. Reading is an exercise not of following and traversing, but of encountering and cutting, in multidimensional activity. Linear syntax is driven by a perspectival mindset: with the full-stop as vanishing point, as a guiding orientation, the sentence organizes itself such that it establishes both a presiding point of view and a readable landscape of proximities and distances (main clauses v. subordinate clauses, clauses v. phrases, etc.). Translating into the tabular is to translate into the planar and thus to dismantle the *given*, 'transobjective', static hierarchy of significations, in order that a mobile, uncertain, subjectivizable ensemble of linguistic percepts might take its place.

25. Tabularity creates a space in which each text can potentially generate its own semiotic. By virtue of what expressive code does a particular poem have four rather than twelve margins? Why are lines spaced in such and such a manner?
26. Tabularity creates the space of the studio in the text (Scott, 2012a: 160–5), informed by the 'enumerative spirit': 'It is a spirit which throws human agency into question, which suspends time by undoing the momentum of syntax; it is the spirit of montage, of manifold *undeclared* syntaxes; it is the spirit of contingency, which poses questions about continuity, function, teleology, epistemology: enumeration does not tell us what type of knowledge we have of things, or what makes things meaningful for us' (Scott, 2012a: 162).
27. Tabularity proposes new geographies for languages (Scott, 2012a: 165–76). 'The route through languages mapped by the translator is the *dérive* [drift] which generates and is generated by psychogeographic impulses and reactions' (Scott, 2012a: 167). As translation transforms *langues* into *langage*, so it engineers and makes possible new patterns of contact between languages and begins to deterritorialize them, to give them a new mobility, a new capacity to re-dispose themselves in relation to each other.

Conclusion

28. When we interpret a text, look for the meaning that seems to do the ST most justice, we always assume it is there. We find what is hidden, not what is absent. But clearly we cannot hope to discover in a text read in 2012 something that was put there in 1560, even if we believe that this was the procedure that reading should take:

    > Whether it is a question of newspapers or Proust, the text has a meaning only through its readers; it changes along with them; it is ordered in accord with codes of perception that it does not control (de Certeau, 1984: 170).

    Let us imagine another reading. I read, I cogitate and daydream, I treasure certain phrases, I misunderstand, I creatively misread, I anticipate, I remember certain fragments of text or narrative in a certain way, I continually picture and associate. This perhaps is a reading for what is absent. We are inclined to believe that the meaning of a text is greater than any individual reader, that the meaning of a text is the sum of all its readers. But the meaning of a text is much less than the textual experience of reading it.
29. If both translation and reading are processes of linguistic experiment, interrogation, disassembly, and if, as we have said, the tabular text is

peculiarly unique and peculiarly reconstructible, then it is also in a state of becoming, an ongoing event, such that each 'performance' of the ST cannot be a recital of it, but must be a continuation or extension of it. The TT is a draft, a work in progress, whereby both translator and reader are trying to advance both the ST and the TT, and their relationship. The process of writing is potentially uninterrupted, more like a diary of a relationship which is an integral part of one's literary life. So each reader can work in this writable space, injecting into it other singularities, so that what emerges is not a consensus, an averaged translation, but an aggregate and organization of specificities and individualities. One might imagine a situation in which, under the accretion of writings, the tabular page finally disappears under its own congestedness (see my remarks on the overwritten text: Scott, 2012a; 2012b). That perhaps is, after all, a fitting end: a collapse of the edifice of translation under the weight of its being put to use.

30. It might be argued that tabular translation involves the translation of the poetics of poetry, or of prose, into a poetics of typography. Meschonnic, who has many misgivings about typographical experimentation, puts it like this:

> La poésie, espace particulier de la page, opposée à la prose, apparaît comme une chose que les pratiques récentes relèguent au passé. Il y a une poétique, à prendre comme ensemble, de la typographie, où la poésie ne se distingue plus
>
> (1982: 328)
>
> [Poetry, a particular use of paginal space, opposed to prose, appears as something which recent practices relegate to the past. There is a poetics, to be taken as a set of features, of typography, within which poetry has no distinctive existence].

But however much its techniques may derive from experimental typographies, tabularity does not aim to found a poetics of typography and thus undermine traditional generical categories (poetry, prose), even though it begins to obliterate the visual distinction between them by pursuing spatialist writing. Its aim is to establish a particular poetics of translation which is made possible or facilitated by typographic variation, and that poetics involves translating *langues* (national languages) into *langage* (the language medium); this naturally entails a reduction of the generical distinction between poetry and prose. But the TT only makes sense in partnership with the ST (and its generical 'wholeness'); and we only submerge *langue* in *langage* in order that there may emerge multilingual versions of the ST, still with their significance for genre intact.

Notes

Prefatory Remarks

1. In choosing Deleuze and Guattari as thinking companions, and in view of the translational techniques developed in the pages following, I realize that I must face the charge Deleuze and Guattari make in relation to the pursuit of multiplicity and hope that I have not played into the hands of a concealed but presiding unity: 'Pour le multiple, il faut une méthode qui le fasse effectivement; nulle astuce typographique, nulle habileté lexicale, mélange ou création de mots, nulle audace syntaxique ne peuvent la remplacer. Celles-ci en effet, le plus souvent, ne sont que des procédés mimétiques destinés à disséminer ou disloquer une unité maintenue dans une autre dimension pour un livre-image. Techno-narcissisme. Les créations typographiques, lexicales ou syntaxiques ne sont nécessaires que si elles cessent d'appartenir à la forme d'expression d'une unité cachée, pour devenir elles-mêmes une des dimensions de la multiplicité considérée; nous connaissons de rares réussites en ce genre' (1980: 33) [To attain the multiple, one must have a method that effectively constructs it; no typographical cleverness, no lexical agility, no blending or creation of words, no syntactical boldness, can substitute for it. In fact, these are more often than not merely mimetic procedures used to disseminate or disperse a unity that is retained in a different dimension for an image-book. Technonarcissism. Typographical, lexical, or syntactic creations are necessary only when they no longer belong to the form of expression of a hidden unity, becoming themselves dimensions of the multiplicity under consideration; we only know of rare successes in this (1988: 22)].

Introduction

1. Whatever one's disagreements with Saussure might be, the distinction he makes between *langage* and *langue* is as fundamental as my own, and

extremely apt to my argument: 'Mais qu'est-ce que la langue? Pour nous elle ne se confond pas avec le langage; elle n'en est qu'une partie déterminée, essentielle, il est vrai. C'est à la fois un produit social de la faculté du langage et un ensemble de conventions nécessaires, adoptées par le corps social pour permettre l'exercice de cette faculté chez les individus. Pris dans son tout, le langage est multiforme et hétéroclite; à cheval sur plusieurs domaines, à la fois physique, physiologique et psychique, il appartient encore au domaine individuel et au domaine social; il ne se laisse classer dans aucune catégorie des faits humains, parce qu'on ne sait comment dégager son unité. La langue, au contraire, est un tout en soi et un principe de classification. Dès que nous lui donnons la première place parmi les faits de langage, nous introduisons un ordre naturel dans un ensemble qui ne se prête à aucune autre classification' (1972: 25) [But what is a language [*langue*]? It is not to be confused with language [*langage*], of which it is only a defined part, essential though it is. It is at once a social product of the faculty of language and a collection of necessary conventions adopted by the social body to allow individuals to exercise this faculty. Taken as a whole, language is multiform and heterogeneous; straddling several spheres, at one and the same time physical, physiological and psychological, it belongs both to the individual sphere and the social sphere; it does not fit into any category of human facts, because its unity is indiscernible. A language, on the other hand, is a self-sufficient whole and a principle of classification. As soon as we give it pride of place among the facts of language, we introduce a natural order into an ensemble which is susceptible of no other classification].

2. Anyone wishing to champion the multilingual against the 'monolingual paradigm' is strongly advised to read Yasemin Yildiz's excellent *Beyond the Mother Tongue: The Postmonolingual Condition* (2012).
3. Marinetti puts it thus: '6. **Abolish all punctuation.** With adjectives, adverbs and conjunctions having been suppressed, naturally punctuation is also annihilated within the variable continuity of a *living* style that creates itself, without the absurd pauses of commas and periods. To accentuate certain movements and indicate their directions, mathematical signs will be used: + – x: = >, along with musical notations' (Rainey, 2005: 16).
4. The 'blind field' is all that is out of shot, off-screen, masked from sight by the frame, both in space and time; that is, the blind field is what lies outside the frame both in spatial extension and in the before and after. My own use of the term derives from Barthes (see 1980: 89–95; 1984: 55–9). Among other things, Barthes proposes that, while both *studium* and the pornographic fully inhabit the framed space, *punctum* and the erotic launch us beyond what can be seen, into the blind field.
5. After Barthes's essay on photography defining it as 'un message *sans code*' (1982b: 13) [a message *without a code*], it is with the utmost circumspection that one should call photography a language. But if one takes into account the discrepancies between the photographic eye and the human

eye (see Scott, 1999: 9–10), photography's mechanisms of production (see Tagg, 1988: 3) and the medium-specific ways in which its meanings shift in relation to time and context, then the suggestion that it is a coded language (*langue*) does not seem unjustified.

Chapter 1: Styles and Margins

1. Madeleine's account of the meeting gives the date as 1 January (Apollinaire, 2005: 27) and Apollinaire's first postcard (16 April 1915) agrees (35); on the other hand, the date on the letter from the poet to Lou, written on the same day, fixes it at 2 January (2010: 74–5) and subsequent scholarship has confirmed this latter date.
2. Apollinaire continued to correspond with Lou alongside his correspondence with Madeleine, despite their fateful last meeting at the Hôtel Terminus in Marseille, 28 March 1915. Apollinaire's final letter to Lou is dated 18 January 1916.
3. Apollinaire also fashioned rings for Lou (see, for example, letter of 8 May 1915 (2010: 348–9)) and addressed her in similarly chivalric terms: 'Gui demande encore une fois à Lou ses couleurs, parce que s'il fallait mourir, il veut mourir sous les couleurs de sa dame comme faisaient les chevaliers' (29 April 1915) (2010: 331) [Gui asks Lou once more for her colours, because if he must die, he would rather do so under the colours of his lady as the knights did] . Nor was he any less pressing in his requests for photographs: 'J'attends tes photos avec une impatience fantastique. J'aimerais bien des photos où on te voit, comme les photos de Desgranges [a photographic studio in Nice], les petites photos c'est gentil, je les aime bien, mais je préfère, tu le comprendras, celles où on voit quelque chose' (26 April 1915) (2010: 321) [I await your photos with enormous impatience. I would like photos which make you clearly visible, like those of Desgranges (...), small photos are nice, I'm fond of them, but I prefer, as you will understand, those in which you can see something].
4. Relevant to this remark, perhaps, are lines from a poem Apollinaire despatched to Lou on 18 April 1915:

   Et parfois je suis tenté de leur montrer ton portrait pour que ces jeunes mâles
   Réapprennent en voyant ta photo
   Ce que c'est que la beauté.
   Mais cela c'est pour moi, c'est pour moi seul
   Moi seul ai droit de parler à ce portrait qui pâlit
   A ce portrait qui s'efface (2010: 297).

   [And sometimes I am tempted to show them your portrait so that these young males/Learn afresh seeing your photo/What beauty is/But it's for me and me alone/I alone have the right to speak to this portrait which grows pale/To this portrait which fades].

The significance of photography's connection with 'beauté' becomes clearer further on in my argument.

5. As Apollinaire puts it in 'Cote 146' (Lou, rather than Madeleine, version):

> Je regarde aussi un portrait en grand chapeau
> Et quelques-uns de mes compagnons ont vu ton portrait
> Et pensant bien que je te connaissais
> Ils ont demandé:
> 'Qui donc est-elle?'
> Et je n'ai pas su que leur répondre
> Car je me suis aperçu brusquement
> Qu'encore aujourd'hui je ne te connais pas bien
> Et toi dans ta photo profonde comme la lumière
> tu souris toujours
>
> (2010: 464–5).

[I also look at a portrait with a large hat/And some of my companions have seen your portrait/And believing that I knew you/They asked/'Who is she then?'/And I didn't know what to reply/Because I suddenly realized/That I don't know you very well even now/And you, in your photograph as deep as light/You go on smiling].

6. 'Ma chérie, je suis fier de ta pudeur à l'égard de tout ce qui n'est pas nous' (26 November 1915) (350) [My beloved, I am proud of your modesty in regard to everything which does not relate to us].
7. All the more surprising, given that Madeleine's letters of the latter months of 1915 clearly match Apollinaire's in their uninhibited display of an erotic imagination (Campa, 2013: 606). Campa's full edition of the Apollinaire-Madeleine correspondence is shortly forthcoming.
8. These lines have a poignant, if indirect, pre-echo in 'C'est…', a poem sent to Lou probably on 23 June 1915:

> C'est la réalité des photos qui sont sur mon cœur que je veux
> Cette réalité seule, elle seule, et rien d'autre
> Mon cœur le répète sans cesse comme une bouche d'orateur et le redit
> A chaque battement
> Toutes les autres images du monde sont fausses
>
> (2010: 451)

[It is the reality of the photos which lie against my heart that I want/This reality alone, alone, and nothing else/My heart repeats it incessantly like an orator's mouth and says it over/At each beat/All the other images of the world are false].

9. e.g. Cecily Mackworth (1961: 200): 'It seems more likely that the amorous

partner of his erotic dreams reappeared in the flesh as he had first seen her in the train between Nice and Marseilles—as a virginal and respectable young girl'; Pierre-Marcel Adéma (1968: 282): 'Désormais à son contact, vivant auprès d'elle, chez elle, il réalise ce qu'avait eu d'excessif son projet. Assez libre dans ses propos et son comportement, du fait de son éducation et du milieu presque colonial où elle vit, Madeleine n'en est pas moins une jeune fille, passionnée certes, mais maîtresse d'elle-même' [From now on associating with her, living in her company, at her home, he realizes what had been excessive about his plan. Fairly free in her talk and behaviour, by dint of her education and the almost colonial milieu in which she lives, Madeleine is no less for that a young girl, passionate certainly, but fully in possession of herself]. Even when we have the added evidence of Madeleine's letters, we shall not be much the wiser (Campa, 2013: 625–7).

10. Throughout these last, difficult, obstructed months of the correspondence, up to the end of 1916, Madeleine remained devoted, patient, forgiving, hopeful (Campa, 2013: 657, 665).
11. Apart from the dispositional differences, there are only two other changes: the singular 'eau vive' of the original has become plural; the 'soleil' of the last line has acquired a capital letter. But it is worth adding that the change in layout has lifted 'Qu'est sa beauté' to the status of refrain where originally it was a periodic line-terminal repetition. My translation, looking to interweave repetitions (with variations of syntactical setting or grammatical class) more insistently, has no place for the structural isolation entailed by refrain, as will be shortly seen.
12. This figure (i) counts as seven the poems presented in the letters as a single cycle entitled 'Le Médaillon toujours fermé', but published as a sequence of individual poems in *Calligrammes*; (ii) does not count 'Le Brancardier' and 'Classe 17', which were subsequently assimilated into 'Chant de l'horizon en Champagne'; (iii) counts the 'Poèmes pour peintures' and the 'Inscriptions pour des gravures' as one each; (iv) includes the four 'poèmes secrets' (5e, 6e, 7e, 8e) contained in the 'Annexes' of Campa's new edition (2005: 457–66).
13. Campa's new biography of Apollinaire provides an example of Madeleine's verse, from a letter dated 27 May 1915, which certainly adds weight to this supposition (2013: 645).

Chapter 2: Choices, Variants and Variation

1. Deleuze and Guattari define the activity of minor languages thus: 'C'est la même chose pour les langues mineures: ce ne sont pas simplement des sous-langues, idiolectes ou dialectes, mais des agents potentiels pour faire entrer la langue majeure dans un devenir minoritaire de toutes ses dimensions, de tous ses éléments. On distinguera des langues mineures, la langue majeure, et le devenir-mineur de la langue majeure' (1980: 134) [The same goes for minor languages: they are not simply sublanguages,

idiolects or dialects, but potential agents of the major language's entering into a becoming-minoritarian of all its dimensions and elements. We should distinguish between minor languages, the major language, and the becoming-minor of the major language (1988: 106]. A minor language is thus not so much a foreign language within the native language as another mode of handling the native language: 'Le mode majeur et le mode mineur sont deux traitements de la langue, l'un consistant à en extraire des constantes, l'autre à la mettre en variation continue' (1980: 135) [The major and minor mode are two different treatments of language, one of which consists in extracting constants from it, the other placing it in continuous variation (1988: 106)].

2. In Leonard Freed's words: 'Also contact sheets are private: they belong to me, whereas photographs, once they are out of my hands, take on a life of their own' (Lubben, 2011: 243).
3. One thinks here of Pissarro's advice to the young painter Louis Le Bail in 1896–7: 'When painting, make a choice of subject, see what is lying at the right and the left, then work on everything simultaneously. Don't work bit by bit, but paint everything at once by placing tones everywhere, with brushstrokes of the right colour and value, while noticing what is alongside' (quoted in Denvir, 1987: 187).
4. One should emphasize that Benjamin's 'aufgefangen sein' here is deeply ambiguous: either it means, as the first translation indicates, 'to be caught', 'to be picked out', 'to be perceived', awareness on the look-out, as it were; or it means, as the second translation indicates, 'to be offset', 'to be counterbalanced', a defensive measure against shock. This latter translation squares better with Benjamin's analysis of the differences between absorbed experience [Erfahrung] and shock-experience [Erlebnis] in 'Über einige Motive bei Baudelaire' [On Some Motifs in Baudelaire]: 'Je größer der Anteil des Chockmoments an den einzelnen Eindrücken ist, je unablässiger das Bewußtsein im Interesse des Reizschutzes auf dem Plan sein muß, je grösser der Erfolg ist, mit dem es operiert, desto weniger gehen sie in die Erfahrung ein; desto eher erfüllen sie den Begriff des Erlebnisses' (1974b: 615) [The greater the shock factor in particular impressions, the more vigilant consciousness has to be in screening stimuli; the more efficiently it does so, the less these impressions enter long experience [*Erfahrung*] and the more they correspond to the concept of isolated experience [*Erlebnis*] (2003b: 319)].

Chapter 3: The Linear and the Tabular

1. Against what one might think of as Apollinaire's natural cosmopolitanism one must set the surprisingly strong nationalistic exhortations of 'L'Esprit nouveau et les poètes'. Or perhaps not so surprisingly. Apollinaire's claims for the primacy of the French in artistic achievement grows partly from his own recent acquisition of French national identity (March 1916), partly from the fact that the lecture was delivered in mid-war (November

1917) and partly from his long-running refutation of claims made by foreign contenders (in particular, the Futurists). But it should also be said that Apollinaire's nationalism fits easily into a vision of a rich, inclusive diversity rather than proud isolationism, and, in that sense, his views chime with those of Victor Segalen and Édouard Glissant: 'Des différences ethniques et nationales naît la variété des expressions littéraires, et c'est cette variété même qu'il faut sauvegarder' (1991: 946) [From ethnic and national differences grows the variety of literary expression, and it is this variety which we must safeguard]. A cosmopolitanism undiversified, without singularities, easily slips into international-parliament-speak: 'Une expression lyrique cosmopolite ne donnerait que des œuvres vagues sans accent et sans charpente, qui auraient la valeur des lieux communs de la rhétorique parlementaire internationale' (1991: 946) [A cosmopolitan lyric expression would only produce poorly defined works, with neither individual note nor structure, which would have the value of the commonplaces of international parliamentary rhetoric].

2. 'Ils [les poètes] veulent être les premiers à fournir un lyrisme tout neuf à ces nouveaux moyens d'expression qui ajoutent à l'art le movement et qui sont le phonographe et le cinéma' (1991: 954) [They [the poets] wish to be the first to provide with a brand new brand of lyricism these new means of expression which add movement to art, that is, the phonograph and cinema].
3. '[. . .] le poète d'aujourd'hui ne méprise aucun mouvement de la nature, et son esprit poursuit la découverte aussi bien dans les synthèses les plus vastes et les plus insaisissables: foules, nébuleuses, océans, nations, que dans les faits en apparence les plus simples: une main qui fouille une poche, une allumette qui s'allume par le frottement, des cris d'animaux, l'odeur des jardins après la pluie, une flamme qui naît dans un foyer' (1991: 951) [[. . .] today's poet does not scorn any of nature's motions, and his mind pursues its discoveries as much in the grandest and most unencompassable of syntheses: crowds, nebulas, oceans, nations, as in the apparently simplest facts: a hand searching through a pocket, a match being struck alight, animal cries, the smell of gardens after rain, a flame kindled in a hearth].
4. Apollinaire's reference to the absence of subject in the new art—'Beaucoup de peintres nouveaux ne peignent que des tableaux où il n'y de sujet véritable. Et les dénominations que l'on trouve dans les catalogues jouent alors le rôle des noms qui désignent les hommes sans les caractériser' (1991: 8–9) [Many of the new painters only paint pictures which have no real subject. And the titles in catalogues are like names which designate individuals without describing them]—is part of his evidence for the pursuit, by the Cubists, of a 'peinture pure'.
5. Point 11 of Marinetti's 'Technical Manifesto of Futurist Literature' (May 1912) runs: '**Destroy the "I" in literature:** that is all psychology. The sort of man who has been damaged by libraries and museums, subjected to a logic and wisdom of fear, is absolutely of no interest anymore. We must abolish

him in literature and replace him once and for all with matter, whose essence must be seized by strokes of intuition [...]' (Rainey, 2005: 17).

6. Linda Dalrymple Henderson has taught us much about the currency of the concept of the fourth dimension in Cubist circles. First, we need to understand that it was not related to Einstein's Special Theory of Relativity (1905), nor to Minkowski's space-time continuum of 1908: '[...] the Cubists were not influenced by Einstein's relativising of simultaneity nor by Minkowski's ideas on "space-time". Instead their "fourth dimension" was an outgrowth of nineteenth-century *n*-dimensional geometry, a fact that provides a valuable insight into the time element in Cubist painting ("space-time") and the resultant juxtaposition of images' (1983: 89–90; see also 1983: 353–65, and 1978: 1–2 and 466–92). Second, the Cubists took their distances from the notion the more it was popularized. Third, in Apollinaire's case, the fourth dimension has to be related both to his interest in Cubism and to his championing of Robert Delaunay's Orphism—that is, both to a low-relief planar geometry and to non-objective colour grids. Fourth, we should remember that, in harnessing the fourth dimension to the new art, theorists and champions were not scrupulous in distinguishing between non-Euclidean geometry and *n*-dimensional geometry.
7. Henderson expresses the distinction between Futurism and Cubism thus: 'With "force-lines" the Futurists transformed the Cubist grid into a dynamic system of vectors' (1983: 110, n. 190).
8. As Henderson puts it: 'But the difficulty of conceiving a fourth dimension also led to the occasional use of the more easily understood idea of time as the fourth dimension' (1983: 9).
9. Henderson produces convincing evidence for Apollinaire's downplaying of the notion of the fourth dimension even in *Les Peintres cubistes* (1913) (1983: 101): the reduction of explicit references to the fourth dimension between his April 1912 *Soirées de Paris* article and its revised version in *Les Peintres cubistes*; his insistence that the concept had only 'un intérêt en quelque sorte historique' (1991: 12) [a so-to-speak historical interest]; his suppression of the name of Maurice Princet from the concluding note. And as his allegiances were already shifting from Cubism to Delaunay, one might suppose that Apollinaire's affair with the fourth dimension was on the ebb. But the likelihood is, as already suggested, that Apollinaire, like other theorists of Cubism (e.g. Gleizes and Metzinger), was more wary of the term and its abuses than of the reconceptualizations of space which underlay it. And the shift of allegiance from Cubism to Delaunay's Orphist colourism did not strain fourth-dimensional thinking as much as might be imagined: Delaunay's notion of 'profondeur', for example, is a significant step beyond three-dimensional notions of depth; and Delaunay also taxes the Cubists with their continued cultivation of perspective despite their claims to inhabit new geometries.
10. Ernst Mach, writing three years after Poincaré's *La Science et l'hypothèse* (1902), traces, in greater detail and with greater vigour, the distinctions

and continuities between physiological space—that is, space perceived according to biological need—and geometric space: 'We distinguish near and remote points in our figures, those at the right from those at the left, those at the top from those at the bottom, entirely by physiological considerations and despite the fact that geometric space is not cognizant of any relation to our body, but only of relations of the points to one another' (2011: 35).

11. That is to say, sounds and voices without identifiable sources. 'Acousmate' is the title given by Apollinaire to two of his early poems (1965: 513, 617), a title glossed by him in his notes as: 'acousmate: bruit de voix ou d'instruments qu'on croit entendre dans l'air' (1965: 1130) [acousmatic: vocal or instrumental sounds that you seem to hear in the air]. These poems are generally reckoned to prefigure Apollinaire's *poèmes-conversations*, poems constituted by snatches of dialogue overheard, usually in café environments.
12. Vertov was to say very much the same thing in 1929, in 'From Kino-Eye to Radio-Eye': 'The school of kino-eye calls for construction of the film-object upon "intervals", that is, upon the movement between shots, upon the visual correlation of shots with one another, upon transitions from one visual stimulus to another' (1984: 90). Among the correlations that Vertov has in mind are the correlations of planes, of foreshortenings, of movements within the frame, of light and shadow, of recording speeds.

Chapter 4: Frames and Blind Fields

1. In another formulation of this difference, Merleau-Ponty writes: 'Alors que le style en chaque peintre vivait comme la pulsation de son cœur et le rendait justement capable de reconnaître tout autre effort que le sien,—le Musée convertit cette historicité secrète, pudique, non délibérée, involontaire, vivante enfin, en histoire officielle et pompeuse' (2008: 101) [Whereas style lived within each painter like his heartbeat, and was precisely what enabled him to recognize every effort which differed from his own, the museum converts this secret, modest, nondeliberated, involuntary, and, in short, living historicity into official and pompous history (1993: 99)].
2. 'Le hors-champ renvoie à ce qu'on n'entend ni ne voit, pourtant parfaitement présent' (Deleuze, 1983: 28) [The out-of-field refers to what is neither seen nor understood, but is nevertheless perfectly present (Deleuze, 1992: 16)].
3. Lying behind these investigations of particular groups of lines is a 'standard' translation of 'Zone' (see Appendix I (vii)). But even this version has already taken a step away from the ST. It breaks Apollinaire's lines down into shorter segments, in the belief that they come out too slackly in English if left as they are; shorter lines increase tension between syntactic segments, and one can exploit the line ending to add suspense and tonal variety—pausing always poses questions about tone. Shorter

lines also encourage the reader to feel for variations in tempo. So I hope that, by adopting this strategy, I am increasing the range of vocal input.

4. See Christian Metz (1990).
5. This itemization might bring to mind László Moholy-Nagy's identification of eight varieties of photographic vision: abstract seeing, exact seeing, rapid seeing, slow seeing, intensified seeing, penetrative seeing, simultaneous seeing, distorted seeing (Passuth, 1987: 327).
6. It is perhaps worth reflecting for a moment on what looks like a sharp division between Deleuze's views and my own. For Deleuze, the subject position is essentially false, something which prevents the release of 'subjectless individuations' (*haecceities*), the events produced by singularities (2007: 315). Within these movements of becoming, processes of subjectivation do indeed occur; but they are transitory interventions and are superseded by the dynamics of the series, the formation, the factory, the assemblage. My own argument for translation as the vehicle of readerly consciousness, of readerly experience, rather than as an account of textual interpretation, unashamedly favours the subjective, argues that the reading subject is the site where the text releases its freight of associative potentiality, achieves performative variety, is re-imagined formally and dispositionally. But, as I have made clear, the subject position supersedes the anecdotal and the impressionistic only by being written back, through translation, into the text. And it is in this being-written-back-into-the-text that the reader-subject becomes an agent of the text, that his/her subjectivity achieves the status both of *available* subjectivity (subjectivation) and 'subjectless individuation'.
7. As possible sources for the poem, Décaudin (1996: 210) also suggests a reminiscence of lines from Baudelaire's 'Recueillement' ('Vois se pencher les défuntes années/Sur les balcons du ciel, en robes surannées') and draws our attention to kinships with the unpublished 'O France, France ma patrie' (Apollinaire, 1965: 855) and with lines from 'L'Anguille' (1965: 356):

   Les yeux dansants comme des anges
   Elle riait elle riait
   Les yeux très bleus les dents très blanches

8. Gordon also observes that it conveys 'the period of the New York speakeasy' (2009: 402).

Chapter 5: The Chromatic and the Acoustic

1. Apollinaire describes this shift thus: 'L'époque constructive de Robert Delaunay commence après la *Ville de Paris*. Les brisures des formes par la lumière créent des plans colorés. Ces plans colorés sont la structure du tableau et la nature n'est plus un sujet de description, mais un prétexte, une évocation poétique d'expression par des plans colorés qui s'ordonnent

par des contrastes simultanés. Leur orchestration colorée crée des architectures qui se déroulent comme des phrases en couleurs et aboutissent à une nouvelle forme d'expression en peinture, à la Peinture pure' (quoted by La Tourette, 1950: 39) [Robert Delaunay's constructive period begins after *La Ville de Paris*. The fracturings of forms by light create coloured planes. These coloured planes are the structure of the picture and nature is no longer a subject of description, but a pretext, a poetic evocation of expression by coloured planes which are organized by simultaneous contrasts. Their coloured orchestration creates architectures which unfold like coloured phrases and produce a new form of expression in painting, Pure Painting].

2. Apollinaire, despite his lyrical propensities, fully espoused these trends and Pierre Francastel seems to me mistaken when he suggests that Apollinaire was perceptually inhibited by an archaizing sensibility: 'Et les malentendus qui sépareront bientôt Delaunay et Apollinaire [...] viendront, au fond, de l'attachement du poète à exprimer sur des modes nouveaux des états de sensibilité anciens' (1957: 24) [And the misunderstandings which were soon to separate Delaunay and Apollinaire would derive, essentially, from the poet's attachment to the expression in new styles of backward-looking states of sensibility].
3. 'Puis, j'aime beaucoup mes vers depuis *Alcools*, il y en a pour un volume au moins et j'aime beaucoup beaucoup "Les Fenêtres" qui a paru à part en tête d'un catalogue du peintre Delaunay' (30 July 1915; 2005: 95) [And then, I'm very fond of the poems I've written since *Alcools*, there are enough for at least one volume and I'm very very fond of 'The Windows' which appeared separately as the opening item in a catalogue for the painter Delaunay]; 'L'un [un paquet] contient deux catalogues de l'Exposition Delaunay en 1913 ou 1914, l'un est à moi, tu me le garderas. [...] Tu y liras un des mes poèmes que j'aime le plus, "Les Fenêtres"' (30 November 1915; 2005: 355) [One package contains two catalogues of the Delaunay Exhibition of 1913 or 1914, one of which is mine and which you should keep for me. [...] You can read in it one of my poems which I love most, 'The Windows'].
4. Francastel is undoubtedly right to claim that Apollinaire's insistence in corralling Delaunay within the circle of Cubism, albeit in the 'impure' sub-category 'cubisme orphique' (1991: 16–17), does an injustice to the true ambitions of his work (1957: 29–30). But in Apollinaire's defence, one should say three things: (i) Francastel himself acknowledges that one 'line' of Delaunay's work belongs to Cubism: 'Delaunay n'a jamais renié le cubisme dont il reste l'un des interprètes les plus complets; c'est lui qui, avec Léger, a conféré au cubisme la qualité de monumentalité' (1957: 42) [Delaunay never renounced Cubism of which he remains one of the most complete interpreters; Delaunay it is who, with Léger, conferred on Cubism the quality of monumentality]; (ii) Apollinaire was looking for a hold-all label under which all new trends in the arts might be mustered—he imagined that Futurism might serve the same purpose;

(iii) in his piece on Picabia, and also in Delaunay's name, he attributed to colour, as we have seen, some of the powers (fourth-dimensional) and the creative autonomy that Delaunay would wish to: 'Il abordait ainsi un art où comme dans celui de Robert Delaunay, la dimension idéale, c'est la couleur. Elle a par conséquent toutes les autres dimensions. [...] La couleur dans cet art est saturée d'énergie et ses extrémités se continuent dans l'espace. La réalité est ici la matière. La couleur ne dépend plus des trois dimensions connues, c'est elle qui les crée' (1991: 45) [He thus engaged with an art in which, as in that of Robert Delaunay, colour is the dimension of the ideal. Consequently it contains all the other dimensions. [...] Colour in this art is saturated with energy and its extremities continue into space. Here reality is matter. Colour no longer depends on the three known dimensions, it is colour that creates them].

5. Delaunay puts it thus: 'Ainsi le cubisme croyant apporter un nouveau langage—expressif—ne faisait qu'apporter une modification extérieure dans un système qu'il n'abolissait pas—mais qu'il soutenait: l'introduction de plusieurs points de vue d'un objet sur la toile ressortissait de la même vision sinon complétée' (Francastel, 1957: 57) [Thus Cubism, believing that it was introducing a new—expressive—language was in fact only producing an external modification in a system which it did not abolish—which it in fact sustained: the insertion of several points of view pertained to the same, albeit incomplete, vision].
6. In Delaunay's words: '*La ligne c'est la limite. La couleur donne la profondeur* (non perspective, *non successive*, mais *simultanée*) *et sa forme et son mouvement* (Francastel, 1957: 110) [*The line describes a limit. Colour opens a depth* (not perspectival, *not successive*, but *simultaneous*) *and its form and its movement*].
7. Apollinaire observes: 'De telles paroles ne se commentent point. Elles veulent être comprises immédiatement et suscitent cette simultanéité qui seule est la création, le reste n'étant qu'énumération, contemplation, étude' (Francastel, 1957: 156–7) [Such words have no need of commentary. They look for immediate comprehension and activate that simultaneity which alone is creation, the rest being no more than enumeration, contemplation, study].
8. Elsewhere, Delaunay writes: 'L'introduction du temps dans la structure du tableau donne la nouvelle affirmation constructive et sa force dans *cette réalité nouvelle*' (Francastel, 1957: 68) [The introduction of time into the structure of the painting provides the new assertion of the constructive and its force in *this brand-new reality*].
9. Delaunay's attitudes to Mallarmé are a little difficult to decipher. Gilles de La Tourette (1950: 15, 32–4, 44), speaking from first-hand contact with Delaunay, is confident of Mallarmé's importance for the painter, and mentions *Fenêtres simultanées* in that connection. Delaunay himself assigns Mallarmé's poetry to the analytic/destructive period of art: 'Avec l'analyse, on ne construit pas. C'est l'époque cahotique [*sic*], dramatique du cubisme. La poésie n'en est pas abstraite. Il y a des rapports entre

cette époque picturale et la Poésie d'un Mallarmé (Tristement dort une mandore au creux néant musicien)' (Francastel, 1957: 96) [With analysis, there is no construction. It is the chaotic/bumpy and dramatic period of cubism. Its poetry is not abstract. There are connections between this pictorial period and the Poetry of a Mallarmé (Sadly sleeps a mandola musician of the hollow void]. It is perhaps worth adding that Francastel is of the view that 'Delaunay n'est pas le descendant de Mallarmé' (1957: 24) [Delaunay is not the descendant of Mallarmé].

10. Stephen Handel drives home the point: 'Acoustic information is usually ambiguous and supports many possibilities. The best perceptual strategy would be to retain as much acoustic information as possible for as long a time as possible to allow surrounding information to influence the percept' (1989: 289).
11. Handel describes the intricate network of overlaps and anticipations that speech-flow is: 'The production system must cheat in order to get all the sounds out rapidly: movements appropriate to several successive sounds must be made simultaneously, and movements necessary to produce future sounds must be started early enough to ensure that the vocal tract will be in the correct position to make those sounds when they are required' (1989: 134).
12. It is safer to speak of tendency, simply because much of Kandinsky's vocabulary has as much to do with sensation as with semantic value.
13. I coin and adapt these words from Steven Feld's 'acoustemology', which he defines thus: 'By acoustemology I wish to suggest a union of acoustics and epistemology, and to investigate the primacy of sound as a modality of knowing and being in the world. Sound both emanates from and penetrates bodies; this reciprocity of reflection and absorption is a creative means of orientation—one that tunes bodies to places and times through their sounding potential. Hearing and producing sound are thus embodied competencies that situate actors and their agency in particular historical worlds' (2003: 226). I would want to extend this vision of 'the reciprocity of reflection and absorption' from the auditory to all the other senses.
14. The story of Apollinaire's relationship with Delaunay has a rather unedifying postscript. When the war broke out, the Delaunays were holidaying in Spain (Fuenterrabia). They stayed on in the Iberian Peninsula, both in Portugal and in Spain (Madrid, Vigo, Barcelona). Campa reports: 'D'abord appelé sous les drapeaux puis déclaré déserteur, Robert fit jouer ses relations et obtint sa réforme au consulat de France à Vigo, le 13 juin 1916' (2013: 511, note 4) [First called up and then declared a deserter, Robert pulled strings and obtained his declaration of unfitness for service from the French consulate at Vigo, June 13, 1916]. Apollinaire referred to Delaunay as a coward (February 7 1915) (Campa, 2013: 537, note 6) and as a 'simultaniste déserteur' (March 13 1915) (1991: 1315). Other, more indulgent accounts skate over the exact circumstances: 'Robert est antimilitariste, et réformé. Aucune obligation, donc, une fois la guerre

déclarée, de revenir en France' (Desanti, 1988: 148) [Robert was antimilitarist, and declared unfit for service. There was thus no obligation, once war had been declared, to return to France]. The Delaunays finally went back to Paris in 1921.

Chapter 6: New Sounds, New Languages

1. For a rich and fascinating treatment of the sources and some of the meanings of 'La Victoire', see Read, 1986.
2. One reason for describing this relationship as dialectical is the way in which the sounds of the body belong to, or are juxtaposed with, cosmic and mythic utterances: e.g. 'Tu dois en avoir assez de faire peur à ce ciel/ Qu'il garde son hoquet' (ll. 15–16); 'Parlez avec les mains faites claquer vos doigts/Tapez-vous sur la joue comme sur un tambour/O paroles/Elles suivent dans la myrtaie/[...]' (ll. 59–62).
3. I borrow this term from Claude Tournadre's analysis of the poem (1973: 171). Tournadre is, however, in no doubt that Apollinaire has little patience with 'bruitism': 'Nous avons donc affaire ici à une parodie des déclarations tapageuses des poètes bruitistes' (1973: 172) [We are thus dealing with a parody of the rowdy declarations of the bruitist poets], but concedes that this is rather too bluntly expressed.
4. In reconnecting 'La Victoire' with the unpublished manuscript poem 'Soldes', Read (1986: 206) reconnects the poet's blindness with that of soldiers returning from the front.
5. On the basis of textual evidence in 'Soldes', Read (1986: 209–10) sees this line as an expression of the capacity of the blind to see into other dimensions, into the depths of consciousness and the heights of aspiration.
6. Read (1986: 211) reminds us of the connections Apollinaire makes elsewhere ('Visée', 'Fusée-signal') between fish and the poetic word.
7. It may be a surprise to find Apollinaire associating his cherished cinema with the mutism to which *langue* condemns language. But just as the sighted and winged need the blind and speaking, for their mutual benefit, so the cinema needs the phonograph to fulfil its promise.
8. Harshav (2004: 204) assigns this move to late 1911.
9. This last colourful detail is mentioned by Wullschlager (2008: 164). Chagall's own account makes no mention of it: 'When lunch was over we staggered back to "La Ruche", licking our lips. [...] Apollinaire enters cautiously, as if he were afraid the whole building might suddenly collapse and bury him in its ruins. [...] Apollinaire sits down. He reddens, puffs out, smiles, and murmurs: "Supernatural...![''] The next day I received a letter, a poem dedicated to me: "Rodztag".' (1989: 112–14). For comments on Chagall's memories of the term 'surnaturel', see Hicken, 2002: 198, note 80.
10. Almost from the outset of his interviews with David Sylvester, Bacon establishes the centrality of accident or chance to his creative procedures and returns periodically to the topic: e.g. 'But there is a possibility that

you get through this accidental thing something much more profound than what you really wanted' (Sylvester, 1987: 17); 'I know that, in my case, I know what I want to do but don't know how to bring it about. And that's what I'm hoping accidents or chance or whatever you like to call it will bring about for me' (Sylvester, 1987: 102); DS: 'You're saying that, in allowing chance to work, one allows the deeper levels of the personality to come across?'/FB: 'I certainly am trying to say that. [...] It seems to come straight out of what we choose to call the unconscious with the form of the unconscious locked around it—which is its freshness' (Sylvester, 1987: 120); 'I always think of myself not so much as a painter but as a medium for accident and chance' (Sylvester, 1987: 140).

11. 'I think the texture of a painting seems to be more immediate than the texture of a photograph, because the texture of a photograph seems to go through an illustrational process onto the nervous system, whereas the texture of a painting seems to come immediately onto the nervous system' (Sylvester, 1987: 57–8).

Conclusion: Repetition, Difference, Representation

1. Deleuze tells us, referring to E. Laroche's *Histoire de la racine nem—en grec ancien* (1949): 'La société homérique ne connaît pas d'enclos ni de propriété des pasturages: il ne s'agit pas de distribuer la terre aux bêtes, mais au contraire de les distribuer elles-mêmes, de les répartir çà et là dans un espace illimité, forêt ou flanc de montagne' (2011: 54, footnote 1) [Homeric society had neither enclosures nor property in pastures: it was not a question of distributing the land among the beasts but, on the contrary, of distributing the beasts themselves and dividing them up here and there across an unlimited space, forest or mountainside (2004a: 85, footnote 6)].

Bibliographical References

Adéma, Pierre-Marcel, 1968. *Guillaume Apollinaire* (Paris: La Table Ronde).

Apollinaire, Guillaume, 1965. *Œuvres poétiques*, ed. Marcel Adéma and Michel Décaudin (Paris: Gallimard).

—, 1966a. *Oeuvres complètes de Guillaume Apollinaire IV*, ed. Michel Décaudin (Paris: André Balland and Jacques Lecat).

—, 1966b. *Calligrammes: Poèmes de la paix et de la guerre (1913–1916)*, pref. Michel Butor (Paris: Gallimard).

—, 1991. *Œuvres en prose complètes II*, ed. Pierre Caizergues and Michel Décaudin (Paris: Gallimard).

—, 1997. *Tendre comme le souvenir* (Paris: Gallimard) (1st pub. 1952).

—, 2005. *Lettres à Madeleine: Tendre comme le souvenir*, ed. Laurence Campa (Paris: Gallimard).

—, 2010. *Lettres à Lou*, ed. Michel Décaudin, new edn rev. and completed by Laurence Campa (Paris: Gallimard).

Apollonio, Umbro (ed.), 1973. *Futurist Manifestos* (London: Thames and Hudson).

Baal-Teshuva, Jacob, 2008. *Marc Chagall 1887–1985* (Cologne: Taschen).

Barthes, Roland, 1970. *S/Z* (Paris: Seuil).

—, 1973. *Le Plaisir du texte* (Paris: Seuil).

—, 1974. *S/Z*, trans. Richard Miller (New York: Hill and Wang).

—, 1980. *La Chambre Claire: Note sur la photographie* (Paris: Cahiers du Cinéma/Gallimard/Seuil).

—, 1982a. 'Le Grain de la voix', *L'Obvie et l'obtus: Essais critiques III* (Paris: Seuil), 236–45.

—, 1982b. 'Le Message photographique', in *L'Obvie et l'obtus: Essais critiques III* (Paris: Seuil), 9–24.

—, 1984. *Camera Lucida: Reflections on Photography*, trans. Richard Howard (London: Fontana-Flamingo).

—, 1994. 'Texte (théorie du)', in Éric Marty (ed.), *Roland Barthes: Œuvres complètes: Tome II 1966–1973* (Paris: Seuil), 1677–89.

Bazin, André, 2002. *Qu'est-ce que le cinéma?* (Paris: Cerf-Corlet) (14th edition).

Beckett, Samuel, 1986. *Collected Poems 1930–1978* (London: John Calder).

Benjamin, Walter, 1974a. 'Das Kunstwerk im Zeitalter seiner technischen Reproduzierbarkeit (Zweite Fassung)', in *Gesammelte Schriften I. 2*, ed. Rolf Tiedemann and Hermann Schweppenhäuser (Frankfurt am Main: Suhrkamp Verlag), 471–508.

—, 1974b. 'Über einige Motive bei Baudelaire', in *Gesammelte Schriften I. 2*, ed. Rolf Tiedemann and Hermann Schweppenhäuser (Frankfurt am Main: Suhrkamp Verlag), 605–53.

—, 1977. 'Kleine Geschichte der Photographie', in *Gesammelte Schriften II. 1*, ed. Rolf Tiedemann and Hermann Schweppenhäuser (Frankfurt am Main: Suhrkamp Verlag), 368–85.

—, 1999. 'Little History of Photography', in *Selected Writings II: 1927–1934*, ed. Michael W. Jennings, Howard Eiland and Gary Smith, trans. Rodney Livingstone et al. (Cambridge, MA: Belknap Press of Harvard University Press), 507–30.

—, 2003a. 'The Work of Art in the Age of its Technological Reproducibility (Third Version)', in *Selected Writings IV: 1938–1940*, ed. Howard Eiland and Michael W. Jennings, trans. Edmund Jephcott et al. (Cambridge, MA: Belknap Press of Harvard University Press), 251–83.

—, 2003b. 'On Some Motifs in Baudelaire', in *Selected Writings IV: 1938–1940*, ed. Howard Eiland and Michael W. Jennings, trans. Edmund Jephcott et al. (Cambridge, MA: Belknap Press of Harvard University Press), 313–55.

Bière-Chauvel, Delphine, 2005. *Le Réseau artistique de Robert Delaunay* (Aix-en-Provence: Publications de l'Université de Provence).

Billy, André, 1923. *Apollinaire vivant* (Paris: La Sirène).

Bobillot, Jean-Pierre, 1993. 'A la fin cou coupé: Travail du vers et subjectivité dans « Zone » d'Apollinaire', *Poétique*, 24, 301–23.

Bohm-Duchen, Monica, 1998. *Chagall* (London: Phaidon).

Bolinger, Dwight L., 1950. 'Rime, Assonance and Morpheme Analysis', *Word*, 6, 117–36.

Bonnefoy, Yves (trans. and ed.), 1995. *William Shakespeare: Vingt-quatre sonnets* (Paris: Thierry Bouchard and Yves Prié).

—, 2000. *La Communauté des traducteurs* (Strasbourg: Presses Universitaires de Strasbourg).

—, 2004. *Shakespeare and the French Poet: including an interview with Yves Bonnefoy*, ed. John Naughton (Chicago: University of Chicago Press).

Borges, Jorge Luis, 2000. *Fictions*, trans. and ed. Andrew Hurley (London: Penguin).

Boschetti, Anna, 2001. *La Poésie partout: Apollinaire, homme-époque (1898–1918)* (Paris: Seuil).

Bull, Michael, and Les Back, 2003. 'Introduction', in Michael Bull and Les Back (eds), *The Auditory Culture Reader* (Oxford: Berg), 1–18.

Burgin, Victor, 2006. 'Possessive, Pensive and Possessed', in David Green and Joanna Lowry (eds), *Stillness and Time: Photography and the Moving Image* (Brighton: Photoworks/Photoforum), 165–76.

Burgos, Jean, 1973. 'Naissance d'un langage: Apollinaire correcteur de lui-même', in Michel Décaudin (ed.), *Apollinaire inventeur de langages: Actes du Colloque de Stavelot (1970)* (Paris: Minard), 22–38.

Campa, Laurence, 2013. *Guillaume Apollinaire* (Paris: Gallimard).

Carroll, John B. (ed.), 1956. *Language, Thought, and Reality: Selected Writings of Benjamin Lee Whorf* (Cambridge, MA: MIT Press).

Chagall, Marc, 1989. *My Life*, trans. Dorothy Williams (Oxford: Oxford University Press) (1st pub. 1965; Russian edn 1947; French trans. by Bella Chagall 1957).

Christin, Anne-Marie, 1995. *L'Image écrite ou la déraison graphique* (Paris: Flammarion).

Clarke, I.F., 1993. *Voices Prophesying War: Future Wars 1763–3749*. 2nd edn (New York: Oxford University Press).

Coke, Van Deren, 1975. 'The Cubist Photographs of Paul Strand and Morton Schamberg', in Van Deren Coke (ed.), *One Hundred Years of Photographic History: Essays in Honor of Beaumont Newhall* (Albuquerque: University of New Mexico Press), 35–42.

Conley, Tim, and Stephen Cain, 2006. *Encyclopedia of Fictional and Fantastic Languages* (Westport, CT: Greenwood Press).

Connor, Steven, 1996. *The English Novel in History 1950–1995* (London: Routledge).

Culler, Jonathan, 1975. *Structuralist Poetics: Structuralism, Linguistics and the Study of Literature* (London: Routledge and Kegan Paul).

Davies, Margaret, 1973. 'L'Avenir dans l'œuvre poétique d'Apollinaire', in Michel Décaudin (ed.), *Apollinaire inventeur de langages: Actes du Colloque de Stavelot (1970)* (Paris: Minard), 141–65.

Debon, Claude, 2004. *'Calligrammes' de Guillaume Apollinaire* (Paris: Gallimard).

—, and Peter Read (eds), 2008. *Les Dessins de Guillaume Apollinaire* (Paris: Buchet/Chastel).

Décaudin, Michel, 1973. 'Apollinaire et les langues', in Michel Décaudin (ed.), *Apollinaire inventeur de langages: Actes du Colloque de Stavelot (1970)* (Paris: Minard), 9–19.

—, 1996. *Le Dossier d'"Alcools"*. 3rd edn (Geneva: Droz; Paris: Minard).

—, 2002. *Apollinaire* (Paris: Librairie Générale Française).

De Certeau, Michel, 1984. *The Practice of Everyday Life*, trans. Steven Rendall (Berkeley: University of California Press).

Delbouille, Paul, 1961. *Poésie et sonorités: La Critique contemporaine devant le pouvoir suggestif des sons* (Paris: Les Belles Lettres).

—, 1984. *Poésie et sonorités II: Les Nouvelles Recherches* (Paris: Les Belles Lettres).

Deleuze, Gilles, 1969. *Logique du sens* (Paris: Minuit).

—, 1983. *Cinéma 1: L'Image-mouvement* (Paris: Minuit).

—, 1990. *Pourparlers* (Paris: Minuit).

—, 1992. *Cinema 1: The Movement-Image*, trans. Hugh Tomlinson and Barbara Habberjam (London: The Athlone Press).

—, 1993. *Critique et clinique* (Paris: Minuit).
—, 1995. *Negotiations: 1972–1990*, trans. Martin Joughin (New York: Columbia University Press).
—, 1997. *Essays Critical and Clinical*, trans. Daniel W. Smith and Michael A. Greco (Minneapolis, MN: University of Minnesota Press).
—, 2003. *Deux Régimes de fous: Textes et entretiens 1975–1995*, ed. David Lapoujade (Paris: Minuit).
—, 2004a. *Difference and Repetition*, trans. Paul Patton (London: Continuum).
—, 2004b. *The Logic of Sense*, trans. Mark Lester with Charles Stivale, ed. Constantin V. Boundas (London: Continuum).
—, 2007. *Two Regimes of Madness: Texts and Interviews 1975–1995*, ed. David Lapoujade, trans. Ames Hodges and Mike Taormina (New York: Semiotext(e)).
—, 2011. *Différence et répétition* (Paris: Presses Universitaires de France) (1st pub. 1968).
—, and Félix Guattari, 1975. *Kafka: Pour une littérature mineure* (Paris: Minuit).
—, and Félix Guattari, 1980. *Mille Plateaux: Capitalisme et schizophrénie II* (Paris: Minuit).
—, and Félix Guattari, 1986. *Kafka: Toward a Minor Literature*, trans. Dana Polan, foreword Réda Bensmaïa (Minneapolis, MN: University of Minnesota Press).
—, and Félix Guattari, 1988. *A Thousand Plateaus: Capitalism and Schizophrenia*, ed. and trans. Brian Massumi (London: The Athlone Press).
—, and Félix Guattari, 1991. *Qu'est-ce que la philosophie ?* (Paris: Minuit).
—, and Félix Guattari, 1994. *What is Philosophy?*, trans. Graham Burchell and Hugh Tomlinson (London: Verso).
Denvir, Bernard (ed.), 1987. *The Impressionists at First Hand* (London: Thames and Hudson).
Desanti, Dominique, 1988. *Sonia Delaunay: Magique magicienne* (Paris: Éditions Ramsay).
Drucker, Johanna, 1996. *The Visible World: Experimental Typography and Modern Art, 1909–1923* (Chicago: University of Chicago Press).
Duro, Paul, 1996. 'Introduction', in Paul Duro (ed.), *The Rhetoric of the Frame: Essays on the Boundaries of the Artwork* (Cambridge: Cambridge University Press), 1–10.
Eco, Umberto, 1995. *The Search for the Perfect Language*, trans. James Fentress (Oxford: Blackwell).
Elkins, James, 2011. *What Photography Is* (New York: Routledge).
Feld, Steven, 2003. 'A Rainforest Acoustemology', in Michael Bull and Les Back (eds), *The Auditory Culture Reader* (Oxford: Berg), 223–39.
Francastel, Pierre (ed.), 1957. *Robert Delaunay: Du cubisme à l'art abstrait*, catalogue by Guy Habasque (Paris: SEVPEN).
Freud, Sigmund, 2002. *The Psychopathology of Everyday Life*, trans. Anthea Bell, intro. Paul Keegan (London: Penguin) (1st pub. 1901).
Gandelman, Claude, 1991. *Reading Pictures, Viewing Texts* (Bloomington, IN: Indiana University Press).

Garfield, Simon, 2010. *Just My Type: A Book About Fonts* (London: Profile Books).

Garnier, Pierre, 1968. *Spatialisme et poésie concrète* (Paris: Gallimard).

Genette, Gérard, 1976. *Mimologiques: Voyage en Cratylie* (Paris: Seuil).

Glissant, Édouard, 1997. *Traité du tout-monde: Poétique IV* (Paris: Gallimard).

Godard, Barbara, 2009. 'Translating Apollinaire after bp Nichol', in Eugenia Loffredo and Manuela Perteghella (eds), *One Poem in Search of a Translator: Rewriting 'Les Fenêtres' by Apollinaire* (Oxford: Peter Lang), 193–221.

Gordon, Bob (ed.), 2009. *1000 Fonts* (Lewes: Ilex).

Gouvard, Jean-Michel, 1996. 'Le Vers d'*Alcools*', in Michel Murat (ed.), *Guillaume Apollinaire: 'Alcools'* (*Littératures Contemporaines 2*) (Paris: Klincksieck), 183–213.

Grammont, Maurice, 1911. *Le Vers français, ses moyens d'expression, son harmonie* (Paris: Édouard Champion) (1st pub. 1904).

Greet, Anne Hyde (trans. and ed.), and S.I. Lockerbie (ed.), 1980. *Guillaume Apollinaire: 'Calligrammes': Poems of Peace and War (1913–1916)* (Berkeley, CA: University of California Press).

Greetham, D.C., 1999. *Theories of Text* (New York: Oxford University Press).

Gullentops, David, 1996. 'Lecture de « Chantre »', in Michel Décaudin (ed.), *Relire 'Alcools'* (Guillaume Apollinaire 19) (Paris: Lettres Modernes/ Minard), 63–80.

Handel, Stephen, 1989. *Listening: An Introduction to the Perception of Auditory Events* (Cambridge, MA: MIT Press).

Harshav, Benjamin (ed.), 2004. *Marc Chagall and His Times: A Documentary Narrative*, trans. Benjamin and Barbara Harshav (Stanford, CA: Stanford University Press).

Henderson, Linda Dalrymple, 1978. *The Artist, 'The Fourth Dimension', and Non-Euclidean Geometry 1900–1930: A Romance of Many Dimensions* (Ann Arbor, MI: University Microfilms, 1978) (PhD Thesis, Yale University, 1975).

—, 1983. *The Fourth Dimension and Non-Euclidean Geometry in Modern Art* (Princeton, NJ: Princeton University Press).

Hicken, Adrian, 2002. *Apollinaire, Cubism and Orphism* (Aldershot: Ashgate).

Hoban, Russell, 2002. *Riddley Walker*, expanded ed. (London: Bloomsbury) (1st pub. 1980).

Ingold, Tim, 2000. *The Perception of the Environment: Essays in Livelihood, Dwelling and Skill* (London: Routledge).

Iversen, Margaret, 2007. 'Following Pieces: On Performative Photography', in James Elkins (ed.), *Photography Theory* (New York: Routledge), 91–108.

Jakobson, Roman, 1956. 'Two Aspects of Language and Two Types of Aphasic Disturbances', in Roman Jakobson and Morris Halle, *Fundamentals of Language* ('S-Gravenhage: Mouton), 53–82.

—, and Linda Waugh, 1979. *The Sound Shape of Language* (Brighton: Harvester Press).

Kracauer, Siegfried, 1965. *Theory of Film: The Redemption of Physical Reality* (New York:Oxford University Press/Galaxy Book).

— , 1995. 'Photography', in *The Mass Ornament: Weimar Essays*, trans. and ed. Thomas Y. Levin (Cambridge, MA: Harvard University Press), 46–63 (1st pub. 1927).

Kristeva, Julia, 1974. *La Révolution du langage poétique: L'Avant-garde à la fin du XIXᵉ siècle: Lautréamont et Mallarmé* (Paris: Seuil).

— , 1984. *Revolution in Poetic Language*, trans. Margaret Waller, intro. Leon S. Roudiez (New York: Columbia University Press).

Larbaud, Valery, 1996. *Les Poésies de A.O. Barnabooth suivi de Poésies diverses et des poèmes de A.O. Barnabooth éliminés de l'édition de 1913*, pref. Robert Mallet (Paris: Gallimard).

La Tourette, F. Gilles de, 1950. *Robert Delaunay* (Paris: Charles Massin).

Lajer-Burcharth, Ewa, 1999. *Necklines: The Art of Jacques-Louis David after the Terror* (New Haven, CT: Yale University Press).

Lipton, Eunice, 1986. *Looking into Degas: Uneasy Images of Women and Modern Life* (Berkeley, CA: University of California Press).

Lockerbie, S.I., 1969. 'Apollinaire: *Alcools: Le Voyageur*', in Peter H. Nurse (ed.), *The Art of Criticism: Essays in French Literary Analysis* (Edinburgh: Edinburgh University Press), 225–39.

Lubben, Kristen, 2011. *Magnum Contact Sheets* (London: Thames and Hudson).

McGann, Jerome, 1991. *The Textual Condition* (Princeton, NJ: Princeton University Press).

Mach, Ernst, 2011. *Space and Geometry: In the Light of Physiological, Psychological, and Physical Inquiry*, trans. Thomas J. McCormack (Watchmaker Publishing) (trans. 1st pub. 1906).

McHugh, Roland, 2006. *Annotations to 'Finnegans Wake'*. 3rd edn (Baltimore, MD: Johns Hopkins University Press).

Mackworth, Cecily, 1961. *Guillaume Apollinaire and the Cubist Life* (London: John Murray).

Magnus, Margaret, 2001. 'What's in a Word? Studies in Phonosemantics', unpublished doctoral dissertation, University of Trondheim, Norway.

Mallarmé, Stéphane, 1998. *Œuvres complètes I*, ed. Bertrand Marchal (Paris: Gallimard).

— , 2003. *Œuvres complètes II*, ed. Bertrand Marchal (Paris: Gallimard).

Marouzeau, Jules, 1965. *Précis de stylistique française*, 5th rev. edn (Paris: Masson).

Mathews, Harry, 2002. 'The Dialect of the Tribe', in *The Human Country: New and Collected Stories* (Normal, IL: Dalkey Archive Press), 7–14.

Merleau-Ponty, Maurice, 1993. *The Merleau-Ponty Aesthetics Reader: Philosophy and Painting*, ed. Galen A. Johnson, trans. and ed. Michael B. Smith (Evanston, IL: Northwestern University Press).

— , 2008. *Signes* (Paris: Gallimard) (1st pub. 1960).

Meschonnic, Henri, 1982. *Critique du rythme: Anthropologie historique du langage* (Lagrasse: Verdier).

Metz, Christian, 1990. 'Photography and Fetish', in Carol Squiers (ed.), *The Critical Image: Essays on Contemporary Photography* (Seattle, WA: Bay Press), 155–64.

Michelson, Annette, 1992. 'The Wings of Hypothesis: On Montage and the Theory of the Interval', in Maud Lavin, Annette Michelson et al., *Montage and Modern Life 1919–1942* (Cambridge, MA: MIT Press), 61–81.

Mullen, R.D., 2000. 'Dialect, Grapholect, and Story: Russell Hoban's *Riddley Walker* as Science Fiction', *Science Fiction Studies*, 27/3, 391–417.

O'Grady, Timothy, and Steve Pyke, 1998. *I Could Read the Sky*, pref. John Berger (London: Harvill Press).

Passuth, Krisztina, 1987. *Moholy-Nagy* (London: Thames and Hudson).

Paterson, Don, 2006. *Orpheus: A Version of Rilke's 'Die Sonette an Orpheus'* (London: Faber and Faber).

Phillips, Christopher, 1992. 'Introduction', in Maud Lavin, Annette Michelson et al., *Montage and Modern Life 1919–1942* (Cambridge, MA: MIT Press), 21–35.

Pilkington, Anthony (ed.), 1993. *Apollinaire:* Alcools (London: Bristol Classical Press) (1st pub. 1970).

Poincaré, Henri, 1952. *Science and Hypothesis*, trans. William John Greenstreet (New York: Dover Publications) (*La Science et l'hypothèse* 1st pub. 1902; this trans. 1st pub. 1905).

— , 1968. *La Science et l'hypothèse* (Paris: Flammarion) (1st pub. 1902).

Proust, Marcel, 1971. *Contre Sainte-Beuve précédé de Pastiches et mélanges et suivi de Essais et articles*, ed. Pierre Clarac with Yves Sandre (Paris: Gallimard).

— , 1987. *À la recherche du temps perdu I*, ed. Jean-Yves Tadié et al. (Paris: Gallimard).

— , 2003. *The Way by Swann's*, ed. and trans. Lydia Davis (London: Penguin).

Rainey, Lawrence (ed.), 2005. *Modernism: An Anthology* (Oxford: Blackwell Publishing).

Rasula, Jed, and Steve McCaffery (eds), 1998. *Imagining Language: An Anthology* (Cambridge, MA: MIT Press).

Read, Peter, 1986. '« La Victoire » d'Apollinaire: contexte, sources et images', in Pierre Brunel, Jean Burgos, Claude Debon and Louis Forestier (eds), *L'Esprit nouveau dans tous ses états – en hommage à Michel Décaudin* (Paris: Minard), 203–14.

Rees, Garnet (ed.), 1975. *Guillaume Apollinaire: 'Alcools'* (London: Athlone Press).

Renaud, Philippe, 1969. *Lecture d'Apollinaire* (Lausanne: L'Âge d'Homme).

Revell, Donald (trans.), 1995. *'Alcools': Poems by Guillaume Apollinaire* (Middletown, CT: Wesleyan University Press).

Roubaud, Jacques, 2000. *Poésie: (récit)* (Paris: Seuil).

Russolo, Luigi, 1986. *The Art of Noises*, trans. and ed. Barclay Brown (New York: Pendragon Press) (1st pub. 1916).

Saenger, Paul, 1997. *Space between Words: The Origins of Silent Reading* (Stanford, CA : Stanford University Press).

Saussure, Ferdinand de, 1972. *Cours de linguistique générale*, ed. Charles Bally and Albert Sechehaye, in collaboration with Albert Riedlinger (Paris: Payot).

—, 1974. *Course in General Linguistics*, ed. Charles Bally and Albert Sechehaye, in collaboration with Albert Riedlinger, trans. Wade Baskin, intro. Jonathan Culler (London: Peter Owen).

Scott, Clive, 1990. *Vers Libre: The Emergence of Free Verse in France 1886–1914* (Oxford: Clarendon Press).

—, 1999. *The Spoken Image: Photography and Language* (London: Reaktion Books).

—, 2000. *Translating Baudelaire* (Exeter: University of Exeter Press).

—, 2006. *Translating Rimbaud's 'Illuminations'* (Exeter: University of Exeter Press).

—, 2009. 'From Linearity to Tabularity: Translating Modes of Reading', *CTIS Occasional Papers*, 4, 37–52.

—, 2012a. *Literary Translation and the Rediscovery of Reading* (Cambridge: Cambridge University Press).

—, 2012b. *Translating the Perception of Text: Literary Translation and Phenomenology* (Oxford: Legenda).

Smith, Bruce R., 2003. 'Tuning into London c. 1600', in Michael Bull and Les Back (eds), *The Auditory Culture Reader* (Oxford: Berg), 127–35.

Steegmuller, Francis, 1973. *Apollinaire: Poet among the Painters* (Harmondsworth: Penguin).

Sylvester, David, 1987. *The Brutality of Fact: Interviews with Francis Bacon* (London: Thames and Hudson).

Tagg, John, 1988. *The Burden of Representation: Essays on Photographies and Histories* (Basingstoke: Macmillan Education).

Tournadre, Claude, 1973. 'A propos de « La Victoire »', in Michel Décaudin (ed.), *Apollinaire inventeur de langages: Actes du Colloque de Stavelot (1970)* (Paris: Minard), 167–80.

Tsur, Reuven, 1992. *What Makes Sound Patterns Expressive? The Poetic Mode of Speech Perception* (Durham, NC: Duke University Press).

Valéry, Paul, 1957. *Œuvres I*, ed. Jean Hytier (Paris: Gallimard).

Vertov, Dziga, 1984. *Kino-Eye: The Writings of Dziga Vertov*, ed. by Annette Michelson, trans. Kevin O'Brien (London: Pluto Press).

Vriesen, Gustav, and Max Imdahl, 1967. *Robert Delaunay: Light and Color* (New York: Harry Abrams).

Wilkie, Christine, 1989. *Through the Narrow Gate: The Mythological Consciousness of Russell Hoban* (Cranbury, NJ: Associated University Presses).

Wollen, Peter, 1989. 'Fire and Ice', in John X. Berger and Olivier Richon (eds), *Other Than Itself: Writing Photography* (Manchester: Cornerhouse Publications), n.p.

Wullschlager, Jackie, 2008. *Chagall: Love and Exile* (London: Penguin).

Yaguello, Marina, 2006. *Les Langues imaginaires: Mythes, utopies, fantasmes, chimères et fictions linguistiques* (Paris: Seuil).

Yildiz, Yasemin, 2012. *Beyond the Mother Tongue: The Postmonolingual Condition* (New York: Fordham University Press).

Zukofsky, Celia and Louis (trans.), 1969. *Catullus (Gai Valeri Catulli Veronensis Liber)* (London: Cape Goliard Press).

Index